SUSE Linux Enterprise - Point of Service 11 Guide

A catalogue record for this book is available from the Hong Kong Public Libraries.

Published in Hong Kong by Samurai Media Limited.

Email: info@samuraimedia.org

ISBN 978-988-8406-63-0

Contents

About this Guide

This guide contains instructions on how to install, manage and deploy SUSE® Linux Enterprise Point of Service. Learn which components constitute a SUSE Linux Enterprise Point of Service environment and how to configure the individual servers and terminals. The guide is intended mainly for system administrators.

Many chapters in this manual contain links to additional documentation resources, available either on the system or on the Internet.

For an overview of the documentation available for your product (and the latest documentation updates), refer to `http://www.suse.com/documentation/` or to the following section.

1 Available Documentation

We provide HTML and PDF versions of our books in different languages.

Find HTML versions of most product manuals in your installed system under `/usr/share/doc/manual` or in the help centers of your desktop. Find the latest documentation updates at `http://www.novell.com/documentation`, where you can download PDF or HTML versions of the manuals for your product.

For more information on the underlying operating system, refer to the SUSE Linux Enterprise Server documentation, available at `http://www.novell.com/documentation/sles11/`.

For information on securing your applications using AppArmor, refer to the Security Guide, available at `http://www.novell.com/documentation/sles11/`.

For an introduction to setting up High Availability environments with SUSE Linux Enterprise, refer to the High Availability Guide, available at `http://www.novell.com/documentation/sles11/`.

2 Feedback

Several feedback channels are available:

Bugs and Enhancement Requests
> For services and support options available for your product, refer to `http://www.suse.com/support/`.
>
> To report bugs for a product component, log into the Novell Customer Center from `http://www.suse.com/support/` and select *My Support > Service Request*.

User Comments
> We want to hear your comments about and suggestions for this manual and the other documentation included with this product. Use the User Comments feature at the bottom of each page in the online documentation or go to `http://www.suse.com/documentation/feedback.html` and enter your comments there.

Mail
> For feedback on the documentation of this product, you can also send a mail to `doc-team@suse.de`. Make sure to include the document title, the product version and the publication date of the documentation. To report errors or suggest enhancements, provide a concise description of the problem and refer to the respective section number and page (or URL).

3 Documentation Conventions

The following typographical conventions are used in this manual:

- `/etc/passwd`: directory names and filenames.

- *placeholder*: replace *placeholder* with the actual value.

- `PATH`: the environment variable PATH.

- `ls`, `--help`: commands, options, and parameters.

- `user`: users or groups.

- Alt, Alt + F1: a key to press or a key combination; keys are shown in uppercase as on a keyboard.

- *File, File > Save As*: menu items, buttons.

- *Dancing Penguins* (Chapter *Penguins*, ↑Another Manual): This is a reference to a chapter in another manual.

Product Overview

SUSE® Linux Enterprise Point of Service is a secure and reliable Linux platform optimized for enterprise retail organizations. Built on the solid foundation of SUSE® Linux Enterprise, it is the only enterprise-class Linux operating system tailored specifically for retail Point of Service terminals, kiosks, self-service systems, and reverse-vending systems.

This section provides an architectural overview of the SUSE Linux Enterprise Point of Service product, along with an overview of server types, images, and the deployment process.

1.1 Architecture

The SUSE Linux Enterprise Point of Service architecture consists of one centralized Administration Server, one or more Branch Servers, and Point of Service terminals. These can be standard PCs running retail check-out applications or specialized point-of-sale machines such as cash registers and customer kiosks (see Figure 1.1, "SUSE Linux Enterprise Point of Service System Architecture" (page 2)). Find a list of system requirements for the individual components in Section 1.2, "System Requirements" (page 3) and an overview of the different server types and their functions in Section 1.3, "Server Types" (page 5).

Figure 1.1: *SUSE Linux Enterprise Point of Service System Architecture*

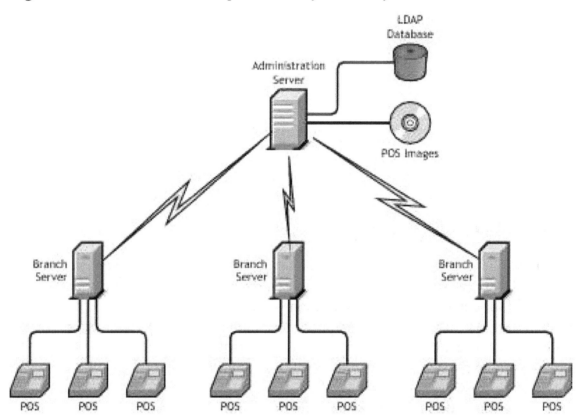

All system information (system structure, image information, the configuration and deployment method for each Branch Server and Point of Service terminal, etc.) is stored in an LDAP database on the Administration Server and may be replicated on Branch Servers. The Administration Server usually also holds the master repository for the images required to boot and configure Point of Service terminals and provides the utilities required to build those images.

NOTE: Creating a Dedicated Image Building Server

However, if you have a large system and want to offload the image building function from the Administration Server, you can also set up a dedicated Image Building Server. For more information, see Chapter 4, *Setting Up the Administration Server* (page 29) and Chapter 3, *Setting Up an Image Building Server* (page 21).

Triggered by the `possyncimages` command (see Section B.3.9, "possyncimages" (page 276), each Branch Server downloads the system information and images required for its local Point of Service terminals from the

Administration Server. The Point of Service terminals, in turn, download their respective images from the Branch Server when they boot.

WARNING: Protecting the Branch Servers

Because Branch Servers contain sensitive information, they must be secured against unauthorized access. Close all unused ports and allow only the root user access to the server console. Refer to Section 9.5, "Securing Your Setup" (page 155) for more details on how to protect your SUSE Linux Enterprise Point of Service setup.

SUSE Linux Enterprise Point of Service is broadly scalable so that a small shop with five Point of Service terminals can be managed just as well as a large chain with a thousand branches. For organizations with several Branch Servers, the link between the Branch and Administration Server is maintained over WAN. During execution of administrative tasks, such as the installation of new Point of Service terminals in a branch, steps must be taken to ensure that the WAN link to the Administration Server is available.

The SUSE Linux Enterprise Point of Service architecture is highly centralized. However, administrative tasks can also be performed on subunits for role-based administration. The Branch Server provides all the services necessary for the operation and management of the Point of Service terminals and the LDAP database can be replicated on the Branch Server. Consequently, the Branch Server and Point of Service terminals can function independently of the Administration Server in the event of server failure or downed connection.

1.2 System Requirements

This section provides a list of minimal hardware requirements for SUSE Linux Enterprise Point of Service.

1.2.1 Administration Server

The following list identifies the system requirements for an Administration Server:

• One server with an x86 or x86-64 processor.

- A minimum of 4 GB hard disk space; recommended 15 GB.

  The required space depends on the size of your images.

- A minimum of 512 MB RAM; recommended 512 MB - 3 GB (at least 512 MB per CPU).

- One network card.

1.2.2 Image Building Server

The following list identifies the system requirements for a dedicated Image Building Server:

- One server with an x86 or x86-64 processor.

- A minimum of 4 GB hard disk space; recommended 25 GB.

  The required space depends on the size of your images.

- A minimum of 512 MB RAM; recommended 512 MB - 3 GB (at least 512 MB per CPU).

- One network card.

1.2.3 Branch Server

The following list identifies the system requirements for a Branch Server:

- One server with an x86 or x86-64 processor.

- A minimum of 4 GB hard disk space; recommended 10 GB.

  The required space depends on the size of the images you distribute to your Point of Service terminals.

- A minimum of 512 MB RAM; recommended 512 MB - 3 GB (at least 512 MB per CPU).

- At least two network cards per server:

  - one network card for the Administration Server's public network,

  - one network card for the Branch Server's private network.

1.2.4 Administration/Branch Server Combination

The following list identifies the system requirements for an Administration/Branch Server combination (Combo Server):

- One server with an x86 or x86-64 processor.

- A minimum of 4 GB hard disk space; recommended 25 GB.

  The required space depends on the size of your images.

- A minimum of 512 MB RAM; recommended 512 MB - 3 GB (at least 512 MB per CPU).

- One network card.

1.3 Server Types

SUSE Linux Enterprise Point of Service is based on SUSE Linux Enterprise and installed as an add-on product. After installation and setup, your SUSE Linux Enterprise Point of Service system includes one centralized Administration Server, one or more Branch Servers, and Point of Service terminals. This section focuses on the server types used in SUSE Linux Enterprise Point of Service and gives an overview of the tasks they run and the services they provide.

1.3.1 Administration Server

The Administration Server is the central administration point for SUSE® Linux Enterprise Point of Service. It is usually located in the main office and is used to manage the Point of Service infrastructure and to host the LDAP database storing the configuration of the Point of Service clients.

The Administration Server provides the following functions:

- Maintaining the master LDAP directory for the Branch Server systems. For more information on the LDAP directory, see Chapter 10, *The LDAP Directory on SUSE Linux Enterprise Point of Service* (page 167).

- Storing the configuration parameters for the Branch Servers.

- Providing an rsync server to distribute the system images and software updates to the Branch Server systems.

For information on installing and configuring the Administration Server, see Chapter 4, *Setting Up the Administration Server* (page 29). Find out more about the Administration Server structure and functions in the following sections.

1.3.1.1 Services

The Administration Server provides two important services in your SUSE Linux Enterprise Point of Service system:

- LDAP is the protocol for accessing the SUSE Linux Enterprise Point of Service directory, which stores all system information.

- rsync is a remote data synchronization service that is used to transfer images from the Administration Server to the Branch Servers.

For the Administration Server to privide services, its firewall needs to allow traffic on the ldap or ldaps ports (389 TCP/UDP and 636 TCP/UDP, respectively) and the rsync port (TCP/UDP 873). For more information, refer to Section 4.2, "Initializing the LDAP Directory with `posInitAdminserver`" (page 32).

1.3.2 Branch Server

The Branch Server provides the network boot and system management infrastructure for the Point of Service terminals. It can also serve as a generic system platform for in-store applications such as database systems and back-ends for Point of Service applications.

The Branch Server provides the following functions:

- DNS services for the local network.

- DHCP to control the network boot process. Instead of setting up the DHCP service on the Branch Server, an external DHCP server can be used. For more information, refer to the list of attributes for `scLocation` elements in Section 10.5.10, "scLocation" (page 212).

- Multicast boot infrastructure for Point of Service terminals.

- Transfer of system images from the Administration Server to the Point of Service terminals.

  The Branch Server uses a software distribution mechanism based on rsync to pull new system images from the Administration Server. It then uses TFTP to push system images and configuration files to the Point of Service terminals. Alternativelly, FTP can be used.

- Management of diskless and disk-based Point of Service terminals. Configuration data is taken from the LDAP directory on the Administration Server.

- System redundancy and failover. A pair of Branch Servers can be configured as a two-node high availability cluster with replicated data.

- NTP, SNMP, logging of syslog output from terminals and other services are not configured using the SLEPOS tools, but can be configured using the standard SLES tools.

For information on installing and configuring the Branch Server, see Chapter 5, *Setting Up a Branch Server* (page 63). Find out more about the Branch Server structure and functions in the following sections.

1.3.2.1 LDAP Branch Server Object

Each Branch Server has a corresponding Branch Server object (`scBranchServer`) in the LDAP directory. This object stores configuration information that is specific to each Branch Server.

For more information on the scBranchServer object, see Chapter 10, *The LDAP Directory on SUSE Linux Enterprise Point of Service* (page 167).

1.3.2.2 LDAP Access

To complete its initial configuration and perform basic functions (such as registering Point of Service terminals and downloading system images and configuration files), the Branch Server must have administrator level access to the LDAP directory. This admin account and password are created by the posInitAdminserver command during the initial configuration of the Administration Server. Once created, this account is not accessible in the LDAP tree.

LDAP communications can be secured with SSL. When you run the posInitAdminserver command, you can enable or disable SSL communication. Note that the firewall running on the Administration Server must allow traffic on the ldap and ldaps ports, 389 TCP/UDP and 636 TCP/UDP, respectively. For more information, refer to Section 4.2, "Initializing the LDAP Directory with posInitAdminserver" (page 32).

The Branch Server mantains a local copy of the branch subtree from the Administration Server LDAP database.

1.3.2.3 Administrative Tasks

Other than emergency handling, no system administration is necessary on the Branch Server. All administrative tasks are controlled from the central Administration Server or are regularly executed by daemons running on the Branch Server. For emergencies and debugging, all administrative functions can be triggered locally or via SSH login by calling commands with few or no parameters.

If you need to update the Point of Service images stored on the Branch Server, you can run possyncimages to manually trigger the rsync update process and download new image files from the Administration Server. For more information, see Section B.3.9, "possyncimages" (page 276).

If you need to update the Point of Service hardware configuration information stored on the Branch Server, run pos dump-all. It regenerates the hardware configuration and config.*MAC* files for all Point of Service terminals found in LDAP. For more information on the pos command, see Section B.3.12, "pos" (page 279). Alternatively, you can trigger terminal updates from the Administration Server by setting scConfigUpdate under the respective `scWorkstation` object to `TRUE` (see Section 10.5.17, "scWorkstation" (page 222)).

For more information on the `pos` command, see Section B.3.12, "pos" (page 279).

1.3.2.4 Services

In SUSE Linux Enterprise Point of Service, Branch Servers provide the services listed in Table 1.1, "Branch Server Services" (page 9).

Table 1.1: *Branch Server Services*

Service	Description
DNS	Every Branch Server runs a DNS master for that branch. The `posldap2dns` command generates the zone files for the BIND name server from the data in the LDAP directory and then reloads the zone files on each Branch Server.
DHCP	A DHCP server can be installed on the Branch Server. The `posldap2dhcp` command generates the `dhcpd.conf` file from branch data in the LDAP directory.
TFTP	The TFTP service on the Branch Server is structured with boot, image, Point of Service, and upload directories. There is a PXE default configuration with which all the Point of Service terminals first load the same initial initrd and the same kernel. For more information, see Section 1.3.2.6, "TFTP Server Directory Structure" (page 10).

Service	Description
	If there is an error with a TFTP action, the service waits 60 seconds, then restarts.
FTP	Alternativelly FTP can be used instead of TFTP. FTP shares same directory structure with TFTP except PXE part. It is recommended on wireless networks not supporting high speed multicast. FTP overcomes the file size limit of TFTP, which enables it to deploy much bigger images.

1.3.2.5 High Availability Configuration

For high availability, Branch Servers can be configured in two-node pairs. The primary node runs all of the scripts and services required to download Branch Server configuration information, synchronize time, and download system images from the Administration Server. The secondary node stays synchronized with the primary, ready to take over and run the scripts and services if the primary fails.

For information on installing a high availability environment, refer to Section 7.2, "SLEPOS High-Availabilty Installation Workflow" (page 112).

1.3.2.6 TFTP Server Directory Structure

SUSE Linux Enterprise Point of Service uses `/srv/tftpboot` as the `tftp_root` path for the TFTP server on the Branch Server. For more information about the file structure, refer to Section A.2, "Branch Server Directory Structure" (page 254).

NOTE: Deletion of Point of Service Control File

The Point of Service control file `hwtype.00:02:55:E8:FA:C9` is deleted (after being moved to `/tftpboot/upload/backup`) and backed up after successful registration in LDAP. For more information, see Section 6.3.3, "The hwtype.*MAC.HASH* File" (page 90).

1.3.3 Special Server Types

Apart from the default implementation shown in Figure 1.1, "SUSE Linux Enterprise Point of Service System Architecture" (page 2), SUSE Linux Enterprise Point of Service allows for a variety of different setups to match your individual requirements. You can create special types of servers, like a dedicated Image Building Server taking load from the Administration Server, or implement POSBranch Servers instead of fully-fledged Branch Servers as described in the following sections.

1.3.3.1 Image Building Server

If your system needs to manage a large number of Point of Service images, you can outsource the image building task to a dedicated Image Building Server. This reduces the processor and memory load required to generate images from the Administration Server and protects the Administration Server and LDAP directory from any possible corruption or user errors that might occur while building Point of Service images.

For information on installing and configuring the Image Building Server, see Chapter 3, *Setting Up an Image Building Server* (page 21).

1.3.3.2 POSBranch Server

For small stores, where the Branch Server only runs the Point of Service infrastructure, the Branch Server can be deployed as a control terminal running on Point of Service hardware. This POSBranch Server configuration is designed for systems that do not run Point of Service applications. However, if the terminal has sufficient memory and disk space, it can run some applications, if required.

In the NLPOS9, the POSBranch Server installation required a special POSBranch image. There is no need for such a specialized POSBranch image any more. Branch servers on Point of Service hardware can be installed as a standard Branch Server, by installing SUSE Linux Enterprise Server 11 and the SUSE Linux Enterprise Point of Service 11 add-on directly on a Point of Service Machine.

NOTE: Access Rights

This implementation of the POSBranch Server allows the Point of Service applications to run under a non-`root` account.

1.4 Images

SUSE Linux Enterprise Point of Service is designed to automate the rollout of Point of Service terminals as much as possible. To assist this automation, the product makes extensive use of image building technology. For each type of terminal, whether it is a non-graphical system or a graphical environment, you can create customized images to be downloaded automatically from the Branch Server when the terminal boots.

1.4.1 KIWI and Image Creator

To create the images for the Point of Service terminals, SUSE Linux Enterprise Point of Service includes both a command line tool (KIWI) and a graphical front-end for KIWI: Image Creator. Install the image building tools by selecting the `SLEPOS Image Server` and the `SLEPOS Images` software patterns in YaST.

When you build images for the Point of Service terminals, all the information required to run a Point of Service terminal—the Linux operating system, drivers, configuration settings, application files, and so forth—can be compiled into a single image file. This file can then be electronically distributed to Point of Service terminals over the network. Additionally, you can generate an ISO version of the image file that can be burned to a CD or copied to a USB stick for manual distribution.

For detailed information on KIWI and Image Creator, refer to Section 8.2, "Building Images with KIWI" (page 132) and Section 8.1, "Building Images with the Image Creator Tool" (page 125).

1.5 SUSE Linux Enterprise Point of Service Deployment

SUSE Linux Enterprise Point of Service requires the following components for a functional system:

- Administration Server,

- Image Building Server,

- Branch Servers,

- Point of Service terminals.

The way in which these components are deployed depends on your system requirements. For example, systems that maintain hundreds of system images might require a dedicated Image Building Server, whereas smaller systems can have the image building utilities installed on the Administration Server. Some customers might install the Administration and Branch Servers on a single box, while others deploy the Branch Server on a Point of Service terminal.

The flexibility of the architecture provides broad scalability so that in large environments components can be distributed to improve system performance, while in smaller environments components can be consolidated to maximize the use of system resources.

1.5.1 Design Guidelines for Large Environments

Every retail environment is different in terms of network speed, server hardware, Point of Service terminal hardware, size of images, frequency of updates, etc. This section presents some design guidelines for large environments.

The recommended maximum number of Point of Service terminals being serviced by a single Branch Server is 100. You can adjust this number up or down depending on how frequently the Point of Service terminals are reimaged and whether you can control when the terminals come online.

NOTE: Time for Booting

For every 100 terminals coming online at the same time, it can take up to 10 minutes for the terminals to download larger graphical images. If the terminals are simply booting from an existing image, it can take 2-3 minutes per 100 terminals.

1.5.2 Installation and Setup

The following summary outlines the general steps required to deploy a SUSE Linux Enterprise Point of Service system. It also identifies the configuration options for each system component and notes where you can go to find detailed instructions.

1 Install the Administration Server using one of the following configurations:

- Install an Administration Server that includes the image building utilities (KIWI and Image Creator) and all the files and directories required to create Point of Service images. For detailed instructions, see Chapter 4, *Setting Up the Administration Server* (page 29).

- Install an Administration Server and a dedicated Image Building Server. For detailed instructions, see Chapter 3, *Setting Up an Image Building Server* (page 21).

- Install an Admin/Branch Server combination.

2 Create the LDAP directory on your Administration Server. For detailed instructions, see Section 4.2, "Initializing the LDAP Directory with `posInitAdminserver`" (page 32).

3 Create the Point of Service images required to deploy your Point of Service terminals.

4 Copy the image files you have created to the appropriate directories on the Administration Server so they will be ready for the Branch Servers to download.

IMPORTANT: Location of the System Images

System images must be located in `/srv/SLEPOS/image/` and boot images must be located in `/srv/SLEPOS/boot/` on the Administration Server before rsync can transmit the images to the Branch Server.

---

5 Create the required LDAP objects for each Branch Server and its Point of Service terminals in the LDAP tree. For detailed instructions, see Section 4.6.1, "Creating Branch Server Objects in LDAP" (page 38).

6 Install the Branch Servers using one of the following configurations:

NOTE: Configuring Admin/Branch Server Combinations

If you install an Admin/Branch Server combination, this step is already completed.

- Install a standard Branch Server. For detailed instructions, see Chapter 5, *Setting Up a Branch Server* (page 63).

- Install a high availability Branch Server cluster of two nodes in an active/passive setup. For general information on how to set up a high availability environment, refer to the High Availability Guide, available from `http://www.novell.com/documentation/sles11/`.

- For stores where the Branch Server is only running the Point of Service infrastructure (i.e. the Branch Server is running no additional applications), the Branch Server can be installed as a control terminal running on Point of Service hardware.

7 After a Branch Server is installed, you must complete the following steps to initialize the Branch Server before attempting to boot its Point of Service terminals:

   7a Run the `posInitBranchserver` command to initialize and configure the Branch Server.

   7b Run `possyncimages` command to download the Point of Service images from the Administration Server to the `/srv/tftpboot` directories on the Branch Server. For detailed instructions, see Section 5.3, "Distributing Images to the Branch Server" (page 71).

7c Start the core script (`posleases2ldap`) as a daemon process on the Branch Server. This script controls all other scripts. For more information, see Section 5.4, "Starting the `posleases2ldap` Core Script" (page 73).

7d If there is a separate Administration Server, start the `posASWatch` command. It checks the availability of the Administration Server, the LDAP synchronization and replication, and the `posleases2ldap` core service. For more information, see Section 5.4, "Starting the `posleases2ldap` Core Script" (page 73).

8 Deploy the Point of Service terminals, following the general instructions in Chapter 6, *Booting Point of Service Terminals* (page 77).

Depending on your network configuration and terminal hardware, you must prepare the Point of Service terminals to boot using one of the following procedures:

- If the Point of Service terminals have access to the network, the terminals can PXE boot and download their image files from the Branch Server. This method is typically used for workstations that are not equipped with a hard disk. For more information on this process, see Section 6.4.1, "Network PXE Boot" (page 94).

- If the Point of Service terminals do not have access to the network, create an isoboot or a oemboot image and deploy the image at the terminal. This method can be used for workstations that either are or are not equipped with a hard disk, and have a CD drive or a USB port. For information on the isoboot process, see Section 6.4.4, "Booting from CD (isoboot)" (page 103)

- If a Point of Service terminal cannot boot from the network or from a CD, it attempts to boot from the hard drive. For more information, see Section 6.4, "Booting the Point of Service Terminal" (page 92).

9 Test your SUSE Linux Enterprise Point of Service installation to ensure that it is functioning correctly. For detailed instructions, see Section 7.1, "Monitoring the Terminal Boot-Up" (page 109).

SUSE Linux Enterprise Point of Service Installation

2

SUSE Linux Enterprise Point of Service is distributed as an add-on product for SUSE Linux Enterprise Server 11 systems. To install SUSE Linux Enterprise Point of Service 11, install the SUSE Linux Enterprise Server 11 base system first. You can choose to install the SUSE Linux Enterprise Point of Service add-on together with your base system during the initial installation process, or you can install the SUSE Linux Enterprise Point of Service add-on on top of an already installed base system at any later time.

2.1 Installation During the Initial Installation Process

To install SUSE Linux Enterprise Point of Service add-on together with your base system during the initial installation process, follow these steps:

1 Start SUSE Linux Enterprise Server 11 installation as usual. For more information, see the SUSE Linux Enterprise Server documentation.

2 To include the SUSE Linux Enterprise Point of Service add-on product, check the *Include Add-On Products from Separate Media* option in the *Installation Mode* dialog in the *System Analysis* step and click *Next*.

3 Click *Add*. If you are installing SUSE Linux Enterprise Point of Service from a CD medium, select *CD* as the source type. If you are installing from a different source, such as NFS or HTTP, choose the appropriate source type. Click *Next*.

4 If you are installing from CD, insert the SUSE Linux Enterprise Point of Service add-on product CD. If you are installing from a different source, provide the necessary source. Click *Continue*.

5 Confirm the SUSE Linux Enterprise Point of Service license agreement and click *Next*.

6 The SUSE Linux Enterprise Point of Service add-on product is displayed in the overview. Click *Next* and continue with the installation as usual.

7 In the *Entering Migration Data* step of the installation, you can enter SLEPOS migration data. Select the appropriate *Path to Archive File* or *Path to Back-up Directory* and click *Next*. For more information about SLEPOS migration, see Chapter 11, *Migration from Older Versions* (page 229).

8 In the *Server Pattern Selection* step of the installation, select the SUSE Linux Enterprise Point of Service patterns appropriate for the type of server you are installing. For Administration Server, select the *Admin Server (AS)* pattern. For Branch Server, select the *Branch Server (BS)* pattern. For Image Building Server, select the *Image Server (IS)* pattern.

You can combine patterns to install a server with multiple functions. For example, for an Administration Server with image building capabilities, select both *Admin Server (AS)* and *Image Server (IS)* patterns. For an Administration Server and Branch Server combination, select both *Admin Server (AS)* and *Branch Server (BS)* patterns.

2.2 Installation On Top of an Already Installed System

To install SUSE Linux Enterprise Point of Service on top of an already installed base system, follow these steps:

1 Start YaST and select *Software > Add-On Products > Add*.

2 Select media type to be used for installation. If you are installing SUSE Linux Enterprise Point of Service from a CD medium, select *CD* as the source type. If you are installing from a different source, such as NFS or HTTP, choose the appropriate source type. Click *Next*.

3 If you are installing from CD, insert the SUSE Linux Enterprise Point of Service add-on product CD. If you are installing from a different source, provide the necessary source. Click *Continue*.

4 Confirm the SUSE Linux Enterprise Point of Service license agreement and click *Next*.

5 In the *Entering Migration Data*, you can enter SLEPOS migration data. Select the appropriate *Path to archive file* or *Path to backup directory* and click *Next*. For more information about SLEPOS migration, see Chapter 11, *Migration from Older Versions* (page 229).

6 In the *Server Pattern Selection* step of the installation, select the SUSE Linux Enterprise Point of Service patterns appropriate for the type of server you are installing. For Administration Server, select the *Admin Server (AS)* pattern. For Branch Server, select the *Branch Server (BS)* pattern. For Image Building Server, select the *Image Server (IS)* pattern.

You can combine patterns to install a server with multiple functions. For example, for an Administration Server with image building capabilities, select both *Admin Server (AS)* and *Image Server (IS)* patterns. For an Administration Server and Branch Server combination, select both *Admin Server (AS)* and *Branch Server (BS)* patterns.

2.3 Upgrading SLEPOS11 to SLEPOS11 SP2

Upgrading SLEPOS11 to SLEPOS11 SP2 consists of two steps:

* upgrading SLES11 to SLES11 SP2,

* upgrading SLEPOS11 to SLEPOS11 SP2.

These two steps can be performed either together or separately. For information on SLES11 upgrade, consult SLES11 SP2 Installation Quick Start guide.

If you want to upgrade SLEPOS11 at the same time as SLES11, check the *Include Add-On Product from Separate Media* option during selection of the installation mode. You will be asked to select the SLEPOS11 SP2 installation source.

If you want to upgrade SLEPOS11 after the SLES11 upgrade, use the YaST *Add-On Products* module and add SLEPOS11 SP2 as an add-on. Network upgrade is not supported in this scenario and results in installation failure during the second installation stage because of DNS resolving failure. You can work around this limitation by switching to a second console (Ctrl + F2), logging in as root and starting DNS server manually with the `rcnamed start` command.

During the upgrade installation, you will be asked to select a SLEPOS pattern. If you do not want to change the installed pattern, just click *Next*.

2.3.1 SLEPOS Configuration After Upgrade

The Administration Server does not need to be configured after upgrading. Only the Branch Server needs reconfiguration after an upgrade. The non-interactive reconfiguration is triggered via the `posInitBranchserver -r -n` command.

Setting Up an Image Building Server

3

Image Building Server is the machine used for building custom image files for Point of Service systems. It is possible to combine the functions of Administration Server and Image Building Server on a single machine. However, if you have a large system and want to offload the image building function from the Administration Server, you can set up a dedicated Image Building Server on a separate machine. It is also recommended to separate the Image Building Server for security reasons. Image building under root privileges can affect the Administration Server.

To install a dedicated Image Building Server, select the *Image Server (IS)* pattern during installation, but not the *Admin Server (AS)* pattern. For more information about the installation process, see Chapter 2, *SUSE Linux Enterprise Point of Service Installation* (page 17).

3.1 Types of Images

To help get you started, SUSE Linux Enterprise Point of Service comes with a set of pre-built image files that you can customize to set up your own system. Every Point of Service terminal requires two images: a boot image and a system image. You can also create your own images using Image Creator or KIWI. For more information, refer to Section 8.1, "Building Images with the Image Creator Tool" (page 125) and Section 8.2, "Building Images with KIWI" (page 132).

3.1.1 Boot Images

The boot images contain the kernel and a bootstrap image (`initrd`), providing the minimum your Point of Service terminals need to initially start up from a bootable CD or USB stick, or from the network (via remote boot technology). The following boot image templates are available:

netboot
> The template creates all the files and directories (including partitioning and boot loader installation) required to boot diskful and diskless terminals from the network over PXE and DHCP. The kernel and the `initrd` are stored at Branch Servers and they are downloaded to terminals using TFTP.
>
> This is the only type of image that supports all SLEPOS features including the wireless support and encryption.

isoboot
> The template creates all the files and directories required to boot diskless and preinstalled disk-equipped systems from CD or DVD. This boot image must be combined with a system image to create a CD or DVD that can be used to boot the Point of Service terminal.
>
> This type of image should be only used for terminals never connected to network and Branch Server.

oemboot
> The oemboot image has same functions as the isoboot image, but is used for booting terminals from USB sticks and similar media. Should be only used for terminals never connected to network and Branch Server.
>
> Additionally, oemboot image can be used for server installation (Branch Server, Administration Server or Combo Server images). It deploys the OEM preload image onto the selected storage device.
>
> The oemboot image does not include features like wireless support or encryption.

3.1.2 System Images

The following system image templates are specially designed for the most common types of retail Point of Service terminals:

Minimal

The `Minimal` image contains only the runtime environment for native-code applications (C and C++) and the ncurses library for non-graphical user interface support. The Minimal image supports only console-based applications. It is stripped down to be as small as possible by using "delete packages" feature. Deleted packages provide other packages with some functionality, that is, as a consequence, not available in the Minimal image by default. If such functionality is needed, depending packages shall be installed. Support includes only building, deployment and booting of the Minimal image. This template will be available only in Image Creator and is considered experimental.

JeOS

The `JeOS` image is slightly larger than the Minimal image, however, it is fully supported.

Graphical

The `Graphical` image includes the features of the `Minimal` image and essential graphical interface capabilities (the X Window System and a lightweight Window Manager), as well as the ability to run Java programs. It supports console-based C/C++ applications, Java programs in a Java2 runtime environment, X11 applications, and basic browser-based applications.

Java web browser plugin must be explicitly enabled. To enable it, the following packages must be included: `java-1_6_0-ibm-alsa`, `java-1_6_0-ibm-devel`, `java-1_6_0-ibm-fonts`, `java-1_6_0-ibm-jdbc`, and `java-1_6_0-ibm-plugin`. They are commented out in the default `config.xml`.

Branchserver

The `Branchserver` image is a specialized image which can be used for deploying a Branch Server instead of using the standard method (installing SLES with the SLEPOS addon and manual configuration of the Branch Server).

The provided image is suitable for online installation, where the terminal images and LDAP data are downloaded from the Administration Server. For offline installation the terminal images and OIF files must be added to the Branch Server image before building.

For more information, see Section 5.6, "Installing a Branch Server Using a Specialized Image" (page 74).

Administration Server and Combo Server
Image templates for fast installation of the Administration Server or the combination of Administration Server and Branch Server are also included.

All system images are based on SUSE Linux Enterprise Server. You can extend Point of Service system images to include add-on features such as:

• Advanced Linux Sound Architecture (ALSA) library for audio support,

• additional device drivers,

• GNOME or KDE desktop environments,

• IBM™ Java technology support,

• Firefox and other Web browsers,

• Samba 3 Client for SMB/CIFS connectivity to Microsoft™ Windows™ servers,

• VNC 4 Remote Control Client for remotely controlling the terminal.

System images that you create are initially stored on the Administration Server (or on the Image Building Server if you have chosen to set up a dedicated Image Building Server). Before you deploy your Point of Service terminals, transmit the system images via rsync to specific directories on the Branch Server from where they can be downloaded to Point of Service terminals at boot time.

When a Point of Service terminal is started for the first time, it performs a PXE boot (or boots from CD or USB stick) and then registers with the Branch Server to obtain the information it needs to download its system image. The TFTP service on the Branch Server automatically delivers the matching system image to the Point of Service terminal.

To make this work as designed, you must create reference objects in the LDAP directory for the types of Point of Service terminals you intend to deploy in your system. For detailed information, refer to Section 4.6.2, "Creating Point of Service Terminal Objects in LDAP" (page 43). Correctly creating and configuring these objects during the installation of the Branch Servers saves you from separately managing the startup of each Point of Service terminal.

3.2 Preparing Source Repositories

The default package repository for image building is provided by a SUSE SMT server. SLEPOS is already preconfigured for an SMT server running on the same machine as the SLEPOS Image Building Server. Once the connection to the SUSE package and update server has been set up, image building will work out of the box.

The SMT server should be installed according to the SMT documentation (`http://www.suse.com/documentation/smt11/`). It can be installed either on the Image Building Server machine (then the image building works out of the box) or on a separate machine available in the network (using HTTP protocol).

The image configuration file `config.xml` contains repository aliases, for example `{SLES 11 SP3 i386}`. These aliases are mapped to repository urls via the `/etc/kiwi/repoalias` file. It is also possible to use the repository URLs directly without aliasing, as in the previous SLEPOS releases. The repository URLs must point to a repository of rpm-md type. `/etc/kiwi/repoalias` has the following format for describing URL aliases:

```
#SLES SP3 repository
{SLES 11 SP3 i386}  http://smt_host/repo/$RCE/SLES11-SP3-Pool/
# SLES SP3 update
{SLES 11 SP3 i386 update}  http://smt_host/repo/$RCE/SLES11-SP3-Updates/
[...]
```

The following SMT channels should be configured: `SLES`, `SLES-Updates`, `SLEPOS`, `SLEPOS-Updates`.

3.2.1 Running SMT on the Image Building Server

SLEPOS is already preconfigured for an SMT server running on the Image Building Server machine. Once the connection to the SUSE package and update server has been set up, image building will work out of the box. No special configuration is necessary.

This is the full list of repositories (in rpm-md format) required for building a SP3 image (`i586` repositories for terminals and `x86_64` repositories for servers):

• `/srv/www/htdocs/repo/$RCE/SLES11-SP3-Pool/sle-11-`*arch*`,`

- `/srv/www/htdocs/repo/$RCE/SLES11-SP3-Updates/sle-11-arch`,

- `/srv/www/htdocs/repo/$RCE/SLE11-POS-SP3-Pool/sle-11-arch`,

- `/srv/www/htdocs/repo/$RCE/SLE11-POS-SP3-Updates/sle-11-arch`.

3.2.2 Running SMT on a Separate Machine

Besides the default of installing the SMT server on the same machine as the Image Building Server, the SMT server can on a separate machine. If a separate machine is used, the local paths to the image repositories must be changed to URLs pointing to the SMT machine, for example:

`/srv/www/htdocs/repo/$RCE/SLE11-POS-SP3-Updates/sle-11-arch`

must be changed to:

`http://server.name/repo/$RCE/SLE11-POS-SP2-Updates/sle-11-arch`

This is the full list of repositories (in rpm-md format) required for building a SP3 image (`i586` repositories for terminals and `x86_64` repositories for servers):

- `http://server.name/repo/$RCE/SLES11-SP3-Pool/sle-11-arch`,

- `http://server.name/repo/$RCE/SLES11-SP3-Updates/sle-11-arch`,

- `http://server.name/repo/$RCE/SLE11-POS-SP3-Pool/sle-11-arch`,

- `http://server.name/repo/$RCE/SLE11-POS-SP3-Updates/sle-11-arch`.

3.2.3 Using SLES and SLEPOS Media Directly to Create an SMT Repository

It is possible to use the SLES and SLEPOS media directly to create an SMT repository. The media can be mounted to a directory or copied. The following example of the image configuration should be changed to point to the used directories. The repository type should be set to `yast2`:

```
<!--   SLE REPOSITORY -->
<repository type="yast2">
 <source path="/var/lib/SLEPOS/dist/SLES-11-SP3-DVD-i586-DVD1"/>
</repository>
<!--   SLEPOS REPOSITORY -->
<repository type="yast2">
 <source path="/var/lib/SLEPOS/dist/SLE-11-SP3-POS-i586-x86_64-DVD1"/>
</repository>
```

It is however strongly recommended to also add the update repositories, using SMT as described above or by creating a plain directory repository manually (for details see KIWI documentation).

NOTE: Configuring Repositories in YaST2 Image Creator

The repository configuration can also be changed in YaST2 Image Creator. In this case, the repository type is detected automatically.

Setting Up the Administration Server

4

The Administration Server is the central administration point for SUSE® Linux Enterprise Point of Service. All system information (system structure, the configuration and deployment method for each Branch Server and Point of Service terminal, image information, and so forth) is stored in an LDAP directory on the Administration Server. The Administration Server is also the central distribution point for the images required to boot and configure Point of Service terminals, and can run the utilities required to build those images. Set up an Administration Server either with or without the image building software.

NOTE: Creating an Image Building Server

The utilities required to build Point of Service images can be installed with the Administration Server or on a dedicated image building server. For more information, see Chapter 3, *Setting Up an Image Building Server* (page 21).

NOTE: Meeting the System Requirements

For a list of system requirements to set up an Administration Server, refer to Section 1.2.1, "Administration Server" (page 3).

4.1 Administration Server Configuration

To configure the Administration Server, follow these steps:

1 Check if the `SLEPOS Administration Server` pattern is installed on the machine to be configured. If it is missing, install it. For more information about installation, see Chapter 2, *SUSE Linux Enterprise Point of Service Installation* (page 17).

If you want to use the Administration Server to build Point of Service images, also select the `Image Server` and `Images` patterns. If you want to use a standalone Image Building Server, these patterns are not needed.

2 Initialize the LDAP server on the Administration Server with the `posInitAdminserver` command. Follow the on-screen instructions. For more information about LDAP initialization, see Section 4.2, "Initializing the LDAP Directory with `posInitAdminserver`" (page 32).

3 Initialize the LDAP database on the Administration Server:

3a Use the `posAdmin` command to add an `organizationalUnit` object as described in Section 4.6.1.1, "Creating organizationalUnit Objects" (page 39).

3b Use the `posAdmin` command to add an `scLocation` object as described in Section 4.6.1.2, "Adding an `scLocation` Object" (page 39).

IMPORTANT: The New `--userPassword` Attribute

The new mandatory attribute `--userPassword` has been introduced in SLEPOS11. This password is needed when configuring a Branch Server.

3c Use the `posAdmin` command to add an `scServerContainer` and `scBranchServer` objects as described in Section 4.6.1.3, "Adding an `scServerContainer` and `scBranchServer` Objects" (page 40).

4 Make sure the rsync port (usually 873) is open on the Administration Server. The rsync port is not open in the default SLES11 installation. You have to add its number in the YaST *Firewall* module under *Allowed Services > Advanced > TCP Ports*.

5 The basic configuration of the Administration Server is now finished. If you want to initialize an offline Branch Server without any internet connection, create an offline installation package, as described in Section 5.2.2.1, "Creating an Offline Installation Package" (page 70).

4.1.1 Changing the Administration Server Password

To change the Administration Server password, edit `/etc/openldap/slapd.conf` and replace both lines containing `rootpw` *old_hashed_password* with a new hashed password. You can get the new hashed password with the `slappasswd` command. Change the password by entering the following commands in the command line:

1 `rcldap stop`

2 `sed -i -e 's;rootpw.*$;rootpw '`slappasswd -c "new_password"`';' /etc/openldap/slapd.conf`:x

3 `rcldap start`

The password stored in `/etc/SLEPOS/adminserver.conf` needs to be changed and reencoded as well. Enter the following command in the command line to change it:

```
sed -i -e 's;POS_ADMIN_PASSWORD=.*
$;POS_ADMIN_PASSWORD='`echo "new_password" | openssl enc
-aes128 -kfile "/etc/SLEPOS/salt.key" -a`';' /etc/SLEPOS/
adminserver.conf
```

4.2 Initializing the LDAP Directory with posInitAdminserver

All system information (system structure, the configuration and deployment method for each Branch Server, available system images, and Point of Service terminal types) is stored in an LDAP directory on the Administration Server.

SUSE Linux Enterprise Point of Service uses the OpenLDAP directory service. The `posInitAdminserver` command defines the LDAP directory schema and the initial records for OpenLDAP. SLEPOS LDAP directory can coexists with other OpenLDAP directories. Certain limitations however still apply. For limitations, see Limitations of Shared OpenLDAP Service (page 34).

To create the SUSE Linux Enterprise Point of Service LDAP directory for OpenLDAP:

1 After installing the Administration Server, log in as `root`.

2 Configure the firewall running on the Administration Server to allow traffic on the LDAP and LDAPs ports, 389 TCP/UDP and 636 TCP/UDP, respectively. Do this by using the YaST Firewall module (`yast2 firewall`).

3 Run `posInitAdminserver`.

4 Specify your organization/company name without spaces or special characters.

5 Specify the two-letter code of your country, `de` for Germany, `us` for United States, `uk` for United Kingdom, and so forth.

6 Specify the alphanumeric LDAP administrator password. The Branch Server uses this account to access the LDAP directory and to run `posAdmin` for adding objects to the LDAP directory.

7 Determine if you want to use SSL when the Branch Server connects to the LDAP directory on the Administration Server. By default, SSL is used.

   • Select Y to use an SSL connection when the Branch Server connects to the LDAP Directory.

   • Select N to disable SSL.

> **IMPORTANT: Securing Your Server Communication**
>
> Using SSL/TLS to secure the connections between Administration Server and Branch Servers is highly recommended.

Administration Server uses YaST CA Management interface for issuing and managing SSL certificates. This provides standardized SLES interface to SSL management and allows viewing and modification of SLEPOS SSL certificates in YaST CA Management module.

> **NOTE: Changing CA Certificate**
>
> When CA certificate is changed, public part must be redistributed to individual Branch Servers and all LDAP servers (on the Administration Server and individual Branch Servers) must be restarted to accommodate this change.

The keys and certificates are located in the `/etc/SLEPOS/keys` directory on both the Administration and Branch Servers.

8 To initialize SUSE Manager integration, confirm `Enable SUSE Manager integration` when asked. After that, SUSE Manager host address, SUSE Manager user name and SUSE Manager password can be entered. The password and user for Administration Server is stored in `adminserver.conf`

The SUSE Manager password for branch users is given by `userPassword` attribute in the appropriate `scLocation`. The user name is derived form its dn path by changing `,cn=` and similar to `.`, for example `cn=mybranch1,ou=myorgunit1,o=myorg,c=us` becomes `mybranch1.myorgunit1.myorg.us`. The SUSE Manager hostname is stored in the `scSUSEManager` attribute of `scHardware`.

Note that terminal images used with SUSE Manager must include the `suse_manager_client_registration` package. In the default `config.xml` it is commented out.

9 If there is an existing Open LDAP database, `posInitAdminserver` asks for password to configuration database for existing OpenLDAP directory. If existing OpenLDAP configuration should not be preserved, enter empty string. The `posInitAdminserver` script will ask for confirmation in this case.

10 `posInitAdminserver` provides a summary of the LDAP directory data based on your input. If all data is correct, press Enter.

If there is something wrong with the input data, abort the installation by pressing Ctrl + C.

11 The command initializes the basic LDAP database structure and performs some tests, then displays a summary of the configuration and test results. When the tests are successfully completed, the command displays a confirmation alert.

NOTE: Limitations of Shared OpenLDAP Service

SLEPOS LDAP directory does not require custom OpenLDAP configuration and can add itself as separate directory. However, the following limitations apply:

- OpenLDAP directory must use configuration database (`cn=config`) as primary configuration (does not use static `/etc/openldap/slapd.conf` configuration file). It is not sufficient to just enable configuration database as ACLs for individual branch locations will not survive OpenLDAP service restart. They can be however recreated by running `posAdmin --refresh`.

- If the existing OpenLDAP configuration is not set to use SSL, SLEPOS can not work with SSL and vice versa. The `posInitAdminserver` script will however detect and use the right CA certificate when SSL is used and it will distribute the certificate to branch locations.

- Existing LDAP directories can not use the same suffix as SLEPOS LDAP directory. SLEPOS use `o=<organization>,c=<country>` by default.

NOTE: Unresolvable Hostname

When `posInitAdminserver` detects that Administration Server's hostname is unresolvable, the script automatically adds it to `/etc/hosts` as `127.0.0.1`.

After you run `posInitAdminserver`, the LDAP directory is initialized on the Administration Server and the LDAP service is available. At this point, you should have a basic tree structure with a root, a Country container, and an Organization container.

You can verify that the LDAP structure is accessible via the `ldapsearch` command. Use a syntax similar to the first example when using SSL. For setups without SSL, use a syntax similar to the second example.

```
ldapsearch -x -H ldaps://administration_server_name -b o=myorg,c=us -s base
 -D cn=admin,o=myorg,c=us -w password
ldapsearch -x -H ldap://administration_server_name -b o=myorg,c=us -s base -
D cn=admin,o=myorg,c=us -w password
```

TIP: Setting the LDAP Debugging Level

Turn on a more verbose output for the `ldapsearch` command by enabling the debug option with `-d1`.

4.3 Creating Point of Service Images

Before you can deploy Point of Service terminals, you must first create image files that contain the operating system and application files required to boot the terminals.

SUSE Linux Enterprise Point of Service provides image templates that can be customized and generated using the Image Creator tool. If you select the Image Server pattern during the Administration Server installation, the image creation utilities (Image Creator and KIWI) are installed on the Administration Server along with all the files and directories required to create Point of Service images. For a detailed, step-by-step introduction to building SUSE Linux Enterprise Point of Service images using Image Creator, refer to Section 8.1, "Building Images with the Image Creator Tool" (page 125).

After you have created the images required for your Point of Service terminals, you must copy the images to the appropriate directories on the Administration Server so that the rsync service can transmit the images to the Branch Server. Depending on whether the Administration Server and the Image Building Server are on the same machine (or whether the images are built on a dedicated Image Building Server), use the different copy procedures outlined in Section 4.5, "Copying the System Image Files" (page 37).

To deploy a new image version, for example an image with updated packages from online repositories, follow these steps:

1 Build new images as described in Section 8.1, "Building Images with the Image Creator Tool" (page 125).

2 Deploy boot images as decribed in Section 4.4, "Copying the Boot Image Files" (page 36).

3 Deploy system images as decribed in Section 4.5, "Copying the System Image Files" (page 37).

4 Synchronize with the Branch Server via the `possyncimages` command (see Section 4.6.2.8, "Activating Images" (page 52) for more information).

4.4 Copying the Boot Image Files

This section explains how to copy the default boot images (initrd and the Linux kernel file) to the appropriate directories on the Administration Server, so they are ready to be transferred to the Branch Servers.

If the images have been built on the same machine, use the `registerImages` command to copy and register them in LDAP.

If the images have been built on a dedicated Image Building Server, use the following command on the Administration Server to copy the images: `registerImages --include-boot` *user@imageserver*`:/var/lib/SLEPOS/system/images/`*image_name*`/`. For more information, see Section 4.7.1, "The `registerImages` Command" (page 55).

Alternativelly, you can copy the images manually using the `cp` command or your favorite file browser, or, if built on a dedicated Image Building Server, `scp`.

4.4.1 Deploying Boot Images with a New Kernel Version

If you build images with a new kernel version, you can preserve old file names and overwrite existing images. In such a case, there is no need to update objects in LDAP database.

Alternatively, you can copy the new kernel and initrd to `/srv/SLEPOS/boot` with new file names (for example `initrd-2.6.27.25.gz` and `linux-2.6.27.25`). In such a case, you must create a new `scDistributionContainer` object (see Section 10.5.7, "scDistributionContainer" (page 208)) and add a new `scPosImage` object to it (see Section 4.5.1, "Deploying New Versions of System Images" (page 37)).

4.5 Copying the System Image Files

System images must be located in the `/srv/SLEPOS/image` directory on the Administration Server. The boot image must be located in `/srv/SLEPOS/boot`. The Branch Servers can then download the image files and deploy them on Point of Service terminals.

If the images have been built on the same machine, use the `registerImages` command to copy and register them in LDAP.

If the images have been built on a dedicated Image Building Server, use the following command on the Administration Server to copy the images: `registerImages --include-boot` *user@imageserver*`:/var/lib/SLEPOS/system/images/`*image_name*`/`. For more information, see Section 4.7.1, "The `registerImages` Command" (page 55).

Alternativelly, you can copy the images manually using the `cp` command or your favorite file browser, or, if built on a dedicated Image Building Server, `scp`.

4.5.1 Deploying New Versions of System Images

If you build new system images, you can preserve old file names and overwrite existing images. In such a case, there is no need to update objects in the LDAP database.

Alternatively, you can copy the new image to a file with a new version number. You must add the new version to the related `scPosImage` in the LDAP database. This can be done via the `scPosImageVersion` attribute of the `scPosImage` object or via a new `scImageVersion` object. (for more information, see Section 4.6.2.8, "Activating Images" (page 52)).

You can also use a new name and version number. In such a case, you must create a new `scPosImage` (see Section 4.6.2.6, "Adding an `scPosImage` Object" (page 51)). If the new image uses a different kernel version, the new `scPosImage` must be added to the corresponding `scDistributionContainer`.

4.6 Creating the Required LDAP Structure

The necessary LDAP objects for branches, terminals, and global roles must be created.

4.6.1 Creating Branch Server Objects in LDAP

Before you can configure and deploy a Branch Server, you must first create the necessary objects in the LDAP directory stored on the Administration Server. All `posAdmin` calls must be executed on the Administration Server. These objects include:

- One or more *organizationalUnit* objects (see Section 4.6.1.1, "Creating organizationalUnit Objects" (page 39)) to represent your organizational structure.

- An *scLocation* object (see Section 4.6.1.2, "Adding an `scLocation` Object" (page 39)) for each site where a Branch Server is located.

- An *scServerContainer* (see Step 1 (page 41)) to contain all the Branch Server objects for a given site.

- An *scBranchServer* object (see Section 4.6.1.3, "Adding an `scServerContainer` and `scBranchServer` Objects" (page 40)) and its associated configuration objects for each Branch Server in your system.

- Additional objects (see Section 4.6.2, "Creating Point of Service Terminal Objects in LDAP" (page 43)) for the Point of Service terminals associated with each Branch Server.

NOTE: LDAP Object Attributes

Each LDAP object has two types of attributes: must and may attributes. The must attributes are required for an object; the may attributes are optional. The tables in this section list only those may attributes that are relevant to SUSE Linux Enterprise Point of Service.

4.6.1.1 Creating organizationalUnit Objects

In a SUSE Linux Enterprise Point of Service system, Organizational Unit (`organizationalUnit`) objects are containers that typically represent regions, divisions, or branches within a company. These objects can be nested to visually represent the structure and organization of your company. Branch location objects are created in `organizationalUnit` containers within the LDAP directory. Use only alphanumeric characters for `ou` objects.

Here is the `posAdmin` command syntax for adding an Organizational Unit object in LDAP (type the command all on one line):

```
posAdmin --base base_context --add --organizationalUnit --ou ou_name [--
description `string´]
```

Section 10.5.1, "organizationalUnit" (page 201) summarizes the Organizational Unit object attributes.

For example, the following command adds the myorgunit Organizational Unit to the LDAP directory and gives it the description "main headquarters":

```
posAdmin --base o=myorg,c=us --add --organizationalUnit --ou myorgunit --
description 'main headquarters'
```

The LDAP context of the newly created `organizationalUnit` is the `ou=myorgunit,o=myorg,c=us` directory.

4.6.1.2 Adding an scLocation Object

An `scLocation` object is typically used to represent a branch office (a site where a Branch Server and Point of Service terminals are located). `scLocation` containers are used to store information about the deployed Branch Servers and Point of Service terminals. This and all other information, which can be modified on the Branch Server, should be stored or referenced in the Location containers to limit the need to grant write privileges to subtrees.

Section 10.5.10, "scLocation" (page 212) summarizes the posAdmin command options for `scLocation` object attributes.

Here is the `posAdmin` command syntax to add an scLocation object in LDAP (type the command all on one line):

```
posAdmin --base
    base_context --add --scLocation --cn
    location_name --ipNetworkNumber
    network_address --ipNetmaskNumber
    subnet_mask --scDhcpRange
    ip_address,ip_address
    --scDhcpFixedRange
    ip_address,ip_address
    --scDefaultGw ip_address --scDynamicIp TRUE |
    FALSE --scDhcpExtern TRUE | FALSE --scWorkstationBaseName
    string --scEnumerationMask
    number --userPassword
    branchpassword
```

The following command adds an `scLocation` named `harbor` to the LDAP directory (type the command all on one line):

```
posAdmin
--base ou=myorgunit,o=myorg,c=us --add --scLocation --cn harbor
--ipNetworkNumber 192.168.1.0 --ipNetmaskNumber 255.255.255.0
--scDhcpRange 192.168.1.10,192.168.1.54
--scDhcpFixedRange 192.168.1.55,192.168.1.88
--scDefaultGw 192.168.1.1
--scDynamicIp TRUE --scDhcpExtern FALSE
--scWorkstationBaseName CR --scEnumerationMask 000
--userPassword branchpassword
```

NOTE: Network Autoconfiguration

In case of network autoconfiguration, scDhcpRange and scDhcpFixedRange parameters can be ommited. For autoconfiguration option when defining ipNetworkMask and ipNetworkNumber, see Section 5.1, "Branch Server Network Configuration" (page 64).

4.6.1.3 Adding an `scServerContainer` and `scBranchServer` Objects

There must be an `scBranchServer` object for every Branch Server in the system. These objects store configuration information that is specific to each Branch Server.

An `scBranchServer` object contains information about hardware, at least one defined network card, and services like FTP, TFTP, DNS and DHCP. It is located with an `scLocation` object in the LDAP tree.

IMPORTANT: Defining the Branch Server Hostname

The location of the `scBranchServer` object in the LDAP directory must correspond to the hostname defined for the Admin/Branch Server during installation. For example, if the hostname is `bs.mybranch.myorgunit.myorg.us`, the `dn` of the `scBranchServer` object would be `cn=bs,cn=server,cn=mybranch,ou=myorgunit,o=myorg,c=us`.

To add an `scBranchServer` object to the LDAP directory with posAdmin, proceed as follows:

1 Before you can add the `scBranchServer` to an `scLocation` object, you must define an `scServerContainer`, using the `--scServerContainer` and common name (`--cn`) options. For example (type the command all on one line):

```
posAdmin
--base cn=mybranch,ou=myorgunit,o=myorg,c=us
--add --scServerContainer --cn server
```

2 In the new `scServerContainer`, add a Branch Server object, using the `--scBranchServer` and common name (`--cn`) options. For example (type the command all on one line):

```
posAdmin
--base cn=server,cn=mybranch,ou=myorgunit,o=myorg,c=us
--add --scBranchServer --cn bs
```

You can also define the reference hardware with the `--scRefServerDn` option, a pointer (Distinguished Name) to the global directory.

3 Add a network interface card (with a static IP address from the subnet defined in the `scLocation` object) using the `--scNetworkcard` option and the `--scDevice` and `--scIpHostNumber` attributes. For example (type the command all on one line):

```
posAdmin --base cn=bs,cn=server,cn=mybranch,ou=myorgunit,o=myorg,c=us
--add --scNetworkcard --scDevice eth0 --ipHostNumber 192.168.1.1
```

Section 10.5.11, "scNetworkcard" (page 216) summarizes the posAdmin command options for `scNetworkcard` attributes.

4 Set up the Branch Server services. At a minimum, define the required DNS, TFTP or FTP, DHCP and posleases services.

NOTE: Using FTP or TFTP

Most current Wi-Fi networks do not support multicast correctly and switch to the lowest available network speed when multicast TFTP is used. Unless you are using accesspoints supporting high speed multicast over Wi-Fi, it is recommended to use FTP instead of multicast TFTP on such networks.

The following example demonstrate how to add the DNS service

```
posAdmin
--base cn=bs,cn=server,cn=mybranch,ou=myorgunit,o=myorg,c=us
--add --scService --cn dns  --ipHostNumber 192.168.1.1
--scDnsName dns --scServiceName dns --scServiceStartScript named
--scServiceStatus TRUE
```

The following example demonstrate how to add the DHCP service:

```
posAdmin
--base cn=bs,cn=server,cn=mybranch,ou=myorgunit,o=myorg,c=us
--add --scService --cn dhcp  --ipHostNumber 192.168.1.1
--scDnsName dhcp --scServiceName dhcp
--scDhcpDynLeaseTime 300 --scDhcpFixedLeaseTime 14400
--scServiceStartScript dhcpd --scServiceStatus TRUE
```

The following example demonstrate how to add the TFTP service:

```
posAdmin
--base cn=bs,cn=server,cn=mybranch,ou=myorgunit,o=myorg,c=us
--add --scService --cn tftp  --ipHostNumber 192.168.1.1
--scDnsName tftp  --scServiceName tftp
--scServiceStartScript atftpd  --scServiceStatus TRUE
```

The following example demonstrate how to add the FTP service:

```
posAdmin
--base cn=bs,cn=server,cn=mybranch,ou=myorgunit,o=myorg,c=us
--add --scService --cn ftp  --ipHostNumber 192.168.1.1
--scDnsName tftp  --scServiceName ftp
--scServiceStartScript pure-ftpd  --scServiceStatus TRUE
```

The following example demonstrate how to add the posleases service:

```
posAdmin
--base cn=bs,cn=server,cn=mybranch,ou=myorgunit,o=myorg,c=us
--add --scService --cn posleases --scDnsName posleases
--scServiceName posleases
--scPosleasesTimeout 10 --scPosleasesChecktime 40
--scPosleasesMaxNotify 6 --scServiceStartScript posleases2ldap
--scServiceStatus TRUE
```

Section 10.5.16, "scService" (page 220) summarizes the posAdmin command options for the scService object attributes.

NOTE: Ommiting ipHostNumber

ipHostNumber attribute can be omitted if service is using same IP address as Branch Server.

4.6.2 Creating Point of Service Terminal Objects in LDAP

The configuration parameters for each Point of Service terminal are stored in the central LDAP directory on the Administration Server. Every Point of Service terminal has its own Workstation object (scWorkstation) in the LDAP tree. The Workstation object is automatically created when a Point of Service terminal registers on the Branch Server. posleases2ldap uses information from the Hardware Reference object (scCashRegister) and Image Reference object (scPosImage) to create the Workstation object. For more information on this process, see Section 6.3.3, "The hwtype.*MAC.HASH* File" (page 90).

Before you can boot the Point of Service terminals, use posAdmin to create the following objects in the LDAP directory (see also Section 10.2, "Using posAdmin to Manage the LDAP Directory" (page 174)):

- An scCashRegister object and its associated configuration objects for each type of Point of Service terminal in your system:

  - scHarddisk or scRamDisk

  - scPxeFileTemplate

- `scConfigFileTemplate` (optional)

- `scConfigFileSyncTemplate` (optional)

- An `scPosImage` object for each client image file that you want the Branch Server to distribute to Point of Service terminals.

  Activate the `scPosImage` objects before you boot the Point of Service terminals. Terminals require an activated `scPosImage` object before they can download the corresponding physical image from the Branch Server. The activation can be achieved either by setting the `scPosImageVersion` attribute of the relevant `scPosImage` object to `active` or by creating a non-disabled `scImageVersion` object. For more information on activating images, see Section 4.6.2.8, "Activating Images" (page 52).

With `posAdmin`, you can add, remove, and modify Point of Service terminal hardware assets such as Point of Service terminals, hard disks, network interface cards, and configuration files with the use of reference objects in the LDAP directory. Hardware reference objects are typically located in the global container in the LDAP directory.

NOTE: LDAP Attributes

Each LDAP object has two types of attributes: must and may attributes. The must attributes are the minimum requirements for an object; the may attributes are optional.

4.6.2.1 Adding an `scCashRegister` Object

An associated object representing the cash register must exist in the LDAP database. This `scCashRegister` object can either represent a specific machine or a generic machine. The generic object is used if a specific image is not found for the given machine. In both cases, the `scCashRegister` must have a hardware subobject like `scRamDisk` or `scHarddisk` which specifies where and how the image should be deployed.

The name of a machine is located in the uploaded `hwtype.MAC.HASH` file under a `HWTYPE` entry. For more information, see Section B.2, "Core Script Process" (page 264).

NOTE: Creating Default `scCashRegister` Objects

To create a default `scCashRegister` object, define the object's
`scCashRegisterName` attribute as `default`. This `scCashRegister`
will then be used to register all machines for which no specific
`scCashRegister` exists.

Define only one default `scCashRegister` object in the Global container.

The `scCashRegister` objects are stored in the Global container so they can be
accessed by all Branch Servers.

NOTE: Defining a System Image for a Point of Service Terminal

A specific system image can be defined in the `scWorkstation`
object. The setting in the `scWorkstation` object overrides the default
image defined in the `scCashRegister` object. For information on this
procedure, see Section 4.6.2.9, "Assigning an Image to a Point of Service
Terminal" (page 53).

Section 10.5.3, "scCashRegister" (page 203) summarizes the posAdmin command
options for `scCashRegister` object attributes.

To add a `scCashRegister` object for a specific machine (for example
with a specific `HWTYPE=cshr4152`), use the command (note the
`scCashRegisterName` name and image reference in `--scPosImageDn`):

```
posAdmin --base cn=global,o=myorg,c=us
--add --scCashRegister --cn cr-test --
scCashRegisterName cshr4152 --scPosImageDn
cn=myGraphical_test,cn=default,cn=global,o=myorg,c=us
```

To add a `scCashRegister` object for a generic machine, use the command (note
`scCashRegister` name being `default`):

```
posAdmin --base cn=global,o=myorg,c=us --
add --scCashRegister --cn cr-test-default --
scCashRegisterName default --scPosImageDn
cn=myGraphical_test,cn=default,cn=global,o=myorg,c=us
```

To add a RAID definition to an existing cash register `raidCR` (under a local role, using one disk specified by id and another by device name), use the following command:

```
posAdmin --DN
 cn=raidCR,cn=myrole,cn=rolecontainer,cn=mybranch,ou=myorgunit,o=myorg,c=us
 --modify --scCashRegister --scRaidScheme '1 /dev/disk/by-id/ata-
ST3160815AS_Z4A1ATWL /dev/sdc'
```

4.6.2.2 Adding an `scRamDisk` Object

The `scRamDisk` object stores configuration information for a Point of Service terminal RAM disk. If no hard disk is available, you must configure a RAM disk for the Point of Service terminal.

Section 10.5.13, "scRamDisk" (page 218), summarizes the posAdmin command options for `scRamDisk` object attributes.

When deploying to the RAM disk of a specific machine, use: `posAdmin --base cn=cshr4152,cn=global,o=myorg,c=us --add --scRamDisk --cn ram --scDevice /dev/ram1`

When deploying to the RAM disk of the generic machine of the previous section, use: `posAdmin --base cn=cr-test-default,cn=global,o=myorg,c=us --add --scRamDisk --cn ram --scDevice /dev/ram1`

The size of the ramdisk is controlled by kernel parameters `ramdisk_size` (default value 400000) and `ramdisk_blocksize` (default value 4096).

4.6.2.3 Adding an `scHarddisk` Object

The `scHarddisk` object stores configuration information for a Point of Service terminal hard disk. The attributes of this object are described in Section 10.5.8, "scHarddisk" (page 210).

When deploying to the harddisk, the partition table must be specified using the `scPartition` objects:

```
posAdmin --base cn=cshr4152,cn=global,o=myorg,c=us
--add --scHarddisk --cn sda --scDevice /dev/sda --scHdSize 10000

posAdmin --base cn=sda,cn=cshr4152,cn=global,o=myorg,c=us
```

```
--add --scPartition --scPartNum 0 --scPartType 83 --scPartMount /srv/SLEPOS
 --scPartSize 1000

posAdmin --base cn=sda,cn=cshr4152,cn=global,o=myorg,c=us
--add --scPartition --scPartNum 1 --scPartType 82 --scPartMount x --
scPartSize 1000

posAdmin --base cn=sda,cn=cshr4152,cn=global,o=myorg,c=us
--add --scPartition --scPartNum 2 --scPartType 83 --scPartMount '/' --
scPartSize 7000
```

Of course, you can also use further attributes of the `scPartition` object. For example, to add the fourth partition with encryption using password *mypassword* and some decription, use:

```
posAdmin --base cn=sda,cn=cshr4152,cn=global,o=myorg,c=us
--add --scPartition --scPartNum 3  --scPartType 83 --scPartMount '/data' --
scPartSize 1000
--scPassword 'mypassword' --description 'partition for classified data'
```

Note that the `scPartNum` attribute is there only to define relative order of the partitions (the first partition with `scPartNum 0`, `scPartType 83` and `scPartMount /srv/SLEPOS` is the service partition).

The minimum size of the service partition sufficient for the wireless operation is 200 MB. However, the service partition is also used for downloading compressed images with multicast option and will be used for other purposes in the future. The recommended size of the service partition is 20 GB.

If booting from the service partition is required (for example when wireless operation or offline deployment is used), `grub` must be included in `initrd`. This can be accomplished by adding `<package name="grub" bootinclude="true"/>` to the `config.xml` file or by adding `grub` to the list of packages to include in boot in via Image Creator.

The service partition cannot be encrypted.

For more information about the `scPartition` object and its attributes, see Section 10.5.20, "scPartition" (page 226). For more information about disk encryption, see Section 9.5.5, "Using Encrypted Partitions on Terminals" (page 159).

When deploying to the hard disk of a generic machine (from example used in Section 4.6.2.1, "Adding an `scCashRegister` Object" (page 44)), simply use `cn=cr-test-default` instead of `cn=cshr4152`.

4.6.2.4 Adding an `scConfigFileTemplate` Object

`scConfigFileTemplate` objects are used when running services, such as the X Window service, that require hardware-dependent configuration files. An `scConfigFileTemplate` object contains the configuration file data that a Point of Service terminal needs in order to run a given service.

To define the `scConfigFileTemplate` object with the `posAdmin` command, you designate the file containing the configuration data as the `--scConfigFileData` parameter. `posAdmin` then extracts the `scConfigFileData` entry of the `scConfigFileTemplate` object.

When a Point of Service terminal registers with a Branch Server or when you run `pos dump-all` or `pos dump-ws` or force update via `scConfigUpdate`, the Branch Server retrieves the configuration data in the `scConfigFileTemplate` object to create a configuration file in `/srv/tftpboot/KIWI/MAC/` directories on the Branch Server. The configuration file name is the same as the `cn` name of the respective LDAP entry.

Using TFTP, the configuration file is then distributed from the Branch Server to the appropriate Point of Services terminals at boot time.

NOTE: Assigning Configuration Files to Point of Services

The `scCashRegister` or `scPosImage` object under which the `scConfigFileTemplate` object is created determines which Point of Service terminals receive the configuration file.

If the `scConfigFileTemplate` object is defined under an `scCashRegister` object, all terminals that correspond to the type defined in the `scCashRegister` object receive the configuration file defined in the `scConfigFileTemplate` object.

If the `scConfigFileTemplate` object is defined under an `scPosImage` object, all terminals that load the system image that corresponds to the `scPosImage` object receive the configuration file defined in the `scConfigFileTemplate` object.

Be aware that in this case the `posAdmin` command does more than just literal insertion of the data specified on the command line. If you want to use some other tool (for example, GQ) to define the `scConfigFileTemplate` object, you must directly add the configuration data as the `scConfigFileData` attribute, not the path to the file containing them. Also keep in mind that the created configuration file name is the `cn` entry of the respective `scConfigFileTemplate` object, so ensure that they are named differently. This can become an issue when, for example, one configuration object is assigned to the scCashRegister and another with the same name to the scPosImage object.

Section 10.5.4, "scConfigFileSyncTemplate" (page 205) summarizes the posAdmin command options for `scConfigFileTemplate` object attributes.

The following example adds a `scConfigFileTemplate` object below the Hardware Reference object, crtype3 (type the command all on one line):

```
posAdmin --base cn=crtype3,cn=global,o=myorg,c=us
--add --scConfigFileTemplate --cn xorg.conf
--scConfigFile /etc/X11/xorg.conf --scMust TRUE
--scBsize 1024 --scConfigFileData /mydata/xorg.conf.1234567
```

Configuration files defined by `scConfigFileTemplate` and `scConfigFileSyncTemplate` objects and referenced on the CONF line in the `config.MAC` file are always checked with respect to the list of deployed configuration files on the terminal (in `/etc/KIWI/InstalledConfigFiles`). This ensures that all defined configuration files exist on the terminal and that the configuration files removed from the CONF line are also deleted from the terminal.

The content of the configuration files is not checked.

4.6.2.5 Adding an `scConfigFileSyncTemplate` Object

`scConfigFileSyncTemplate` objects are used when running services that require hardware-dependent configuration files, for example, the X Window service. The `scConfigFileSyncTemplate` object points to the configuration file that a Point of Service terminal needs to run a given service. This object differs from `scConfigFileTemplate` objects because the configuration data is not stored in the object; the object points to a configuration file outside the LDAP directory.

When a Point of Service terminal registers with a Branch Server, or you run `pos dump-all`, or `pos dump-ws` or force update via `scConfigUpdate`, the Branch Server first uses rsync to synchronize the configuration files in the `/srv/SLEPOS/config` directory on the Administration Server which the same directory on the Branch Server and then copies relevant configuration files, as specified in the `scConfigFileSyncTemplate` objects from the `/srv/SLEPOS/config` directory to the `/srv/tftpboot/KIWI/`*MAC*`/` directory. The filenames are changed to the respective `cn` names of the corresponding `scConfigFileSyncTemplate` LDAP entries.

IMPORTANT: Location of Configuration Files

Any configuration files referenced in the `scConfigFileSyncTemplate` object must be located in the `/srv/SLEPOS/config/` directory on the Administration Server, otherwise they will not be transferred to the Branch Server.

Using TFTP, the configuration file is then distributed from the Branch Server to the appropriate Point of Service terminals at boot time.

NOTE: Assigning Configuration Files to Point of Service Terminals

The `scCashRegister` or `scPosImage` object under which the `scConfigFileSyncTemplate` object is created determines which Point of Service terminals receive the configuration file.

If the `scConfigFileSyncTemplate` object is defined under an `scCashRegister` object, all terminals that correspond to the type defined in the `scCashRegister` object receive the configuration file designated in the `scConfigFileSyncTemplate` object.

If the `scConfigFileSyncTemplate` object is defined under an `scPosImage` object, all terminals that load the system image that corresponds to the `scPosImage` object receive the configuration file designated in the `scConfigFileSyncTemplate` object.

Also keep in mind that the created configuration file name is the `cn` entry of the respective `scConfigFileTemplate` object. Make sure they are named. This can become an issue when for example, one configuration object is assigned to the scCashRegister and another with the same name to the scPosImage object.

Section 10.5.4, "scConfigFileSyncTemplate" (page 205), summarizes the posAdmin command options for `scConfigFileSyncTemplate` object attributes.

The following example adds an `scConfigFileSyncTemplate` object below the Hardware Reference object, crtype3 (type the command all on one line):

```
posAdmin
--base cn=crtype3 ,cn=global,o=myorg,c=us
--add --scConfigFileSyncTemplate --cn xorg.conf
--scConfigFile /etc/X11/xorg.conf --scMust TRUE --scBsize 1024
    --scConfigFileLocalPath /srv/SLEPOS/config/xorg.conf.cr3
```

4.6.2.6 Adding an `scPosImage` Object

All system images that you want to distribute to Point of Service terminals must have a corresponding `scPosImage` object in the LDAP directory. These objects are typically organized within Distribution Container objects under the Global container in the LDAP tree.

NOTE: Referring to Boot Images

Boot images do not have `scPosImage` objects; they are referenced in the `scInitrdName` attribute in the `scDistributionContainer` object.

After the installation and configuration of SUSE Linux Enterprise Point of Service, an `scPosImage` object is automatically added to the Default Distribution Container for the Minimal image. However, this LDAP entry is only intended to serve as an example. You must manually add an `scPosImage` object for each system image you want to distribute to Point of Service terminals.

IMPORTANT

The reference objects for SUSE Linux Enterprise Point of Service images should be created in the Default Distribution Container. It references the current kernel version included and the default booting image in the product and therefore, should store all the `scPosImage` objects for SUSE Linux Enterprise Point of Service images.

Section 10.5.12, "scPosImage" (page 216), summarizes the posAdmin command options for `scPosImage` object attributes.

The following commands add a `scPosImage` object into the default container (and set its version via the `scImageVersion` object):

```
posAdmin
--base cn=default,cn=global,o=myorg,c=us --add --scPosImage --cn myMinimal
--scImageName myTestMinimal --scDhcpOptionsRemote /boot/pxelinux.0 --
scDhcpOptionsLocal LOCALBOOT
```

```
--scImageFile myMinimal.i686 --scBsize 8192

posAdmin --base cn=myMinimal,cn=default,cn=global,o=myorg,c=us
--add --scImageVersion --scDisabled FALSE --scVersion 3.4.2
```

If you already have specified another container as scDistributionContainer, you can also add an scPosImage object to this other container (anothercontainer in this case):

```
posAdmin
--base cn=anothercontainer,cn=global,o=myorg,c=us --add --scPosImage --
cn myMinimal
--scImageName myTestMinimal --scDhcpOptionsRemote /boot/pxelinux.0 --
scDhcpOptionsLocal LOCALBOOT
--scImageFile myMinimal.i686 --scBsize 8192

posAdmin --base cn=myMinimal,cn=anothercontainer,cn=global,o=myorg,c=us
--add --scImageVersion --scDisabled FALSE --scVersion 3.4.2
```

If you want to add a new image version to an existing scPosImage object, see Section 4.6.2.8, "Activating Images" (page 52).

4.6.2.7 Adding an scDistributionContainer Object

Each collection of system images built against a specific kernel and initrd must have a corresponding scDistributionContainer object in the LDAP dabase. Therefore, if deploying a system image built against a new kernel or initrd version, a new scDistributionContainer object must be created.

The scInitrdName attribute of the scDistributionContainer object references the appropriate boot images.

4.6.2.8 Activating Images

Each image can be available in several versions. Each image version can be either enabled (active) or disabled (passive). If there are more enabled versions of one image, the highest version is used. If there is no enabled version of the image, no terminals can download and use the image.

The version (and activation) data for each image can be stored on two different places in the LDAP database – in the scPosImageVersion attribute of the relevant scPosImage object and in the scImageVersion objects placed under it. The scPosImageVersion attribute can hold information about multiple versions, while the scImageVersion object holds information about one version (but it supports more features, such as image encryption). More `scImageVersion` objects can be created to store information about multiple versions.

The `scPosImageVersion` attribute is considered deprecated and it may become unsupported in the future. For more information, see Appendix C, *Deprecated Elements* (page 287). If the `scPosImageVersion` attribute and the `scImageVersion` objects are used together, the data are combined. In case of a conflict, `scImageVersion` takes precedence.

For more information about the `scPosImage` object and its `scPosImageVersion` attribute, see Section 10.5.12, "scPosImage" (page 216). For more information about the `scImageVersion` object, see Section 10.5.19, "scImageVersion" (page 226).

A convenient way to add the `scImageVersion` object offers the `registerImages --ldap` command. For more information, see Section 4.7.1, "The `registerImages` Command" (page 55).

To add version `2.4.2` manually with `posAdmin` using the `scImageVersion` object, run the following command:

```
posAdmin --base cn=minimal,cn=default,cn=global,o=myorg,c=us
--add --scImageVersion --scDisabled FALSE --scVersion 3.4.2
```

To activate the new image version on a Branch Server, use `possyncimage; pos dump-all`.

To deactivate an image activated by the `scImageVersion` object, use the following command:

```
posAdmin --modify --scImageVersion --scDisabled TRUE --DN
scVersion=3.4.2,cn=minimal,cn=default,cn=global,o=myorg,c=us
```

To deactivate an image activated by the `scPosImageVersion` attribute, use the following command:

```
posAdmin --modify --multival --scPosImage --scPosImageVersion
'3.4.2;active=>3.4.2;passive' --DN
cn=minimal,cn=default,cn=global,o=myorg,c=us
```

4.6.2.9 Assigning an Image to a Point of Service Terminal

You can manually assign a specific image to a Point of Service terminal through its `scWorkstation` object.

The following command assigns 'myMinimal' image
`2.0.4` to the `CR001 scWorkstation` object in the
`cn=`*mybranch*`,ou=`*myorgunit*`,o=`*myorg*`,c=`*us* location (type the command
all on one line):

```
posAdmin
--modify --scWorkstation
--scPosImageDn cn=myMinimal,cn=default,cn=global,o=myorg,c=us
--scPosImageVersion 2.0.4
--DN cn=CR001,cn=mybranch,ou=myorgunit,o=myorg,c=us
```

When you explicitly assign an image name (`scPosImageDn`) and its version
(`scPosImageVersion`) in the `scWorkstation` entry, the version and active/
passive status information in the corresponding `scPosImage` image object in the
global container is ignored. However, if you only assign the image name, the version
information in the `scPosImage` image object is used.

The `scWorkstation` object is automatically created in the LDAP directory the
first time you boot a Point of Service terminal. The `posleases2ldap` daemon
detects new registration (`hwtype.MAC(.HASH)`) files uploaded by terminals and
creates appropriate hardware configuration files (`config.MAC`), along with the
corresponding `scWorkstation` object.

4.6.2.10 Removing Images

To remove the image assigned to a workstation, run the following command (type
the command all on one line):

```
posAdmin
--modify --scWorkstation --scPosImageDn --scPosImageVersion
--DN cn=CR001,cn=mybranch,ou=myorgunit,o=myorg,c=us
```

4.7 Copying Images to the Administration Server rsync Directory

Before the rsync service can transmit the images to the Branch Server, system image
files must be located in the `/srv/SLEPOS` directory on the Administration Server.
Client images must be located in the `/srv/SLEPOS/image` directory and the boot
images must be located in `/srv/SLEPOS/boot`.

The registerImages command is provided for copying system image files to the /srv/SLEPOS directory on the Administration Server. This command also provides functions for compressing the images, adding them to LDAP and installing boot images. These procedures can also be performed manually.

4.7.1 The registerImages Command

An image can be registered with the registerImages *path/to/image/ file* command. New versions can be installed later using the registerImages --delta *name_of_installed_base_image path/to/image/ file* command. This generates delta files containing only the necessary changes and thus saving bandwidth when images on Branch Server are updated via possyncimages.

System image names must follow the kiwi convention: *name.arch-N.N.N* and *name.arch-N.N.N*.md5.

For example, you can install an image and register it in LDAP using this command:

```
registerImages --ldap --move --gzip
--kernel /var/lib/SLEPOS/system/images/minimal-3.1.5/initrd*.kernel \
--initrd /var/lib/SLEPOS/system/images/minimal-3.1.5/initrd*.splash.gz \
/var/lib/SLEPOS/system/images/minimal-3.1.5/minimal.i686-3.1.5
```

You can install a new image and create the appropriate delta later, using this command:

```
registerImages --delta minimal.i686-3.1.5 --ldap --move /var/lib/SLEPOS/
system/images/minimal-3.1.6/minimal.i686-3.1.6
```

For a list of options used by the registerImages command, see Section B.3.10, "registerImages" (page 277).

4.7.2 Using registerImages with Remote Files and Tarballs

To use registerImages with remote files, use the following syntax:

```
registerImages [ --kernel [scp:][user@]host:remote_kernel_file --initrd
 [scp:][user@]host:remote_initrd_file ] [scp:][user@]host:temote_image_file
```

```
registerImages [ --kernel http://remote_kernel_file --initrd http://
remote_initrd_file ] http//:remote_image_file
```

`ssh` will ask for a password. Alternativelly it can be configured to use password-less login. For more information see the ssh documentation.

To use `registerImages` with directories or tarballs (produced by Kiwi or SUSE Studio), use the following syntax:

```
registerImages [ --include-boot ] local_directory
registerImages [ --include-boot ] local_tarball
registerImages [ --include-boot ] [scp:][user@]host:remote_directory
registerImages [ --include-boot ] [scp:][user@]host:remote_tarball
registerImages [ --include-boot ] http:remote_tarball
```

With the `--include-boot` option, the kernel and initrd are extracted directly from the tarball or directory (instead of specifying it directly with the `--kernel` and `--initrd` options).

4.7.3 Manually Copying Images to the Administration Server's rsync Directory

The system images can also be copied to the Administration Server's rsync directory manually.

4.7.3.1 Copying System Images to the Administration Server's rsync Directory

The following example demonstrates how to put a previously extended Graphical system image in the Administration Server's rsync directory so it can be received, on request, by the Branch Server:

1 Copy the extended Graphical system image:

```
cp /srv/SLEPOS/image/Graphical-2.0.4-2004-12-05 \
   /srv/SLEPOS/image/graphical-2.0.4
```

2 Copy the corresponding Graphical image MD5 checksum file:

```
cp /srv/SLEPOS/image/Graphical-2.0.4-2004-12-05.md5 \
```

```
/srv/SLEPOS/image/graphical-2.0.4.md5
```

4.7.3.2 Copying Boot Images to the Administration Server's rsync Directory

The following example demonstrates how to copy the first and second stage boot images to the Administration Server's rsync directory so they can be received, on request, by the Branch Server:

NOTE

Point of Service terminals boot two images, a first stage image (`initrd.gz`) and a second stage image (`linux`). For more information, see Section 6.4, "Booting the Point of Service Terminal" (page 92).

---

1 Copy the initrd-netboot image as `initrd.gz`:

```
cp /srv/SLEPOS/image/initrd-netboot-suse-
SLES11.architecture-image_version.splash.gz \
    /srv/SLEPOS/boot/initrd.gz
```

2 Copy the kernel image as `linux`:

```
cp /srv/SLEPOS/image/initrd-netboot-suse-
SLES11.architecture-image_version.kernel.kernel_version-flavour /srv/
SLEPOS/boot/linux
```

4.8 Simple Administration GUI

SLEPOS11 SP2 introduces a simple administration GUI, `posAdmin-GUI`. Goal of the `posAdmin-GUI` is to help with the creation of Branch Server, role, image and cashregister objects. Using posAdmin-GUI, the administrator can avoid typing long `posAdmin` commands and benefit from a nicer user interface and check data immediately.

The posAdmin-GUI uses YaST libraries, therefore ncurses, GTK and Qt user interfaces are available.

To start posAdmin-GUI, use the `posAdmin-GUI` command. If you start it on an already configured Administration Server, the `adminserver.conf` configuration file is parsed and used to fill organization and country entries. You can also start posAdmin-GUI with the `posAdmin-GUI` *slepos-xml-file* command. The provided SLEPOS XML is parsed and all available data are loaded.

NOTE: posAdmin-GUI Limitations

posAdmin-GUI can only be used for importing new objects into the LDAP database. It does not allow any modification of existing objects and it is not possible to rename existing objects or to add, remove, or change their attributes. Only creating new objects is supported.

posAdmin-GUI does not load data from the existing LDAP database.

The posAdmin-GUI interface has four main sections: the *BranchServer Configuration*, *Images Configuration*, *CashRegisters Configuration*, and *Finalize*. To navigate between them, click the tabs in the top of the window or the *Next* and *Back* buttons in the bottom right corner. Whenever you try to navigate between the tabs, the entered data are checked for consistency.

Use the *Advanced Mode* button to toggle the display of advanced configuration options like IP/DNS mapping functions or RAID schemes.

Use the *Default* button to revert all configurations to the default state. If posAdmin-GUI was called with a provided XML file, data from the file will be reloaded.

4.8.1 BranchServer Configuration

The *BranchServer Configuration* tab defines all Branch Server-related data. The values defined on this tab are used for defining the relevant `scLocation` object and its attributes (as described in Section 10.5.10, "scLocation" (page 212).

In the upper section (*BranchServer Configuration*), enter the name of the Branch Server using the *Country*, *Organization*, *Organizational Unit*, and *Location* (`scLocation`) values. If you need to add nested organizational units, click *Add Nested OU*. Enter the *BranchServer Access Password* in the appropriate field.

In the middle section (*BranchServer Details*), check whether an external DHCP server should be used and whether global and/or local roles should be used.

In the lower section (*BranchServer Advanced Configuration*), available only when the *Advanced Mode* is toggled on, enter the *IP Mapping Function*, *DNS Mapping Function*, *Associated Domain*, *Enumeration Mask*, and *Workstation Base Name*.

To configure Branch Server services, click *BranchServer Services Configuration*. For more information, see Section 4.8.1.1, "BranchServer Services Configuration" (page 59).

To configure Branch Server networking, click *BranchServer Network Configuration*. For more information, see Section 4.8.1.2, "BranchServer Network Configuration" (page 59).

4.8.1.1 BranchServer Services Configuration

To configure Branch Server services, click the *BranchServer Services Configuration* button.

To add a new service, select *add new service* in the *List of Registered Services*. Enter *Service Name*, *Service DNS Name*, *Name of Service Script in /etc/init.d/*, and *Service Specific Parameters*. The *Service Specific Parameters* field can contain optional parameters of the scService object.

For example, *Service Specific Parameters* for posleases service can contain:

```
scPosleasesMaxNotify=6
scPosleasesTimeout=10
scPosleasesChecktime=40
```

To enable the service, activate the *Service Enabled* option. Save the configuration by clicking the *Add Service* button.

To modify a service, select it in the list, modify any value and click *Update Service*. To delete a device, select it in the list and click *Delete Service*.

When the services configuration is finished, click *Return to BS Configuration*.

NOTE: Ommiting posleases Service

The posleases can be ommited. Then the object is generated during the Branch Server initialization with default values (see Section B.3.2, "posInitBranchserver" (page 267)).

4.8.1.2 BranchServer Network Configuration

To configure Branch Server network, click the *BranchServer Network Configuration* button.

Enter *BranchServer Hostname*, *BranchServer Network Address*, *BranchServer Network Mask*, *BranchServer Default Gateway*, *DHCP Fixed IP Range*, and *DHCP Dynamic IP Range*.

The *BranchServer Network Cards* list contains all configured Branch Server network cards. To add a new card, select *add new network card* in the list, enter *NIC Device Name* (for example `eth1`) and *NIC IP Address*, and click *Add Device*. To modify a device, select it in the list, modify any value and click *Update Device*. To delete a device, select it in the list and click *Delete Device*.

When the network configuration is finished, click *Return to BS Configuration*.

4.8.2 Images Configuration

The *Images Configuration* tab lists all registered local and global images. Select an image in the list to edit its properties. Save any changes by clicking the *Update Image* button. To delete an image from the list, click *Remove Image from List*. To add a new image, select *<add new image>* in the list and click *Add Image*.

For each image, select whether it is a *Global Image* or *BranchServer Local Image*. Enter *Image Name*, *Image Version*, and the path to the *Image File*.

If the *Advanced Mode* is activated, you can enter *Image Password* and *DHCP Options* and blockize.

For each image a list of configuration templates and its management is available.

4.8.3 CashRegisters Configuration

The *CashRegisters Configuration* tab lists all known local and global POS terminals (CashRegisters), as well as terminals defined by their roles. Select a terminal in the list to edit its properties. Save any changes by clicking the *Update CashRegister* button. To delete a terminal from the list, click *Remove CR from List*. To add a new terminal, select *<add new CR>* in the list and click *Add CashRegister*.

For each terminal, select whether it is a *Global CR* or *Local CR*. If global and/or local roles are enabled and roles are registered in the *BranchServer Configuration* tab, you can also select *Role CR* for a terminal defined by its role. In such a case, select the needed role from the list of known roles on the right.

Enter *CashRegister Name* and select the *Associate Image* from the list of images registered in the *Images Configuration* tab.

If the *Advanced Mode* is activated, you can enter *Raid Scheme* definition and/or enable disk journaling.

For each terminal, lists of associated disks and configuration templates and their management are available.

4.8.4 Finalization

Use the *Generate configuration* button to create the SLEPOS XML file. Before generating the file, the configured data are checked. You will be asked where to save the generated XML file.

If the *Update LDAP after generation* option is checked, the `posAdmin --import --type XML --file generated_xml_file` command is automatically called after the XML file is generated.

If the *Generate OIF after LDAP modify* option is checked, the `posAdmin --generate --base branchserver_DN` command is automatically called after the XML file is imported into the LDAP database.

Setting Up a Branch Server

5

The Branch Server provides the network boot and system management infrastructure for the SUSE® Linux Enterprise Point of Service terminals as well as a generic system platform for instore applications, such as database systems and back-ends for the Point of Service applications.

The Branch Server can be installed in two modes, online or offline. The online installation mode requires an internet connection to the Administration Server. If no internet connection to the Administration Server is available, use the offline installation mode.

If you intend to set up a high-availability Branch Server, check out the High Availability Guide, available from `http://www.novell.com/documentation/sles11/`.

NOTE: Setting Up a POSBranch Server

In the NLPOS9, a specialized POSBranch image was needed to setup a Branch Server running on Point of Service hardware. There is no need for such a specialized POSBranch image now. The Branch Server can now be directly installed on POS hardware.

NOTE: System Requirements

For a list of system requirements to set up an Branch Server, refer to Section 1.2.3, "Branch Server" (page 4).

Before configuring a Branch Server, check if the following conditions are met:

- The `Branch Server` pattern must be installed on the machine to be configured. If it is missing, install it. For more information about SLEPOS11 installation, see Chapter 2, *SUSE Linux Enterprise Point of Service Installation* (page 17).

- The Administration Server and its LDAP database must be configured and initialized as described in Chapter 4, *Setting Up the Administration Server* (page 29). For more information about LDAP database configuration and initialization, see Section 4.2, "Initializing the LDAP Directory with `posInitAdminserver`" (page 32).

- Either internet connection to the Administration Server or the offline installation package must be available. If an internet connection is available, follow the procedure described in Section 5.2.1, "Online Branch Server Configuration" (page 66). If the offline installation package is available, follow the procedure described in Section 5.2.2, "Offline Branch Server Configuration" (page 68).

5.1 Branch Server Network Configuration

SLEPOS offers three ways to configure the network on a Branch Server:

1. LDAP-based,

2. Branch Server-based,

3. predefined defaults.

5.1.1 LDAP-Based Network Configuration

The Branch Server network is configured based on the settings defined in LDAP. This mode is selected when all of the following conditions are met:

1. The Branch Server's object scLocation attributes ipNetworkNumber and ipNetworkMask differ from 0.0.0.0.

2. Either one scNetworkcard is defined under scLocation object or one NIC is left unconfigured on Branch Server.

3. scNetworkcard attribute scDevice matches one of the Branch Server's NIC.

4. scNetworkcard attribute ipHostNumber differs from 0.0.0.0.

`posInitBranchServer` then automatically updates network configuration and basic DNS configuration. When `posInitBranchServer` is about to overwrite a manual configuration, user confirmation is requested. If it is running in noninteractive mode, permission to overwrite is granted automatically.

5.1.2 Branch Server-Based Network Configuration

The Branch Server's NICs are manually configured on the Branch Server. This mode is selected when all of the following conditions are met:

1. Branch Server's object scLocation attributes ipNetworkNumber and ipNetworkMask equal 0.0.0.0.

2. One scNetworkcard is defined under scLocation object and its scDevice attribute matches one of the manually configured NICs on the Branch Server, or there is only one manually configured NIC on the Branch Server, which matches one of scNetworkCards scDevice attributes.

3. scNetworkcard attribute ipHostNumber equals 0.0.0.0.

`posInitBranchServer` then updates the LDAP configuration to match the current BranchServer configuration and updates the basic DNS configuration.

5.1.3 Predefined Network Configuration

The Branch Server's NICs are configured according to the SLEPOS defaults. This mode is selected when all of the following conditions are met:

1. Branch Server's object scLocation attributes ipNetworkNumber and ipNetworkMask equal 0.0.0.0.

2. One scNetworkcard is defined under scLocation object and its scDevice attribute matches one unconfigured NIC on the Branch Server, or there is only one unconfigured NIC on the Branch Server, which matches one of the scNetworkCards scDevice attributes.

3. scNetworkcard attribute ipHostNumber equals 0.0.0.0.

When basically no information about the network is set, `posInitBranchServer` configures NICs and updates LDAP databases with a configuration based on SLEPOS defaults:

```
scLocation attributes:
  scNetworkNumber   = '192.168.1.0'
  scNetworkMask     = '255.255.255.0'
  scDhcpRange       = '192.168.1.10,192.168.1.54'
  scDhcpFixedRange  = '192.168.1.55,192.168.1.88'
  scDefaultGw       = '192.168.1.1'
scNetworkcard attribute
  ipHostNumber = '192.168.1.1'
```

5.2 Configuring Branch Server with the posInitBranchserver Command

The `posInitBranchserver` command is provided for the Branch Server configuration.

5.2.1 Online Branch Server Configuration

The following procedure describes the installation process of a SUSE Linux Enterprise Point of Service11 Branch Server if an Internet connection to the Administration Server is used:

1 Execute the `posInitBranchserver` command.

The `posInitBranchserver` command asks for the installation mode to be used. For the default online installation enter 1 or just press Enter.

2 Provide the required information. Enter the organization/company name (`organization`), organizational unit (`organizationalUnit`) and location/branch name (`scLocation`) as initialized on the Administration Server (and as specified in the LDAP database). Enter the resolvable and connectible name or the IP address of the Administration Server. Enter the Branch Server password defined when the `scLocation` object was created using `posAdmin` on the Administration Server.

It is possible to use nested organizational units, for example:
`cn=mybranch,ou=mysuborgunit,ou=myorgunit,o=myorg,c=us.`

To enter nested organizational units to `posInitBranchserver`, use the dot notation: `mysuborgunit.myorgunit`.

3 The script checks resolvability of the Administration Server IP address and tries to download Administration Server certificates. The certificates are then used for automatic establishment of encrypted SSL communication. If no certificates are found, an unencrypted communication is used.

IMPORTANT: Administration Server's rsync Port Must Be Open

Make sure the rsync port (usually 873) is open on the Administration Server. The rsync port is not open in the default SLES11 installation. You have to add it by entering its number in the YaST *Firewall* module under *Allowed Services > Advanced > TCP Ports*.

IMPORTANT: Branch Server's tftp Port Must Be Open

Make sure the tftp port (usually 69) is open on the Branch Server. This port is not open in the default SLES11 installation. You have to add it by adding its number in the YaST *Firewall* module under *Allowed Services > Advanced > TCP Ports*. If ftp is used, the ftp ports must be open.

If an Administration Server certificate is found, you are asked to acknowledge its fingerprint and validate it.

4 The script asks if you want to create and use a local branch LDAP database on the Branch Server. It contains a copy of the subtree from the Administration Server LDAP database which corresponds to this Branch Server. This is part of the SUSE Linux Enterprise Point of Service11 offline functionality feature. The recommended default setting is `yes`.

If your choice is `yes`, the script initializes a local branch LDAP database. If your choice is `no`, enter the hostname or IP address of an already initialized LDAP database.

5 The script issues a command to start LDAP SyncRelp replication to create a copy of the branch subtree from the Administration Server's LDAP database.

6 If everything is in order, the script finds the Branch Server domain in the Administration Server's LDAP database and prints information about the found domain.

7 The script asks for a final confirmation before it configures and starts the core Branch Server services.

8 If everything is in order, the script finishes successfully. If an error occurs, it is reported and logged in syslog.

NOTE: Aborting the Command

If you select `no` in any configuration step (except when selecting not to use a local branch LDAP), the script deletes all its intermediate data and exits.

5.2.2 Offline Branch Server Configuration

The following procedure describes the installation process of a SUSE Linux Enterprise Point of Service 11 Branch Server if no Internet connection to the Administration Server is used:

1 Preferably, execute `posInitBranchserver -f` *pathToOfflineInstallationFile*. You can also execute the `posInitBranchserver` command without options and select 2 when asked for the installation mode to be used.

2 Provide the required information. Enter the organization/company name (`organization`), organizational unit (`organizationalUnit`) and location/ branch name (`scLocation`) as initialized on the Administration Server (and as specified in the LDAP database). Enter the resolvable and connectible name or the IP address of the Administration Server. Enter the Branch Server password defined when the `scLocation` object was created using `posAdmin` on the Administration Server.

If an offline installation file was provided in the first step, the default values from the file are used.

3 In the offline installation mode, the script does not check resolvability of the Administration Server IP address. Server certificates are copied from the offline installation file, if present.

If an Administration Server certificate is found, you are asked to acknowledge its fingerprint and validate it. SSL communication is then automatically established. If no certificate is found, unencrypted communication is used.

4 The script asks if you want to create and use a local branch LDAP database on the Branch Server. It contains a copy of the subtree from the Administration Server LDAP database which corresponds to this Branch Server. This is a part of the SUSE Linux Enterprise Point of Service11 offline functionality feature. The recommended default setting is `yes`.

If you select `yes`, the script initializes a local branch LDAP database. If you select `no`, enter the hostname or IP address of an already-initialized LDAP database.

5 The script initializes the local branch LDAP database using the `ldapadd` command from the offline installation file.

6 In offline installation mode, it is not yet possible to find the Branch Server domain. Therefore, if there is no Internet connection, the attempt fails and the script terminates. However if there is a connection to the Administration Server, the script finds the Branch Server domain in the Administration Server's LDAP database and prints information about the found domain.

7 The script asks for a final confirmation before it configures and starts the core Branch Server services.

8 If everything is in order, the script finishes successfully. If an error occurs, it is reported and logged in syslog.

NOTE: Aborting the Command

If you select `no` in any configuration step (except when you select not to use a local branch LDAP), the script deletes all its intermediate data and exits.

NOTE: Administration and Branch Server Combination

If the Administration and Branch Servers are being configured on a single machine, no certificates are used and the SSL communication is disabled.

Also, there is no local branch LDAP database created, as the offline functionality is not needed.

5.2.2.1 Creating an Offline Installation Package

If you want to initialize an offline Branch Server without any Internet connection, create an offline installation package:

1 To create an offline installation package, use:

```
posAdmin
--base scLocationDN
--generate
```

For example, for the `cn=mybranch,ou=myorgunit,o=myorg,c=us` branch, use:

```
posAdmin
--base cn=mybranch,ou=myorgunit,o=myorg,c=us
--generate
```

2 The generated offline installation package is located in the `/var/share/SLEPOS/OIF/scLocationDN.tgz` file. For the company mentioned earlier, the file name would be `/usr/share/SLEPOS/OIF/mybranch.myorgunit.myorg.us`.

5.2.2.2 Transferring System Image Files

If there is no network connection between Administration Server and Branch Server, the system image files must be copied from the Administration Server to the Branch Server manually.

Boot images must be copied from the `/srv/SLEPOS/boot/` directory on the Administration Server to the `/srv/tftpboot/boot/` directory on the Branch Server and then put to production using the `possyncimages --local` command.

System images and their associated MD5 checksum files must be copied from `/srv/SLEPOS/image/` on the Administration Server to `/srv/tftpboot/image` on the Branch Server and then put to production using the `possyncimages --local` command.

5.2.3 Changing the Branch Server Password

Before attempting to change the Branch Server password, ensure that the following conditions are met and understood:

- The Branch Server is already initialized.

- The Branch Server is in online mode and the Administration Server's LDAP is available.

- The Branch Server's local LDAP will be restarted during the procedure.

When you are ready to proceed with changing the password, call `posInitBranchServer -p` or `posInitBranchServer --chpasswd`.

You will be asked to enter the old Branch Server password then the new Branch Server password twice. After changing the password, the system will perform a password validation and inform you of the result.

In case of problems, see Section 12.3.3, "Problems with Changing the Branch Server Password" (page 241).

5.3 Distributing Images to the Branch Server

If you want to create a new image or change an image version, run the `possyncimages` command at the Branch Server. This transfers new or updated images to the Branch Server after the images have been added to the Administration Server's RSYNC directory.

IMPORTANT: rsync Service and LDAP Objects

The rsync service must be properly configured and running on the Administration Server for the `possynimages` command to run. For more information, see Section 4.6.1.3, "Adding an `scServerContainer` and `scBranchServer` Objects" (page 40).

Additionally, each system image has an associated `scPosImage` object in LDAP. The object's `scPosImageVersion` attribute should be set to active or a relevant `scImageVersion` object must be created to keep track of the most recent image version and state before `possyncimages` transfers the images to the Branch Server. For more information, see Section 4.6.2.8, "Activating Images" (page 52).

The basic process is as follows:

1 Via the PID file, the `possyncimages` command initially checks if an instance is already running.

2 The image files are then copied from the Administration Server to the Branch Server. Boot images are copied from the `/srv/SLEPOS/boot/` directory on the Administration Server to the `/srv/tftpboot/boot/` directory on the Branch Server. System images and their associated MD5 checksum files are copied from `/srv/SLEPOS/image/` to `/srv/tftpboot/image`.

`possyncimages` downloads the base images first but later prefers downloading the deltas instead of full images. Full images are recreated on the Branch Server in `/srv/SLEPOS`.

During this process, the TFTP server must be stopped or otherwise prevented from transmitting the image files to clients.

For more information on the `possyncimages` command, see Section B.3.9, "possyncimages" (page 276).

After executing the `possyncimages` command, verify the result by checking the contents of the following directories:

- `/srv/tftpboot/image`

- `/srv/tftpboot/boot`

5.3.1 Controlling the List of Images Downloaded by Branch Server

The `scLocation` object can have a multivalue `scSynchronizedImagesDn` attribute, which contains a list of `scPosImage` or `scCashRegister` DNs. The `possyncimages` command downloads only the listed images or the images used on listed terminals. If one `scPosImage` object points to multiple image versions, the command downloads all active ones. An empty list means that all images have been downloaded. The list can be edited with `posAdmin`.

5.4 Starting the posleases2ldap Core Script

Start the core script (`posleases2ldap`) as a daemon process on the Branch Server. The core script is responsible for registering any new Point of Service terminals at the LDAP directory and transferring image install notification data to the LDAP directory on the Administration Server.

- To verify that `posleases2ldap` is currently running, execute the following command:

  `rcposleases2ldap status`

- To manually start the `posleases2ldap` service, execute the following command:

  `rcposleases2ldap start`

- To ensure the Branch Server automatically starts the core script at boot time, execute the following command:

  `insserv posleases2ldap`

5.5 Starting the posASWatch Service

The `posASWatch` command checks if the Administration server is available. It also checks the status of LDAP Sync replication and the `posleases2ldap` core service. The service is started with the `rcposASWatch start` command and stopped with the `rcposASWatch stop` command. To check the service status, use the `rcposASWatch status` command.

IMPORTANT: Start the Service Manually

To ensure that local LDAP contains valid data (if the Branch Server and Administration Server are installed on different machines), you need to start the service after the Branch Server is restarted. The service is *NOT* configured to start automatically by default. If the service is not running and the network connection to the Administration Server is down, the Branch Server is unable to function properly.

To ensure that the Branch Server starts the `posASWatch` command automatically at boot time, execute the `insserv posASWatch` command.

NOTE: When the `posASWatch` Service is Not Required

The `posASWatch` service is needed when the network connection to the Administration Server is down. If the Administration Server is never used or the Administration Server and the Branch Server are combined on one machine, this service is not required. When the machine hosting both servers is configured and an attempt to start the service is made, the service will exit with an error message.

5.6 Installing a Branch Server Using a Specialized Image

Instead of installing Branch Servers using the standard method (installing SLES with the SLEPOS addon and manual configuration of the Branch Server), it is possible to build a Branch Server image using Image Creator or KIWI.

The image building process is the same as for terminal images. The image boot defaults to "oemboot" with the "install_stick" option. The result is an USB image, which offers installation to a hard disk during first boot. Other boot methods can be configured according to the KIWI manual.

The provided image is suitable for the online installation, where the terminal images and LDAP data are downloaded from the Administration Server. For offline installation, the terminal images and OIF files must be added to the Branch Server image before building. The OIF files of one or more branches must be added to the

`/usr/share/SLEPOS/OIF` of the image (`/var/lib/SLEPOS/system/images/branchserver-3.4.0/root/usr/share/SLEPOS/OIF`). You can also copy the terminal images from Administration Server's `/srv/SLEPOS` to `/var/lib/SLEPOS/system/images/branchserver-3.4.0/root/srv/SLEPOS`.

When the Branch Server image boots, it is necessary to configure one network interface card for connecting to the Administration Server, the other one can remain unconfigured. Then it offers offline installation based on the selected OIF file or online installation.

Booting Point of Service Terminals

6

Point of Service terminals are the end point in the SUSE® Linux Enterprise Point of Service architecture. They provide customer service functions or bank teller workstations.

For booting special images (for example for BIOS update), see Section 7.3, "Booting Special Images on Terminals" (page 114).

6.1 Conditions to Add a Point of Service Terminal

The process of adding a Point of Service terminal to a SUSE Linux Enterprise Point of Service system consists of these four steps:

1. The POS machine connected to the Branch Server is started and downloads the boot image.

2. The POS machine uploads the `hwtype.`*`MAC.`*`HASH` file (for example `hwtype.00:11:25:A7:D6:0D`) into the `/srv/tftpboot/upload` directory.

3. The `posleases2ldap` command uses this file and the information in the LDAP database to create the `config.`*`MAC`* file (for example `config.00:11:25:A7:D6:0D`) in the `/srv/tftpboot/KIWI` directory.

4. The POS machine uses the information in the `config.MAC` file to load the correct image and boot up.

The third step is the most important part of this process. The following conditions must be met to complete it successfully:

- The `hwtype.MAC.HASH` file must be present in the `/srv/tftpboot/upload` directory.

NOTE: Configuration Without an External DHCP Server

If no external DHCP server is used, the terminal must get the IP address from the DHCP server on the Branch Server (its MAC address must be listed in the `/var/lib/dhcp/db/dhcpd.leases` file).

This occurs when the system was set by `posInitBranchserver` with `EXT_DHCP=FALSE` in the LDAP database under `scLocation` corresponding to this Branch Server.

- The correct image file and its checksum file must be located on the Branch Server in the `/srv/tftpboot/image` directory. These files must be downloaded from the Administration Server in advance. For more information, see Section 5.3, "Distributing Images to the Branch Server" (page 71).

Example 6.1: *Example Image and Checksum Files*

```
/srv/tftpboot/image/myGraphical_test.i686-3.1.4
/srv/tftpboot/image/myGraphical_test.i686-3.1.4.md5
```

- An associated object representing the used image file must exist in the LDAP database.

Image objects are typically located in the global container under the default `scDisributionContainer`. To add the image to the default `scDisributionContainer` use these commands:

```
posAdmin --base cn=default,cn=global,o=myorg,c=us
--add --scPosImage --cn myGraphical
--scImageName myTestGraphical
--scDhcpOptionsRemote /boot/pxelinux.0 --scDhcpOptionsLocal LOCALBOOT
--scImageFile myGraphical_test.i686
--scBsize 8192
```

```
posAdmin --base cn=myGraphical,cn=default,cn=global,o=myorg,c=us
--add --scImageVersion --scDisabled FALSE --scVersion 3.4.2
```

However, each set of system images built against a specific Linux kernel and initrd
must have their own corresponding scDistributionContainer object in
the LDAP database. Therefore, if you are adding a system image built against
a new Linux kernel version or initrd, it is necessary to create the corresponding
scDisributionContainer object.

- An associated object representing the cash register must exist in the LDAP
  database. This scCashRegister object can either represent a specific machine
  or a generic machine. The generic object is used if a specific image is not found
  for the given machine. In both cases, the scCashRegister must have a
  hardware subobject like scRamDisk or scHarddisk, which specifies where
  and how the image should be deployed.

The name of a machine is located in the uploaded hwtype.MAC.HASH file under
the HWTYPE entry.

To add a scCashRegister object for a specific machine (with
HWTYPE=cshr4152) use the command:

```
posAdmin --base cn=global,o=myorg,c=us
--add --scCashRegister --cn cr-test --
scCashRegisterName cshr4152 --scPosImageDn
cn=myGraphical,cn=default,cn=global,o=myorg,c=us
```

Note the scCashRegisterName name and image reference in --
scPosImageDn).

When deploying to a hard disk (detected on terminal as /dev/sda device) of this
specific machine, use these commands:

```
posAdmin --base cn=cshr4152,cn=global,o=myorg,c=us
--add --scHarddisk --cn sda --scDevice /dev/sda --scHdSize 9000

posAdmin --base cn=sda,cn=cshr4152,cn=global,o=myorg,c=us
--add --scPartition --scPartNum 0 --scPartType 82 --scPartMount x --
scPartSize 1000

posAdmin --base cn=sda,cn=cshr4152,cn=global,o=myorg,c=us
--add --scPartition --scPartNum 1 --scPartType 83 --scPartMount '/' --
scPartSize 7000
```

When deploying to a RAM disk of this specific machine, use this command:

```
posAdmin --base cn=cshr4152,cn=global,o=myorg,c=us --
add --scRamDisk --cn ram --scDevice /dev/ram1
```

To add a scCashRegister object for a generic machine use this command:

```
posAdmin --base cn=global,o=myorg,c=us --
add --scCashRegister --cn cr-test-default --
scCashRegisterName default --scPosImageDn
cn=myGraphical,cn=default,cn=global,o=myorg,c=us
```

(Note the scCashRegisterName name.)

When deploying to a harddisk of a generic machine, use these commands:

```
posAdmin --base cn=cr-test-default,cn=global,o=myorg,c=us
--add --scHarddisk --cn sda --scDevice /dev/sda --scHdSize 9000
```

```
posAdmin --base cn=sda,cn=cr-test-default,cn=global,o=myorg,c=us
--add --scPartition --scPartNum 0 --scPartType 82 --scPartMount x --
scPartSize 1000
```

```
posAdmin --base cn=sda,cn=cr-test-default,cn=global,o=myorg,c=us
--add --scPartition --scPartNum 1 --scPartType 83 --scPartMount '/' --
scPartSize 7000
```

When deploying to a RAM disk of the generic machine, use this command:

```
posAdmin --base cn=cr-test-
default,cn=global,o=myorg,c=us --add --scRamDisk --cn
ram --scDevice /dev/ram1
```

- The posleases2ldap process is started and running.

If all conditions are fulfilled, the new config.MAC is created or overwritten and the uploaded file hwinfo.MAC deleted at the time the posleases2ldap checks the upload directory.

The generated config.MAC file should contain lines reflecting the values in the LDAP database. The IP address is the address of the TFTP service specified in ipHostNumber under the TFTP scService object in the scBranchserver in the relevant scLocation.

If deploying to a hard drive, the following lines should be present:

```
IMAGE=/dev/sda2;myGraphical_test;3.1.4;192.168.90.1;8192
PART=1000;82;x,8000;83;/
DISK=/dev/sda
```

If deploying to a RAM disk, the following line should be present:

```
IMAGE=/dev/ram1;myGraphical_test;3.1.4;192.168.90.1;8192
```

NOTE: Booting with Roles

If roles are used, the booting process is different. See Section 9.3, "API Description" (page 151) for more details.

6.2 Hardware

Point of Service terminals are implemented in a variety of hardware. The primary difference of Point of Service hardware is whether the terminal has an internal hard drive or other persistent media (such as a flash drive), or whether the terminal is diskless. A system that has a hard disk can be configured to store the image on a disk partition instead of a RAM disk so it can boot from the hard disk if it cannot boot over the network.

6.2.1 Hardware Configuration Files

Point of Service terminal hardware configuration information is either stored in LDAP, as `scConfigFileTemplate` objects, or on the Administration Server as a file in the `/srv/SLEPOS/config/` directory and get distributed via rsync. These hardware configuration files must have a corresponding `scConfigFileSyncTemplate` object in the LDAP directory.

NOTE: Point of Service Configuration Files

The hardware configuration files discussed in this section should not be confused with `config.MAC` Point of Service configuration files. The `config.MAC` files contain the parameters required to configure a Point of Service terminal during a network PXE or hard disk boot. For more information, see Section 6.3.1, "The config.MAC File" (page 83).

The `scConfigFileTemplate` and `scConfigFileSyncTemplate` objects are located in LDAP under the `scPosImage` or `scCashRegister` objects. In addition to providing Point of Service hardware configuration information, they specify which configuration file a Point of Service terminal should download from the Branch Server at boot time. For information on creating these objects in the LDAP directory, see Section 4.6.2.4, "Adding an `scConfigFileTemplate` Object" (page 48) or Section 4.6.2.1, "Adding an `scCashRegister` Object" (page 44).

The Branch Server initially acquires the hardware configuration information for its local Point of Service terminals in one of the following ways:

- `posleases2ldap` reads the configuration information stored in the `scConfigFileTemplate` object in LDAP and creates a configuration file in the `/srv/tftpboot/KIWI/`*MAC*`/` directory on the Branch Server. The hardware configuration file is then distributed to the appropriate Point of Service terminal at boot time.

- `posleases2ldap` reads where the configuration file is located in the `scConfigFileSyncTemplate` object, then triggers an rsync call to download the configuration file from the Administration Server. The configuration file is stored in the `/srv/tftpboot/KIWI/`*MAC*`/` directory on the Branch Server so it can be distributed to the appropriate Point of Service terminal at boot time.

You do not have to do anything to initiate these processes except to start the `posleases2ldap` service on the Branch Server after installation.

However, if the terminal's hardware configuration information changes after its initial registration, you must manually run either `pos dump-all` or `pos dump-ws --workstation` *name or MAC* to update the hardware configuration information on the Branch Server. These commands regenerate the hardware configuration and `config.`*MAC* files for all Point of Service terminals found in LDAP.

For more information on the `pos` command, see Section B.3.12, "pos" (page 279).

6.2.2 Graphical Display Configuration

The graphics controller depends on the model type, so it can be derived from static tables. Some Point of Service terminals can use multihead X configurations. The corresponding `xorg.conf` files are manufacturer-specific and are not provided as part of the SUSE Linux Enterprise Point of Service software package.

6.2.3 Using a Terminal with Multiple Network Interfaces

SLEPOS now supports terminals having more than one network interface (for example WiFi and LAN or more than one LAN). During registration and subsequent boots, the list of all interfaces is retrieved and LDAP updated (attribute `macAddress` of the `scWorkstation object`). This ensures that `config.MAC` files, MAC directories and specific pxe files are correctly created (or linked) for all interfaces, so the machine can freely use any of then to boot.

MAC interfaces cannot be directly interchanged between workstations, because the workstation is identified by them. To accomplish this, a two step procedure is needed: the MAC(s) of the interface(s) to be exchanged must first be deregistred, by removing the interface(s) from the machine(s) and rebooting the machine(s). The `posleases2ldap` script then removes the MAC(s) from the workstation's LDAP data. After that, they can be reused, so the interface(s) can be moved into another machine(s).

6.3 Point of Service Configuration Files

Each Point of Service terminal has its own configuration file which it loads at boot time. This configuration file determines which hardware drivers and images are loaded on the Point of Service terminal. The following sections describe the configuration files for a Point of Service terminal booted from the network or CD, and the configuration file used to register new Point of Service terminals.

6.3.1 The config.*MAC* File

The `config.MAC` files (where *MAC* is the MAC address of the specific terminal) contain the parameters required to configure a specific Point of Service terminal during a network PXE or hard disk boot. Each Point of Service terminal has its own `config.MAC` file on the Branch Server.

When the Branch Server connects to the Administration Server, it logs into the LDAP directory, accesses the configuration parameters for its registered Point of Service terminals, and stores the information locally as ASCII configuration files (`config.MAC`) in the `/srv/tftpboot/KIWI` directory. At boot time, each Point of Service terminal connects to the Branch Server over TFTP and loads its associated `config.MAC` file.

There is no need to manually create the Point of Service configuration files. When a new Point of Service terminal comes online, its configuration file is automatically created from LDAP entries on the Administration Server.

For more information on this process, see Section 6.3.3, "The hwtype.*MAC.HASH* File" (page 90) and Section B.2, "Core Script Process" (page 264).

To modify a Point of Service configuration file, you must modify the terminal's entries in LDAP and then run the `pos dump-all` command on the Branch Server.

For more information, see Table 10.1, "posAdmin: General Command Line Options" (page 176).

The format of the `config.MAC` file is as follows:

```
IMAGE=device;image;version;srv_ip;bsize;compressed,...,
CONF=source;dest;srv_ip;bsize,...,source;dest;srv_ip;bsize
PART=size;id;mount,...,size;id;mount
JOURNAL=ext3
DISK=device
```

Here is a sample `config.MAC` file:

```
IMAGE=/dev/sda2;minimal.i686;3.5.4;192.168.1.1;4096;compressed
CONF=/KIWI/00:30:05:1D:75:D2/ntp.conf;/etc/
ntp.conf;192.168.1.1;1024;d6b12b7c552ca4cff978fffc0776ab92,
/KIWI/00:30:05:1D:75:D2/xorg.conf;/etc/X11/xorg.conf;
192.168.1.1;1024;ae3b70560b72ab39688b7dba330b766d
PART=500;82;swap,2000;83;/
DISK=/dev/sda
.
.
.
```

The following list provides a detailed description of each parameter in `config.MAC` and its variables.

config.MAC Configuration File Parameters

`IMAGE=`

Specifies which image (*image*) should be loaded with which version (*version*) and to which storage device (*device*) it should be linked.

Multiple image downloads are possible, but the first listed image must be the main system image. If the hard drive is used, a corresponding partitioning must be performed.

device

The storage device to which the image is linked, for example, `/dev/ram1` for a RAM disk, `/dev/sda2` for a hard disk, or `/dev/md1` for RAID.

RAM devices should not be confused with hard disk devices, which use a partition table. On a Point of Service terminal, the partition `sda1` is used for the Linux swap partition and `sda2` defines the root file system (`/`). On the RAM disk device, `/dev/ram0` is used for the initial RAM disk and cannot be used as storage device for the system image. It is recommended to use `/dev/ram1` for the RAM disk.

When RAID is in use, devices have to be referenced as `/dev/md*number*`, starting from zero (not from one as usual when RAID is not used). The `posleases2ldap` script automatically takes care of this if the RAID configuration `scRaidScheme` of the used `scCashRegister` is detected.

image

The name of the image to load on the Point of Service terminal.

version

The version of the image to load on the Point of Service terminal.

srv_ip

The server IP address for the TFTP download.

This variable must always be included in the `IMAGE=` parameter.

bsize

The block size for the TFTP download. If the block size is too small according to the maximum number of data packages (32768), linuxrc automatically calculates a new block size for the download. The maximum block size is 65464 Bytes.

This variable must always be included in the `IMAGE=` parameter.

`compressed`

Specifies that the boot process uses a compressed image. If the `compressed` variable is not included, the standard boot process is used.

The boot fails if you specify `compressed` but the image is not compressed. It also fails if you do not specify `compressed` and the image is compressed.

IMPORTANT: Image Compression

The name of the compressed image must contain the `.gz` suffix and must be compressed with `gzip`.

`CONF=`

Specifies the configuration files to download to the Point of Service terminal. The data is provided in a comma-separated list of *source*:*target* configuration files.

source

The path to the source configuration file on the TFTP server.

dest

The directory on the Point of Service terminal to which you want to download the source configuration file.

srv_ip

The server IP address for the TFTP download, which must always be included in the `CONF=` parameter.

bsize

The block size for the TFTP download. If the block size is too small according to the maximum number of data packages (32768), linuxrc automatically calculates a new block size for the download. The maximum block size is 65464 Bytes. This variable must always be included in the `CONF=` parameter.

md5sum

Contains the md5sum hash of the configuration file.

PART=

Specifies the partitioning data provided in a comma-separated list.

The first element of the list defines the service partition. This partition is used for administration purposes, such as storing the encrypted image before the installation, downloading a new image in the background, or local booting for the wireless terminals.

The second element of the list defines the swap partition. The third element defines the root partition. Each element must include the size (*size*), the type (*id*), and the mount point (*mount*).

NOTE: Formatting Partitions

The fourth and following partitions are not formatted automatically. If these partitions already exist and contain meaningful data, they are not changed in any way and all data on these partitions is preserved. This is useful to keep data between updates. To force formatting of these partitions, increase the size of the third (root) partition.

It is also possible to force formatting of the data partitions (including the service partition, but not the root partition) by using the POS_FORMAT_DATA_PART kernel parameter. By default, data partitions are formatted only when fsck fails with an uncorrectable error. If POS_FORMAT_DATA_PART=yes, data partitions are also formatted if the requested filesystem type is changed. If POS_FORMAT_DATA_PART=force, data partitions are formatted during each boot.

---

size

The size of the partition in MB. If you want the partition to take all the space left on a disk, use a lowercase letter x as the size specification.

id

The partition type: S for swap, L for all others.

mount

The partition mount point, for example: /home.

IMPORTANT: Service Partition

The first (service) partition must be mounted as /srv/SLEPOS.

IMPORTANT: Swap Partition

The swap partition must not contain a mount point. Use a
lowercase letter x instead.

JOURNAL=

> Specifies a journaling file system. The value for this parameter must be set to
> ext3 because that is the only journaling file system SUSE Linux Enterprise
> Point of Service supports.
>
> If you have an existing ext2 image, you can change the file system by setting a
> flag in the scCashRegister or the scWorkstation objects rather than
> recreating the image. If ext3 is specified in either of the LDAP objects, the Point
> of Service terminal extends the file system to ext3 when the image is deployed.
>
> The JOURNAL= parameter is only evaluated if the DISK= parameter is set.

DISK=

> Defines the device through which the hard disk can be addressed, for example: /
> dev/sda. This parameter is only used with PART.

RAID=

> Defines the raid configuration, according to the scRaidScheme attribute of the
> used scCashRegister (in the same format, but separated with semicolons ;).
> When applied, the image device is automatically written on the IMAGE line as /
> dev/md*number*. Only raid1 is supported by KIWI.
>
> Note, that dmraid fake-raid controllers are also supported.

RELOAD_IMAGE=

> If set to yes, this parameter forces the configured image to be loaded from the
> server even if the image on the disk is up-to-date.
>
> If you run pos dump-all or use another method to regenerate the
> config.*MAC* file, it overwrites this optional parameter, which is mainly used
> for debugging purposes. This parameter is only pertinent on disk-based systems.

RELOAD_CONFIG=

> If set to a non-empty string, this parameter forces the config.*MAC* file to be
> loaded from the server.

If you run `pos dump-all` to regenerate the `config.MAC` file, it overwrites this optional parameter, also mainly used for debugging purposes and pertinent only on disk-based systems.

`HWTYPE=`

Hardware type of the terminal, used to determine correct `scCashRegister` object for registration (compared to `scCashRegisterName`).

`POS_HWTYPE_HASH=`

Hash of the hwtype file used for registration (or a message explaining that `pos dump-all` or another method was used).

`KERNELVER=`

The content of `scKernelVersion` of the `scDistributionContainer` containing the used image.

`KERNELMATCH=`

The content of `scKernelMatch` of the `scDistributionContainer` containing the used image.

`KERNELEXP=`

The content of `scKernelExpression` of the `scDistributionContainer` containing the used image.

`WORKSTATION_LDAP_IP=`

IP of the workstation in the LDAP database when the config file was created.

`POS_KERNEL_PARAMS_HASH_VERIFY=`

Hash of additional kernel parameters supplied by `scPxeFileTemplatescPxeFile`.

`PART_PASSWORDS=`

Contains a comma separated list of passwords for the encrypted partition(s). For data partitions, the password is taken from the `scPassword` attribute of the associated `scPartition` object (under the used `scHarddisk`). For the root partition, it contains the password of the system image, according to the `scPassword` attribute of the used `scImageVersion` object.

Specifying * as partition password means that a random password is generated on each boot. This is useful for swap partitions.

`POS_ID=`

Contains the assigned ID.

```
POS_ROLE=
```
Contains the assigned role.

```
POS_HWTYPE_ERR_HASH=
```
Identifies the API client to which the message in `POS_ERR=` applies.

```
POS_ERR=
```
Error message if setting of the role or ID failed or if there was some other general problem preventing the creation of a valid and current config.*MAC*.

```
SUSEMANAGER=
```
Contains semicolon separated hostname to the SUSE Manager and the terminal's SUSE manager registration key.

6.3.2 KIWI isoboot Configuration Files

For more information on creating an isoboot image, see Section 8.2.1, "Understanding the KIWI Configuration" (page 133).

6.3.3 The hwtype.*MAC*.*HASH* File

When a Point of Service terminal comes online for the first time, it does not have a `config.`*MAC* file on the Branch Server. To create this file for the terminal, the system must first register the Point of Service terminal in LDAP. This is done through the Point of Service control file, `hwtype.`*MAC*.*HASH* (where *MAC* is the MAC address of the specific terminal). The Point of Service control file contains the information required to create the terminal's workstation object (`scWorkstation`) in LDAP and determine which image and configuration settings should be included in the terminal's configuration file (`config.`*MAC*).

When role-based mode is active (see Section 9.2.1, "Creating the `scRole` Object" (page 148)) od `scIDPool` is not empty (see Section 9.1, "Using Terminals with IDs" (page 147)), the terminal returns hwtype file with added hash suffix which helps to determine whether the `config.`*MAC* file (via `POS_HWTYPE_HASH` entry) was created as a result of this request. Also, `posleases2ldap` now reads the role and id requests and reacts according to the role-based scheme when creating the resulting `config.`*MAC*.

The Point of Service control file is formatted as follows:

```
HWTYPE=hardware type
HWBIOS=bios version
IPADDR=current IP address of the terminal
POS_ROLE=role selected on the terminal (role based mode)
POS_ID=id selected on the terminal
```

The process used to create the `config.MAC` file from the `hwtype.MAC.HASH` file is as follows:

1. During the Point of Service boot process, the hardware type and BIOS version are detected.

2. Using this information, the `posleases2ldap` command creates the control file `hwtype.MAC.HASH`.

   For more information, see Section B.3.7, "posleases2ldap" (page 274).

3. The linuxrc program uploads `hwtype.MAC.HASH` to the Branch Server's upload directory `/srv/tftpboot/upload`.

NOTE: Uploading the Control File

The control file is uploaded to the TFTP server only when no configuration file (`config.MAC`) exists.

---

4. The hardware type identified in the `hwtype.MAC.HASH` file is compared to the `scCashRegister` objects in the LDAP directory.

   If a match is found, the information in `scCashRegister` and its associated objects is used to create the Point of Service terminal's `scWorkstation` object in LDAP and its `config.MAC` file in the Branch Server's `/srv/tftpboot/KIWI` directory. After the `config.MAC` file is created, the `hwtype.MAC.HASH` file is deleted.

   If the hardware type is unknown, the information in the default `scCashRegister` object is used to create the Point of Service terminal's `scWorkstation` object and `config.MAC` file.

IMPORTANT: Default `scCashRegister` Object

This safety net feature works only if you have configured a designated default `scCashRegister` object in the LDAP directory. For information on defining a default `scCashRegister` object, see Section 4.6.2.1, "Adding an `scCashRegister` Object" (page 44).

For a detailed review of the core scripts involved in this process, see Section B.2, "Core Script Process" (page 264).

When changing the ID or role, the client uploads the `upload/ hwtype.MAC.HASH` file. For more information, see Section 9.3.3, "Changing ID and/or Role" (page 152).

6.4 Booting the Point of Service Terminal

IMPORTANT: Creating LDAP Objects Before Booting

You must create `scCashRegister` and its associated objects before you can boot the Point of Service terminals. For more information, see Section 4.6.2.1, "Adding an `scCashRegister` Object" (page 44).

Typically, when you boot a Point of Service terminal, it will first try to boot from CD or USB-stick. If a CD or USB device is not available, the terminal attempts a network PXE boot. If the network is not available, it boots from the hard drive. You can override this order with the BIOS settings.

The first time you boot the Point of Service terminals, the `posleases2ldap` daemon creates a workstation object (`scWorkstation`) and hardware configuration files for the Point of Service terminals that register on the Branch Server. For more information on this process, see Section 6.3.3, "The hwtype.MAC.HASH File" (page 90).

Figure 6.1, "Point of Service Terminal Boot Process" (page 93) provides a simplified overview of the Point of Service boot process for a network PXE boot, a hard disk boot, and a CD boot.

Figure 6.1: *Point of Service Terminal Boot Process*

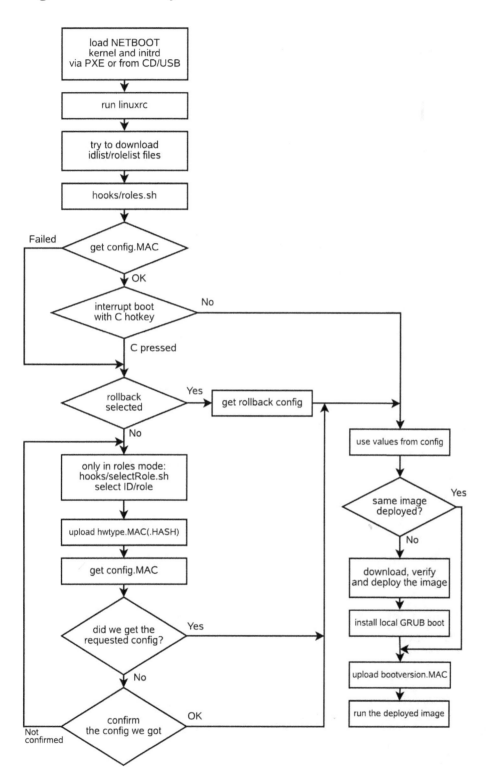

Detailed information about each boot process is provided in the following sections.

6.4.1 Network PXE Boot

To boot Point of Service terminals from the network, the following conditions must be met:

- The terminal must have a network connection to the Branch Server.

- While the TFTP service is set up and started automatically by the `posInitBranchserver` command, you must make sure to open the TFTP port in the firewall on the Branch Server. If the FTP service is used, the FTP port must be open. For more information on Branch Server configuration, see Chapter 5, *Setting Up a Branch Server* (page 63).

- The terminal must have an associated `scCashRegister` object in the LDAP directory. For more information, see Section 4.6.2, "Creating Point of Service Terminal Objects in LDAP" (page 43).

- The Point of Service boot images must be located in the `/srv/tftpboot/boot/` directory on the Branch Server and the system images must be located in the `/srv/tftpboot/image/` directory.

- The Point of Service system images must have an associated `scPosImage` object in the LDAP directory. The image must be activated. For more information on activating images, see Section 4.6.2.8, "Activating Images" (page 52). For more information, see Section 4.6.2.6, "Adding an `scPosImage` Object" (page 51).

If these conditions are met, the Point of Service terminal can successfully boot from the network.

The following is a detailed description of what takes place when a Point of Service terminal boots from the network:

1. The Point of Service terminal makes a DHCP request.

2. In the boot configuration file, which defaults to `pxelinux.cfg/default`, the boot parameters are defined. There is specified where the kernel and the initrd are located. The terminal downloads these files.

   The initrd (or initrd.gz) becomes the first bootstrap environment.

3. The Point of Service terminal downloads the Linux kernel from the `netboot` image which consists of several files (the Linux kernel and a symbolic link, the initrd, and the initrd's md5sum), for example:

```
initrd-netboot-suse-SLES11.i686-2.1.1.splash.gz
initrd-netboot-suse-SLES11.i686-2.1.1.kernel.3.0.8-0.11-default
initrd-netboot-suse-SLES11.i686-2.1.1.kernel
initrd-netboot-suse-SLES11.i686-2.1.1.splash.md5
```

The naming scheme of the kernel is `initrd-netboot-suse-SLES11.`*`architecture-image_version`*`.kernel.`*`kernel_version-flavour`*. The Linux kernel is used to PXE boot the Point of Service terminals.

4. Using PXE network boot or boot manager (GRUB), the Point of Service terminal boots the initrd (for example, `initrd-netboot-suse-SLES11.i686-2.1.1.splash.gz`) which it receives from the Branch Server.

   If no PXE boot is possible, the Point of Service terminal tries to boot via hard disk, if accessible.

5. The `linuxrc` script begins.

6. The file systems required to receive system data are mounted, for example the `/proc` file system.

7. The Point of Service hardware type (`hwtype`) is detected.

   The Point of Service hardware manufacturer provides a program to do this. The first time the Point of Service terminal boots, this information is used to register the Point of Service terminal and create the terminal's `config.`*`MAC`* file. This information is also used to determine which configuration files the terminal should use.

8. The Point of Service BIOS version (`hwbios`) is detected. The Point of Service hardware manufacturer provides a program to do this.

9. Network support is activated. The required kernel module is determined from a static table by selecting the entry corresponding to the hardware type. If no known hardware type is detected, a default list of modules is used and types are tried one after the other. Forcing loading a driver is possible using boot parameters such as `kiwikernelmodule=ide-disk`.

10The module is loaded using `modprobe`. Any dependencies to other modules are resolved at that time.

11The network interface is set up via DHCP.

12After the interface has been established, the DHCP variables are exported to the `/var/lib/dhcpcd/dhcpcd-eth0.info` file and the contents of DOMAIN and DNS are used to generate an `/etc/resolv.conf` file.

13The TFTP server address is acquired.

During this step, a check is made to determine whether the hostname `tftp.`*DOMAIN* can be resolved. If not, the DHCP server is used as the TFTP server.

Forcing another TFTP server is possible with a kernel parameter such as `kiwitftp=`*IP_ADDRESS* or if you set this kernel parameter in the `pxelinux.cfg/default` file.

14The idlist and the first available rolelist (`rolelist.`*MAC*, `rolelist.`*hwtype*, `rolelist.default`) is downloaded and the role mode is activated.

The Point of Service configuration file, `config.`*MAC*, is loaded from the Branch Server's `/srv/tftpboot/KIWI` directory over TFTP.

If the Point of Service terminal boots for the first time, its `config.`*MAC* file does not exist yet. The Point of Service terminal must first register on the system.

If the role mode is activated and it is the first boot, the role and ID menu is displayed. If the role mode is activated but it is not the first boot, the `Press C to change ID/role` message is displayed. If the C key is pressed, the role and ID menu is displayed.

A new Point of Service terminal registers as follows:

a. A Point of Service control file (`hwtype.`*MAC.HASH*) is uploaded to the TFTP server's upload directory: `/srv/tftpboot/upload`.

The `hwtype.`*MAC.HASH* file indicates the Point of Service hardware type and the BIOS version. The `hwtype.`*MAC.HASH* file is uploaded during first boot or when the role or ID is changed. If role mode is activated, the `hwtype.`*MAC.hash* is uploaded (for more information, see Section 9.3,

"API Description" (page 151). The system uses this information to create the terminal's `config.`*`MAC`* file. For more information on this process, see Section 6.3.3, "The hwtype.*MAC.HASH* File" (page 90).

    b. After the upload, the Point of Service terminal renews the DHCP lease file (`dhcpcd -n`).

    c. The Point of Service terminal attempts to load its new `config.`*`MAC`* file from the TFTP server.

    d. If the `config.`*`MAC`* file is not yet available, the Point of Service terminal waits several seconds before repeating the two previous steps.

15. When the `config.`*`MAC`* file loads, the system begins an analysis of its contents.

    For more information about the content and file format of the `config.`*`MAC`* file, refer to Section 6.3.1, "The config.*MAC* File" (page 83).

16. The `PART` line in the `config.`*`MAC`* file is analyzed.

    If there is a `PART` line in the configuration file, a check is made using the image version to see whether any local systems need to be updated.

    - If no system update is required, no image download occurs and the Point of Service terminal boots from the hard drive.

    - If a system update is required, the Point of Service terminal's hard disk is partitioned according to the parameters specified in the `PART` line.

17. Indicated images are downloaded with multicast TFTP.

18. If the image is compressed, it is copied then decompressed.

19. The image checksums are verified. If they do not match, the images are downloaded again.

20. The `CONF` line in the Point of Service configuration file is evaluated.

    All the indicated files are loaded from the TFTP server and stored in a `/config/` path. For more information about KIWI configuration, see Section 8.2.1, "Understanding the KIWI Configuration" (page 133).

21. All the userland processes based on the boot image (`dhcpcd -k`) are terminated.

22 The system image is mounted.

23 The configuration files stored in the `/config/` path are copied to the mounted system image.

24 If this is a new image, an `Image Install Notification` occurs. If the terminal boots successfully, this information will be synchronized to the LDAP directory.

   a. The *bootversion.MAC* file is created in `/srv/tftpboot/upload`.

   b. `posleases2ldap` transfers the information to the `scNotifiedImage` attribute in the `scWorkstation` object in LDAP.

25 The system switches to the mounted system image.

26 The root file system is converted to the system image using `pivot_root`.

   All the required configuration files are now present because they have been stored in the system image or have been downloaded via TFTP.

   The file systems that are mounted read-only can be stored in cramfs-compressed RAM file systems to save Point of Service RAM resources.

27 The boot image is unmounted using an exec umount call.

28 When linuxrc or the exec call terminates, the kernel initiates the init process, which starts processing the boot scripts as specified in `/etc/inittab`.

6.4.2 Booting System Images with Kexec

System images can also be booted using Kexec. The advantage of using Kexec is the possibility to use a boot image kernel and system image kernel with different versions. There is no need to reboot on the first installation of the terminal. Also, it allows the standard SLES boot process. The disadvatage is the slower boot with forced Kexec.

Kexec is used by default when the kernel version does not match. Kexec can also be forced by setting FORCE_KEXEC to a non-empty string on the boot kernel command line. For more information about setting kernel command-line parameters, see Section 9.6, "Specifying Kernel Command Line Options for Selected Terminals" (page 162).

When using Kexec, the system image must contain the `kexec-tools` package.

The booting procedure with Kexec follows these steps:

1 The boot image (kernel+initrd) is started from PXE.

2 the system image is downloaded and deployed.

3 The configuration (initrd, grub) for the kernel from the system image is generated.

4 The kernel from the system image is started with Kexec, then the standard SLES boot process continues.

6.4.3 Booting Scenarios Using Netboot Image

This section describes the typical booting scenarios using the netboot image.

Figure 6.2: *Booting Scenarios Using Netboot Image*

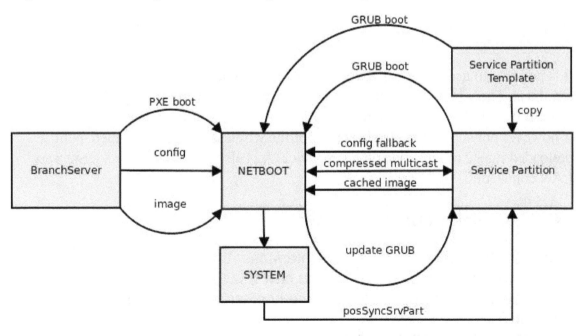

6.4.3.1 Normal PXE Boot (without a service partition)

This is the typical booting scenario using the netboot image with terminals connected over wired network and service partition is not used:

1 PXE boot from Branch Server

2 Init network

3 Download config from Branch Server

4 Download image from Branch Server

5 Install GRUB on system image

6 Image boot

In case of the Branch Server failure, the procedure is as follows:

1 PXE boot from Branch Server fails

2 GRUB boot from system image

6.4.3.2 WiFi boot (using a service partition)

It is possible to use wireless networks (Wi-Fi) to connect wireless SLEPOS terminals. The wireless support must be added when building images. The wireless support is included only in the netboot image – PXE booting via wireless networks is however not supported. The first boot of the wireless can be performed using a preloaded image or an image on a USB stick. It is also possible to use a temporary LAN connection.

NOTE: Multiple Network Interfaces

If a terminal uses multiple network interfaces (LAN and wireless, for example), a new record in LDAP and new `config.MAC` is created for each interface. All interfaces have the same hostname and IP address assigned by DHCP.

NOTE: Multicast Over Wireless Networks

Most current Wi-Fi networks do not support multicast correctly and switch to the lowest available network speed when multicast TFTP is used. Unless you are using accesspoints supporting high speed multicast over Wi-Fi, it is recommended to use FTP instead of multicast TFTP on such networks.

---

1 GRUB boot from service partition template

2 Init network (WiFi)

3 Download config from the Branch Server

4 Install/update GRUB on service partition

5 Download image from the Branch Server

6 Image boot

A normal WiFi boot proceeds as follows:

1 GRUB boot from service partition

2 Init network (WiFi)

3 Download config from the Branch Server

4 Install/update GRUB on service partition

5 Check/download image from the Branch Server

6 Image boot

6.4.3.3 Boot with Reduced Network Load

1 Boot from PXE or service partition

2 Init network (WiFi)

3 Download config from the Branch Server

4 If the service partition contains the required image, it is used.

5 Image boot

6 Change terminal configuration via the roles API or `pos dump-all`

7 Run `posSyncSrvPart` on the terminal

8 Reboot the terminal, the process starts from the beginning

6.4.3.4 Offline Deployment

First boot proceeds as follows:

1 GRUB boot from service partition template

2 Network initialization fails

3 Download config from service partition template

4 Disk partitioning, the service partition template is copied to the service partition

5 Install GRUB on the service partition

6 Deploy image from the service partition

7 Image boot

The next boots proceed as follows:

1 GRUB boot from service partition template

2 Network initialization fails

3 Download config from service partition

4 Check deployed image

5 Image boot

If the terminal becomes connected to the Branch Server, the boot proceeds as follows:

1 GRUB boot from service partition

2 Init network

3 Download config from the Branch Server

4 Install/update GRUB on service partition

5 Check/download image from the Branch Server

6 Image boot

6.4.4 Booting from CD (isoboot)

If you are unable to electronically distribute Point of Service images over your network, you must manually distribute the images using isoboot images. For more information on creating an isoboot image, see Section 8.1, "Building Images with the Image Creator Tool" (page 125).

The behavior of Point of Service terminals booting from CD is similar to Point of Service terminals that receive the first and second stage boot images over the LAN from a Branch Server. The following is a general description of what takes place when a Point of Service terminal boots from CD:

1. The system image is installed to a RAM or hard disk on the Point of Service terminal.

   The partition information resides in the KIWI `config.xml` file located on the CD.

2. The installed system image is booted from the RAM or hard disk on the Point of Service terminal.

Depending on the system image that resides on the boot CD (Minimal or Graphical), you should note the following restrictions:

- The Graphical image should only be used for Point of Service systems with storage media such as hard disk or flash medium. Otherwise, the Point of Service system must be upgraded with enough RAM to hold the system image.

- There must be enough available RAM on diskless Point of Service terminals to load the first and second stage boot images. Otherwise the terminal returns a kernel panic error.

NOTE: Onboard VGA Memory Consumption

Keep in mind that onboard VGA reduces the Point of Service terminal's available RAM.

6.4.5 Image Install Notification

When the Branch Server distributes a new image to a Point of Service terminal, the system provides notification that the image was successfully installed on the Point of Service terminal. The notification is stored in the scWorkstation object in the LDAP directory on the Administration Server.

When the image is successfully installed on the Point of Service terminal, the linuxrc script running on the Point of Service terminal creates the *bootversion.MAC* file in the /srv/tftpboot/upload directory on the Branch Server. The posleases2ldap process then transfers the information to the scNotifiedImage attribute in the scWorkstation object in LDAP and deletes the *bootversion.MAC* file. The notification string is extended to also contain time and md5 hash of the config file used (see Section 10.5.17, "scWorkstation" (page 222).

The /srv/tftpboot/upload/bootversion.*MAC* file, in addition to image name (first line) and image version (second line) can contain a hash of the mentioned config.*MAC* file and a rollback flag:

```
POS_CFG_HASH=41c08da9b4bdc1179506f4f0324b3821
POS_ROLLBACK=1
```

The POS_ROLLBACK flag indicates whether this is a rollback request (POS_ROLLBACK=1) or notification (POS_ROLLBACK=0 or not present).

In both cases, the information in the bootversion.*MAC* file is inserted into LDAP, into the `scNotifiedImage` parameter. It can contain up to `IMAGE2LDAP_MAX_NOTIFY_IMAGES` entries, the default is 4.

In case of a rollback request, a stored `config.`*MAC* file (`/srv/tftpboot/KIWI/rollback.config.`*MAC.hash*) is copied back to `/srv/tftpboot/KIWI`.

Not only `config.`*MAC* but all relevant files are saved to be used with rollback:

* The associated configuration files (described in the CONF variable of the `config.`*MAC* file) are stored as `/srv/tftpboot/KIWI/rollback/config/`*config_file.hash*.

* The associated PXE file, a specific PXE (01-M-A-C format) or the default PXE, is stored in `/srv/tftpboot/KIWI/rollback/boot/pxe.`*hash* (specific and default). Both the specific and the default PXE files are recovered as a specific PXE file, otherwise the current default PXE file, possibly shared between many terminals, would be overwritten.

* The kernel and initrd files (boot images) are stored as `/srv/tftpboot/KIWI/rollback/boot/`*kernel.hash* and `/srv/tftpboot/KIWI/rollback/boot/`*initrd.hash*. These files are not recovered with their original names to protect the current kernel and initrd possibly shared by other terminals.

If rollback files are no longer used (they are not referenced in any rollback `config.MAC.hash` file), they are deleted. The oldest rollback `config.MAC.hash` file is deleted if the number of rollback configurations exceeds the maximum number defined in `scNotifiedImage` under the relevant `scWorkstation`.

If a different kernel or initrd is present in the rollback data, it is not used immediatelly after this rollback is selected, but only after reboot after a bootversion file is uploaded back to the server. The kernel parameters in the pxe file are included in the first boot, but only those used later in the booting process (after the rollback occurs) are applied. The associated configuration files are included and used, even during the first boot in which the rollback selection occured.

For terminals, the rollback information is stored in the `/srv/tftpboot/KIWI/rollback.`*MAC* files. To keep them, the files are synchronized in every posleases2ldap cycle according to the scNotifiedImage parameters and the respective scWorkstation objects. If scNotifiedImage contains an invalid reference or a reference without the respective /srv/tftpboot/KIWI/ rollback.*MAC* file present, it is ignored and not included in the rollback list.

6.5 Selecting a Boot Image Using Menu on a Terminal

If a terminal has a list of IDs, roles or a rollback list, it offers a possibility to change its configuration during boot. The Branch Server must be configured to use roles. For more information, see Section 9.2, "Using Terminals with Roles" (page 148).

6.5.1 Changing the ID of a Booting Terminal

To change the ID of the terminal during its boot, follow these steps:

1 Wait for the terminal to print the Press C to change configuration message. Press **C** quickly to prevent a timeout.

2 Using the cursor keys, select *Change ID/Role* from the menu and press **Enter**.

3 Using the cursor keys, select the requested ID and press **Enter**.

4 Press **Enter**. The booting sequence continues with the selected ID.

6.5.2 Changing the Role of a Booting Terminal

To change a role of the terminal during its boot, follow these steps:

1 Wait for the terminal to print the Press C to change configuration message. Press **C** quickly to prevent a timeout.

2 Using the cursor keys, select *Change ID/Role* from the menu and press **Enter**.

3 Using the cursor keys, select the requested role and press Enter.

4 Press Enter. The booting sequence continues with the selected role.

6.5.3 Performing a Rollback

During boot of a terminal, if some previous configurations have already been used on the terminal, it is possible to enter the rollback menu and choose one of the four most recent configurations.

If an older image is selected, it should be used until the `pos dump-all` is used.

1 Wait for the terminal to print the `Press C to change configuration` message. Press C quickly to prevent a timeout.

2 Using the cursor keys, select *Rollback* from the menu and press Enter.

3 Using the cursor keys, select the requested image and press Enter.

4 Press Enter. The booting sequence continues with the selected image.

Managing SUSE Linux Enterprise Point of Service

7

7.1 Monitoring the Terminal Boot-Up

To verify and test your SUSE Linux Enterprise Point of Service installation:

1 Attach a Point of Service client to the Branch Server network.

2 Verify the list of properly registered workstations with the `pos ws-list` command.

You can also verify if the necessary LDAP objects have been created manually by using the `ldapsearch` command. For example (setup without SSL):

```
ldapsearch -x -H ldap://administration_server_name -b base_context -s
 base -D dn_of_admin_user -w password
```

For setups with SSL, use:

```
ldapsearch -x -H ldaps://administration_server_name -b base_context -s
 base -D dn_of_admin_user -w password
```

3 Verify the following LDAP object settings:

- The `scCashRegister` object matching the model type of the Point of Service terminal must exist in the LDAP database, for example: `IBMSurePOS300Series`.

- There must be an `scPosImage` object for each image in the `/srv/tftpboot/image/` directory on the Branch Server. The `scPosImageDn` attribute within each object must correspond to an existing Point of Service image.

For further information how to modify and add LDAP entries for your specific SUSE Linux Enterprise Point of Service system environment, see Chapter 10, *The LDAP Directory on SUSE Linux Enterprise Point of Service* (page 167).

4 Verify that the Point of Service system images and their corresponding MD5 checksum files are available in the `/srv/tftpboot/image/` directory on the Branch Server.

5 Verify that the `initrd.gz` and `linux` images are available in the `/srv/tftpboot/boot/` directory on the Branch Server.

6 Power up the Point of Service client and watch the Branch Server log messages using the following command:

```
tail -f /var/log/messages
```

7 While the Point of Service client is booting, check if there are tftpd entries.

For example:

```
.. bs1 tftpd[31434]: Serving /boot/pxelinux.0 to 192.168.2.15:2070
.. bs1 tftpd[31435]: Serving /boot/pxelinux.cfg/C0A8020F to
   192.168.2.15:57217
.. bs1 tftpd[31436]: Serving /boot/pxelinux.cfg/C0A8020 to
   192.168.2.15:57090
.. bs1 tftpd[31437]: Serving /boot/pxelinux.cfg/C0A802 to
   192.168.2.15:56963
.. bs1 tftpd[31438]: Serving /boot/pxelinux.cfg/C0A80 to
   192.168.2.15:56836
.. bs1 tftpd[31439]: Serving /boot/pxelinux.cfg/C0A8 to
   192.168.2.15:56709
.. bs1 tftpd[31440]: Serving /boot/pxelinux.cfg/C0A to
   192.168.2.15:56582
.. bs1 tftpd[31441]: Serving /boot/pxelinux.cfg/C0 to
   192.168.2.15:56455
```

```
.. bs1 tftpd[31442]: Serving /boot/pxelinux.cfg/C to 192.168.2.15:56328
.. bs1 tftpd[31443]: Serving /boot/pxelinux.cfg/default to
 192.168.2.15:56201
.. bs1 tftpd[31444]: Serving /boot/linux to 192.168.2.15:56202
.. bs1 tftpd[31445]: Serving /boot/initrd.gz to 192.168.2.15:56203
.. bs1 dhcpd: DHCPDISCOVER from 00:06:29:e3:02:e6 via eth0
.. bs1 dhcpd: DHCPOFFER on 192.168.2.15 to 00:06:29:e3:02:e6 via eth0
.. bs1 dhcpd: DHCPREQUEST for 192.168.2.15 (192.168.2.1) from
 00:06:29:e3:02:e6 via eth0
.. bs1 dhcpd: DHCPACK on 192.168.2.15 to 00:06:29:e3:02:e6 via eth0
.. bs1 tftpd[31454]: Serving CR/config.00:06:29:E3:02:E6 to
 192.168.2.15:32768
.. bs1 tftpd[31455]: Fetching from 192.168.2.15 to upload/
hwtype.00:06:29:E3:02:E6
```

The Point of Service terminal performs a PXE boot to receive the Linux kernel and its first stage boot image, `initrd.gz`. For detailed information on the Point of Service boot process, see Section 6.4, "Booting the Point of Service Terminal" (page 92).

8 Check the `hwtype.MAC.HASH` file in the `/srv/tftpboot/upload` directory (for example, `hwtype.00:06:29:E3:02:E6`). This file contains the information required to create the terminal's workstation object (scWorkstation) in LDAP and determine which image and configuration settings should be included in the terminal's configuration file. For more information, see Section 6.3.3, "The hwtype.*MAC.HASH* File" (page 90).

9 See if the Point of Service client is able to boot the second stage image. This is the system image configured in LDAP (scPosImage) and downloaded from the `/srv/tftpboot/image/` directory on the Branch Server (for example, the browser-2.0.4 image).

10 If everything proceeds normally, the Point of Service terminal boots and you see the login prompt.

If the boot is successful, the `config.MAC` for the terminal is written to the `/srv/tftpboot/KIWI/` directory on the Branch Server. For example, if a terminal's MAC address is 00:06:29:E3:02:E6, the `config.00:06:29:E3:02:E6` file will be located in the `/srv/tftpboot/KIWI/` directory. Additionally, the scWorkstation object for the Point of Service terminal is created in the LDAP directory.

7.2 SLEPOS High-Availabilty Installation Workflow

SLEPOS relies on SUSE Linux Enterprise Server High Availabilty Extension to facilitate active-passive high availability scenario. Following workflow assume basic knowledge of SLE-HAE configuration. For SLE-HAE details see the SLE-HAE User Guide. Both primary and secondary nodes are assumed to have SLE-HAE and SLEPOS extensions installed.

Before configuring high-availabiltyit is necessary to prevent all slepos services (ldap, dhcp, etc.) from starting via traditional initscripts. All services are handled by RA (resource agent). Initialization of services via traditional way will prevent RA from initialization and can potentially prevent shared storage from mounting.

Init scripts can be disbled via `chkconfig` *service* `off` or via `yast runlevel-editor`.

To configure the primary node, follow these steps:

1 Configure networking (virtual IP for HA services) as defined in SLE-HAE User Guide (RA ocf:hearbeat:IPaddr2).

2 Configure shared storage (e.g. drbd) as defined in SLE-HAE user guide. The following directories should be on the shared storage and linked back:

```
/var/lib/SLEPOS
/var/lib/branchldap
/var/lib/named
/var/lib/dhcp
/etc/named.d/ldap_generated
```

3 Configure syncing using csync2 as defined in SLE-HAE User Guide and add the following configuration files to synchronize:

```
include /etc/SLEPOS/*;
include /etc/drbd.d;
include /etc/drbd.conf;
include /etc/named.conf;
include /etc/dhcpd.conf;
include /etc/openldap/*;
include /etc/sysconfig/atftpd;
include /etc/sysconfig/named;
```

```
include /etc/sysconfig/dhcpd;
include /etc/sysconfig/ldap;
include /etc/sysconfig/openldap;
include /etc/named.d/forwarders.conf;
```

4 Configure resource agents and slepos resource group containing `lsb:posleases, ocf:heartbeat:slapd, osc:heartbeat:named, lsb:atftp, ocf:heartbeat:Pure-FTPd` services:

```
primitive aftp lsb:atftpd \
    operations $id="aftp-operations" \
    op monitor interval="15" timeout="15"
primitive dhcpd ocf:heartbeat:dhcpd \
    operations $id="dhcpd-operations" \
    op monitor interval="10" timeout="20" \
    params config="/etc/dhcpd.conf" interface="eth1"
primitive pureftp ocf:heartbeat:Pure-FTPd \
    operations $id="ftp-operations" \
    op monitor interval="60s" timeout="20s" \
    params script="/usr/sbin/pure-config.pl" conffile="/etc/pure-ftpd/
pure-ftpd.conf" pidfile="/var/run/pure-ftpd.pid"
primitive named ocf:heartbeat:named \
    operations $id="named-operations" \
    op monitor interval="30" timeout="30" \
    params named_config="/etc/named.conf" named_rootdir="/var/lib/named"
 named_user="named"
primitive openldap ocf:heartbeat:slapd \
    operations $id="openldap-operations" \
    op monitor interval="60s" timeout="20s" \
    params config="/etc/openldap/slapd.conf" slapd="/usr/lib/openldap/
slapd" services="ldap://127.0.0.1:389" bind_dn="<branch server ldap
 DN>" password="<branch server LDAP password" user="ldap" group="ldap"
 watch_suffix="<SLEPOS LDAP suffix>"
primitive posaswatch lsb:posASWatch \
    operations $id="posaswatch-operations" \
    op monitor interval="15" timeout="15"
primitive posleases lsb:posleases2ldap \
    operations $id="posleases-operations" \
    op monitor interval="15" timeout="15"
primitive virtual_ip ocf:heartbeat:IPaddr2 \
    params ip="<virtualIP>" broadcast="<broadcast_address>" nic="<bonded
 device>" iflabel="<num_identifier_of_alias>" \
    op monitor interval="10s"
group pos virtual_ip mount_mnt openldap named dhcpd aftp pureftp
 posaswatch posleases \
    meta target-role="Started"
```

Do not forget to add configuration for shared storage (e.g. `ocf:linbit:drbd`) and its collocation with SLEPOS services group (pos) and order in which services are activated.

5 Initialize the Branch Server normally.

6 Check the directories moved in step 2 if they are still linking back to the shared storage. If not, repeat step 2.

7 Start HA (openais).

To configure the primary node, follow these steps:

1 COnfigure network interfaces.

2 Link directories to shared storage (see step 2 of the primary node configuration).

3 Join cluster and sync configuration as defined in SLE-HAE user guide (for example `sleha-join`).

7.3 Booting Special Images on Terminals

It is possible to boot special non-SLEPOS images on terminal, for example images provided by hardware vendor to update BIOS on terminals.

To setup booting of this image files via pxe menu, use the follwoing command:

```
pos sync pxe-bootmenu set --imagespath path
```

The optional `--imagespath` option contains the path to the directory containing files to add into menu, they will be copied into the `boot/ext` subdirectory. If this option is not supplied, only bios boot images currently existing in `boot/ext` will be used.

The optional `--force` option allows to overwrite existing backup files.

In order for the pxe menu to not be reverted back, `posleases2ldap` must be stopped, and no `pos dump` command can be run. Rebooting of the Branch Server should also be avoided for pxe menu to stay intact, since the Branch Server automatically starts the posleases2ldap service.

To restore the previous state, use `pos sync pxe-bootmenu undo`. The optional `--force` option allows to overwrite the current file by backups (for specific pxe, default is always overwritten). The images copied into `boot/ext` directory are not removed by undo command, should be deleted manually if no more needed.

7.4 Remotely Managing Point of Service Terminals with admind and adminc

In a SUSE® Linux Enterprise Point of Service system, `admind` and `adminc` enable you to perform tasks like shutdown, configuration reload, or application restart on multiple Point of Service terminals from a single location.

7.4.1 admind

The daemon admind allows simple commands to be executed on Point of Service terminals from a remote location. Using it with adminc, an administrator can perform tasks like shutdown, configuration reload, or application restart on multiple Point of Service terminals from a single location. admind is typically started by the xinetd super-server, but can be run as a regular service.

IMPORTANT: admind with Limited Authentication Only

admind does not provide strong authentication. Its level of security is adequate only for systems that boot from the network, thus relying on the integrity of the network infrastructure (DHCP and DNS in particular). Authentication is provided through verification of the hostname and user against a list in the configuration file.

---

admind writes its diagnostics via syslog to `/var/log/messages`.

7.4.1.1 Command Line Options

`admind` has the following command syntax:

```
admind [-vIP] [configfile] [options]
```

Table 7.1, "admind Command Line Options" (page 116) summarizes the admind command line options.

Table 7.1: *admind Command Line Options*

Option	Description
-I (uppercase i)	Does not require admind to look up identities to authenticate the calling user. This option is not recommended because it poses a security risk to your system.
-P	Does not require admind to verify the hostname. This option is not recommended because it poses a security risk to your system.
-v	Provides verbose output to syslog.

7.4.1.2 admind.conf

The standard configuration information for admind is located in /etc/SLEPOS/ admind.conf. The file format typically appears as follows:

```
S=hostname1
S=hostname2
U=username1
U=username1
X:0=init 0
X:6=init 6
X:r=/etc/init.d/rc/POSApplication restart
(...)
```

Option	Description
-S	Defines a valid server. The names of the connecting servers are compared against this list. Short names can be used and are expanded for the local domain.

Option	Description
-U	Defines a valid username on the connecting machine.
-X	Defines the fixed commands. Each command has a single letter or digit key (X: [0-9a-zA-Z]).

Executed commands are expected to terminate and deliver a return value. Long-running commands or commands that do not terminate must be wrapped in a script that executes the command in the background.

7.4.2 adminc

adminc distributes commands to Point of Service terminals running admind. It sends a command string to the list of IP addresses. adminc attempts to connect to clients in parallel up to a specified maximum number.

adminc can also be used to start (wake) a series of terminals designated by MAC address.

7.4.2.1 Command Line Options

adminc has the following command syntax:

```
adminc [--port] portno
       [--parallel] maxparallel
       [--commands] keys IP [IP*]
adminc [--wake] MAC [MAC*]
```

summarizes the available options for adminc.

Table 7.2: *adminc Command Line Options*

Option	Description
--port	The port number that admind listens to. The default is 8888.

Option	Description
`--parallel`	The maximum number of parallel sessions to start. The default is 8.
`--commands`	The command keys to be sent to clients. The command keys are specified in the client's `admind.conf` file.
`--wake MAC` *MACes*	The wake command starts the designated clients. Clients are designated by their MAC addresses.

7.4.2.2 adminc Examples

```
adminc --command 0 192.168.99.11 192.168.99.12 192.168.99.13
Node: 192.168.99.11   Exit Code: 0
Node: 192.168.99.12   Exit Code: 65280
Node: 192.168.99.13   Exit Code: 0
```

7.4.3 posGetIP

posGetIP is a helper script that is used in conjunction with adminc. It finds all addresses for Point of Service terminals that are managed by the local Branch Server. This tool must be run on the Branch Server. The output is a list of addresses, one line each.

Both IP and MAC addresses can be listed. The default is to list the IP addresses. It finds its server base by looking at the IP addresses that are configured on the local machines. `/etc/SLEPOS/branchserver.conf` is used to find the LDAP connection information.

7.4.3.1 Command Line Options

posGetIP has the following command syntax:

```
posGetIP [--ip|noip] [--mac]
```

Table 7.3, "posGetIP Command Options" (page 119) summarizes the available posGetIP command options.

Table 7.3: *posGetIP Command Options*

Option	Description
`--ip`	Prints the IP addresses of all Point of Service terminals that are managed by the local Branch Server. This option is enabled by default.
`--noip`	Provides a screen dump of the Point of Service terminals that are managed by the local Branch Server. This option does not print the IP addresses of the terminals managed by the current Branch Server.
`--mac`	Prints the MAC address of all Point of Service terminals that are managed by the local Branch Server.

7.4.3.2 posGetIP Examples

```
adminc --command 6 `posGetIP`
adminc --wake `posGetip --mac --noip`
```

7.4.4 Installing admind on a Point of Service Terminal

The following sections outline how to add admind to a terminal system image.

1 Use the Image Creator tool to start this procedure.

For information about using Image Creator, see Section 8.1, "Building Images with the Image Creator Tool" (page 125).

2 To start the xinetd service on the Point of Service terminal, activate the *Scripts* tab. In the *Image Configuration Script* box, add after the line `suseActivateDefaultServices`:
```
suseInsertService xinetd
```

3 Create the `admind.conf` file in the `/usr/share/kiwi/image/` `SLEPOS/`*`image_name-version`*`/root/etc` directory.

4 Set the configuration parameters in the `admind.conf` file.

4a Set the *`branch.local`* parameter to the fully qualified hostname of the Administration or Branch Server, on which you want to run adminc. This allows the terminals to trust the designated box. If you are running adminc from multiple stations, they must be included in this list. For example:
```
S=branch.local
S=branch2.local
S=localhost
```

4b Add all users with rights to execute commands on Point of Service terminals. For example:
```
U=root
U=tux
```

4c Add any additional commands you want to execute on the POS terminals. For example:
```
X:0=/sbin/init 0
X:3=/sbin/init 3
X:5=/sbin/init 5
X:6=/sbin/init 6
X:p=/sbin/poweroff
X:r=/sbin/reboot
```

5 Build the image with the `--extend` option to include the `setup.admind` file.

NOTE

The `setup.admind` file is located in the `/usr/share/kiwi/SLEPOS/` `templates/addons/` directory. It references the RPMs required to add the admind utility to a standard client image.

---

6 Distribute the image to your Point of Service terminals.

7.4.5 Installing the admind Client on Administration and Branch Servers

To install admind on an Administration or Branch Server, follow these steps:

1 Install the `admind-client` RPM on the Administration or Branch Server: Start YaST, *Software > Software Management*, and select `admind-client` for installation.

NOTE

It may also be necessary to install the `tcpd`, `xinetd`, and `pidentd` RPMs.

---

2 Start identd using YaST: *System > System Services (Runlevel)* and enable identd.

7.5 Backup and Restore

All system information (system structure, the configuration and deployment method for each Branch Server and Point of Service terminal, image information, and so forth) is stored in an LDAP directory on the Administration Server. This information must be backed up regularly to avoid data loss in case of storage failure and administration errors. The following sections discuss several methods for backing up and restoring the LDAP directory in SUSE® Linux Enterprise Point of Service so you can decide which method suits your needs best.

WARNING: Risk of Data Loss

Before starting to reconfigure your SUSE® Linux Enterprise Point of Service system, take precautions against data loss and execute at least a logical online backup to a local file as described in Section 7.5.3, "Online Backup" (page 122).

7.5.1 Offline Physical Backup

An offline backup must be executed on the Administration Server and does not put any load on the LDAP server. The drawback is that the LDAP server is not available during the time of the backup.

To perform a physical file backup of the LDAP directory, follow these steps:

1 Stop the LDAP server with `rcldap stop`.

2 Copy all the files in the /var/lib/ldap/ directory to an archive directory using cp, tar or any other command line tool for archiving or compressing files.

3 After the copy completes, start the LDAP server with rcldap start.

Procedure 7.1, "Restoring an Offline Backup" (page 123), describes how to restore a physical backup.

7.5.2 Offline Logical Backup

To perform a logical backup of the LDAP directory (database dump):

1 Stop the LDAP server with rcldap stop.

2 Run the following command:

```
slapcat > "ldap.$(date '+%F-%T')"
```

This generates a file in LDAP Data Interchange Format (LDIF file) named ldap. *datetime* where *datetime* is the current date and time. LDIF files are structured ASCII files that can be viewed, for example, with less. The resulting output file can be archived, backed up on offline media, and restored with the slapadd command as described in Section 7.5.4, "Restoring Data" (page 123).

3 After the backup completes, start the LDAP server with: rcldap start.

Procedure 7.1, "Restoring an Offline Backup" (page 123) describes how to restore a logical backup.

7.5.3 Online Backup

An online backup uses the LDAP server to extract all data. This has the advantage that the server is available at all times and the backup can be stored to a remote machine that has an LDAP client, using an authenticated LDAP bind. Of course, the LDAP communication can also be secured with SSL.

1 To create an LDIF file similar to the one created during an offline logical backup, proceed as follows:

```
ldapsearch -x -D adminDN❶ -w adminPassword❷ -H ldap://LDAPServer/❸ -
b baseDN❹ > "ldap.$(date '+%F-%T')"
```

- ❶ DN of the administrator user (for example, cn=admin, o=*myorg*, c=*us*).
- ❷ The administrator password (for example, secret).
- ❸ LDAP server name or IP address.
- ❹ Base DN (distinguished name) of the LDAP structure (for example, o=*myorg*, c=*us*).

2 To use LDAP with SSL, enter the following instead:

```
ldapsearch -x -D adminDN -w adminPassword -H ldaps://LDAPServer/ -
b baseDN > "ldap.$(date '+%F-%T')"
```

Procedure 7.2, "Restoring an Online Backup" (page 123) describes how to restore an online backup.

7.5.4 Restoring Data

Procedure 7.1: *Restoring an Offline Backup*

To restore offline backups, you need to stop the LDAP server and restart it afterwards.

1 Stop the LDAP server with rcldap stop.

2 If you did a physical file backup, restore the files in /var/lib/ldap by copying them back or extracting them from the archive you created.

If you did a logical backup, run the slapadd command to restore the logical database dump:

```
slapadd -l backupfile
```

where *backupfile* is the file created by slapcat.

3 Run /usr/lib/SLEPOS/posACLUpgrade.pl to regenerate missing LDAP ACL.

4 Start the LDAP server with rcldap start.

Procedure 7.2: *Restoring an Online Backup*

To restore an online backup, the LDAP server must be running.

1 In case the LDAP database has been corrupted, remove the database files in `/var/lib/ldap/` before restoring the online backup. The LDAP server is able to run with an empty database.

2 Restore the backup file created via `ldapsearch` with either the command:

```
ldapadd -x -D adminDN -w adminPassword -H ldap://LDAPServer -f backupfile
```

or for secure LDAP communication with SSL:

```
ldapadd -x -D adminDN -w adminPassword -H ldaps://LDAPServer -f backupfile
```

3 Run `/usr/lib/SLEPOS/posACLUpgrade.pl` to regenerate missing LDAP ACL.

Building SLEPOS Images

8

SUSE Linux Enterprise Point of Service uses KIWI as the main tool for creating Point of Service system images. YaST also provides Image Creator, a GUI front-end to KIWI for easy image building. It is recommended to use this graphical front-end to build system images.

8.1 Building Images with the Image Creator Tool

Image Creator, the recommended graphical front-end to build images, can be started from YaST by choosing *Miscellaneous > Image Creator*.

When Image Creator is started, the Image Creator Configuration Overview dialog is shown. It lists image configurations saved in the `/var/lib/SLEPOS/system` directory. You can add, delete, or edit configurations by using the appropriate buttons in the dialog. Images can be built from a newly added configuration or from a configuration opened by *Edit*.

Figure 8.1: *The Image Creator Configuration Overview*

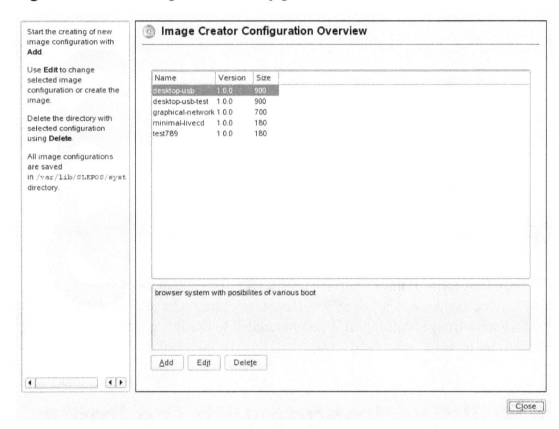

NOTE: Logging in as `root` User

In order to be able to log in as `root` on the terminal, you need to create the `root` user and assign a password to it in the *Users* tab.

NOTE: Creating Images from Scratch

Only image templates shipped with SUSE Linux Enterprise Point of Service are supported. If you want to prepare your own image from scratch, the SLE-11-SDK product must be used and the `kiwi-desc-*` packages installed. There is no L3 support available for the SLE-11-SDK product.

IMPORTANT: Building 32-bit Images on 64-bit Machines

SLEPOS terminals need 32bit images. If you want to build 32bit images on a 64bit machine, the Subscription Management Tool (SMT) must be used for repository management. It is also recommended to use SMT for SLE update repositories (SLES-11-Updates, SLE-11-POS-Updates). For SMT configuration, see Subscription Management Tool Guide.

If SMT is configured, add repositories in Image Creator. Press *Add* > *Specify URL* and enter the repository URL, for example: `http://smt.mycompany.us/repo/$RCE/SLES11-Updates/sle-11-i586/`.

The `linux32 kiwi` command has to be used when building 32bit images on 64bit machines.

8.1.1 Creating an Image Based on Templates

To create a new image configuration from a template shipped with SUSE Linux Enterprise Point of Service follow these steps:

1 Click *Miscellaneous > Image Creator* in the YaST Control Center.

2 In the Image Creator Configuration Overview dialog, press *Add*. The *Image Preparation* dialog appears.

3 Enter the name of the new configuration in the *KIWI Configuration*.

4 Select *Base on Template* and choose the template to use from the list. If you want to re-use a previously created configuration, select *Base on Existing Configuration* and choose the directory with the configuration to use.

5 Select the *Image Type* you want to create. To create a bootable live CD with a system image, choose *Live ISO Image*. To create a bootable USB stick with a system image, choose *USB Stick Image*. If you need to boot clients from the network using PXE/DHCP and then download a system image from the network, select *Network Boot Image*.

6 The path in which the directory with the image will be created is set in the *Output Directory*. The default value is determined by the template and you can leave it as it is.

7 Package repositories used for creating the image are listed in the *Package Repository* table. The templates include paths to copies of the SUSE Linux

Enterprise Server and SUSE Linux Enterprise Point of Service source media located in the default distribution directory `/var/lib/SLEPOS/dist/`.

To add a new repository, click *Add*, select the type of the repository and enter the required information. If the image building server is on the same architecture as the terminals (i586), it is possible to use update repositories defined in the operating system. To add a system repository, configure the update repository according to the SLES Administration Guide and use *Add From System* in Image Creator.

It is also possible to manually add selected packages to the `/var/lib/ SLEPOS/system/`*image_name*`/repo/` directory.

8 Click *Next* to proceed with creating the image configuration. Image Creator now downloads the repository metadata. This action may take some time. If the configured repositories are not valid, Image Creator will report that.

9 In the Image Configuration dialog, add `root` and other needed users. Otherwise, you can use the default values defined in the template. To edit the settings, see Section 8.1.7, "Image Configuration Settings" (page 130). Click *Finish*.

10 You are asked if the image should be created now. To create the image, select *Yes*. If you choose *No*, the image configuration will be saved but no image will be built.

11 A window showing logs opens. After successfully creating the image, click *OK*. The path to the directory containing the new image is shown. Click *OK*.

8.1.2 Building Network Boot Images

In environments where the available network infrastructure is suitable to boot SUSE Linux Enterprise Point of Service terminals over LAN, you can use network boot images and boot clients using PXE/DHCP. Network boot images are built together with any system image when the *Network Boot Image* option in Image Creator is selected. If you want to create a system image with a network boot image using Image Creator, follow these steps:

1 Start Image Creator and create an image as described in Section 8.1.1, "Creating an Image Based on Templates" (page 127). Select *Network Boot Image* as *Image Type*.

2 Manually copy all the created files including the MD5 checksum files to the `/srv/SLEPOS/boot/` and `/srv/SLEPOS/image/` directories on the administration server. For more information, see Section 4.4, "Copying the Boot Image Files" (page 36) and Section 4.5, "Copying the System Image Files" (page 37).

8.1.3 Building Bootable CD Images with a System Image

In environments where no suitable network infrastructure is available to boot SUSE Linux Enterprise Point of Service terminals over the LAN, you can use bootable live CDs containing system images. To create such images using Image Creator, follow these steps:

1 Start Image Creator and create an image as described in Section 8.1.1, "Creating an Image Based on Templates" (page 127). Select *Live ISO Image* as *Image Type*.

2 After the image creation is completed, burn the created image to CD using any CD burning application, for example Nautilus in GNOME or k3b in KDE.

8.1.4 Building Bootable CD Images without a System Image

If the terminals are not able to boot from network over the PXE/DHCP but the network is present, CDs without a system image can be used to boot the client system. The system image is downloaded from the network after the boot process. To create such images using Image Creator, follow these steps:

1 Start Image Creator and create an image as described in Section 8.1.1, "Creating an Image Based on Templates" (page 127). Select *Network Boot Image* as *Image Type*.

2 Change to the directory containing the created image.

3 The ISO image should now be created using KIWI.

```
kiwi --bootcd path_to_the_initrd
```

For example:

```
kiwi --bootcd initrd-netboot-suse-
SLES11.i686-2.1.1.splash.gz
```

4 After the image creation is completed, burn the created ISO image to CD using any CD burning application, for example Nautilus in GNOME or k3b in KDE.

8.1.5 Building Server Images in Image Creator

For building server images (for Administration Server, Branch Server or Combo Server) with Image Creator, a 64bit Image Building Server is necessary. The *32bit Architecture Image* option in Image Creator should be unchecked when building these images.

8.1.6 Adding Installable Documentation in RPM Format

To include documentation packages in RPM format in your images, follow this procedure:

1 Create a new image with Image Creator.

2 Finish the image settings and quit the Image Creator without building the image.

3 In the `/var/lib/SLEPOS/system/`*image_name*`/config.xml` file, remove the line containing `<rpm-excludedocs>True</rpm-excludedocs>`.

4 Return to the Image Creator, edit the last image, and start building the image.

8.1.7 Image Configuration Settings

In the *Image Configuration* tab, adjust the configuration of the software in the resulting image. In the relevant fields, set the *Version* of the image and its *Size* in the selected *Units*. If the *Additive* option is active, the value entered in *Size* is added to the size of the selected packages. The set value is the minimal free space on the image.

To add or remove a pattern or a package from the *Installed Software* list, click *Change*. Packages in the *Ignored Software* list are removed from any patterns to be installed, but they remain installed and are available to be selected as individual packages or dependencies. Packages in the *Packages to Delete* list are always uninstalled from the target image without any dependency checking. To put packages on a list, click in the list window and write the name of the packages with one name per line.

NOTE: Package Versions and Taboos

Image Creator does not support package version selection and it installs the newest package version all time. Taboos are also not supported.

NOTE: Deleted Dependencies

If you add any package to a template-based image, make sure that it does not depend on any packages set to be deleted. Remove these packages with dependencies from the *Packages to Delete* list, because otherwise the added software will not work.

In the *Description* tab, enter information about the *Author* of the image including *Contact* information and image *Specification*.

In the *Users* tab, create users that need to be available in the target system. For each user, specify *Login Name*, *Full Name*, *Password*, *Home Directory* and *UID*. In *Group Name* and *GID*, specify the group to which the users belong.

NOTE: Conflicting User Groups

If the GID of any user group specified in this dialog conflicts with a GID of any group created by selected packages in post-installation scripts, image building will fail. In such a case, use different GIDs.

In the *Scripts* tab, you can adjust configuration scripts that are used to build the image.

The *Directories* tab contains two tables. In the *Directory with System Configuration* table, you can specify directories to copy to the root directory of the resulting system.

For example, add a directory with configuration files. In the second table, *Directory with Scripts*, add scripts to the `config` directory to run after the installation of all the image packages.

8.2 Building Images with KIWI

KIWI is a full-blown imaging suite that allows you to configure, build, and deploy your own operating system images. The KIWI workflow is divided into three distinct stages:

Preparing the Image Configuration (Physical Extend)
Determine which packages are installed on your image and which configuration files are included with the image. Create a directory holding the contents of the new file system from a software package source such as SUSE Linux Enterprise Server and create an image description file, (`config.xml`). The resulting infrastructure is referred to as the *physical extend*. For a detailed description of the image configuration procedure, refer to Section 8.2.2, "Preparing the Image Configuration" (page 137).

Creating the Image (Logical Extend)
The image itself is created using the data gathered in the *physical extend*. The resulting image is called *logical extend*. The image creation process does not require user interaction, but can be fine-tuned by modifying the `images.sh` script that is called during the creation process. For a detailed description of the image creation procedure, refer to Section 8.2.3, "Creating the KIWI Image" (page 139).

Deploying the Image
The final image can be deployed using various different methods. SUSE Linux Enterprise Point of Service supports PXE net boot, live system images, and USB stick images.

TIP: Using SUSE Linux Enterprise Point of Service Image Templates

SUSE Linux Enterprise Point of Service provides several templates that may be used to create new images. All the delivered templates are stored in the `/usr/share/kiwi/image/SLEPOS/` directory. When using these templates, copy contents of the directory that contains the respective configuration to a new subdirectory in `/var/lib/SLEPOS/system/`.

8.2.1 Understanding the KIWI Configuration

KIWI configurations as used in SUSE Linux Enterprise Point of Service should always reside in `/var/lib/SLEPOS/system/image_name`. The main configuration file that contains the most important aspects of the image description is called `config.xml` and resides in `/var/lib/SLEPOS/system/image_name/config.xml`. A typical image configuration directory for SUSE Linux Enterprise Point of Service can include the following items:

`config.xml`

This file is used to define the image type, base name, repositories used to build the image, profiles, options, and the package/pattern list. The wireless support is also enabled here. For a more detailed example of a typical SUSE Linux Enterprise Point of Service `config.xml`, refer to Example 8.1, "An Example `config.xml` Image Description" (page 134).

`config.sh`

`config.sh` is an optional image configuration script. It is executed at the end of the installation of the image after the `chroot` command is used to switch to the image. It can be used to configure the image system by activating or deactivating services.

`images.sh`

`images.sh` is an optional clean up script that runs before the image creation process is started and the logical extend is created. It removes files that are only needed while the physical extend exists.

`config`

The `config` directory is an optional directory that may contain shell scripts to be executed after all packages have been installed. You could, for example manipulate a package to remove parts that are not needed for the operating system by adding the relevant script to the `config` directory. Make sure the name of your bash scripts resembles the package name specified in `config.xml`.

`repo`

The `repo` directory is an optional directory that could hold any RPM packages that do not originate from one of your preconfigured repositories, but which you want to add manually. Just place the RPMs in this directory and reference them by `<package name="your_package">` in the `config.xml` file.

root
> The `root` directory contains files, scripts and directories to customize the image after the installation of all packages.

cdboot
> The `cdboot` directory is an optional directory holding all the data needed to create a bootable CD. It includes the `isolinux.cfg`, `isolinux.msg`, and `isolinux.sh` files needed to build an ISO image from a pre-built CD tree. This subdirectory is needed for any image of the type `initrd-isoboot`.

TIP: For More Information

Refer to the KIWI package documentation under `/usr/share/doc/packages/kiwi/kiwi.pdf` for a detailed listing of all configuration files and directories available for KIWI (Section 1.3 *The KIWI Image Description*).

Example 8.1: *An Example config.xml Image Description*

```
<?xml version="1.0" encoding="utf-8"?>
<image name="POS_Image_Graphical4" displayname="POS_Image_Graphical4"
 schemaversion="5.2">❶
  <description type="system">❷
    <author>Admin User</author>
    <contact>noemail@example.com</contact>
    <specification>POS image builder software - configuraton for graphical
image</specification>
  </description>
  <preferences>❸
    <type checkprebuilt="true" boot="netboot/suse-SLES11" fsnocheck="true"
filesystem="ext3" compressed="true" image="pxe">
      <pxedeploy server="192.168.100.2" blocksize="4096">
        <partitions device="/dev/sda">
          <partition type="82" number="1" size="5"/>
          <partition type="83" number="2" mountpoint="/" target="true"/>
        </partitions>
      </pxedeploy>
    </type>
    <type boot="isoboot/suse-SLES11" image="iso"/>
    <type boot="oemboot/suse-SLES11" filesystem="ext3" installiso="true"
image="oem"/>
    <version>4.0.0</version>
    <packagemanager>zypper</packagemanager>
    <rpm-check-signatures>false</rpm-check-signatures>
```

```
    <rpm-force>false</rpm-force>
    <boot-theme>studio</boot-theme>
    <timezone>UTC</timezone>
    <hwclock>localtime</hwclock>
    <defaultdestination>/var/lib/SLEPOS/system/images</defaultdestination>
    <defaultroot>/var/lib/SLEPOS/system/chroot</defaultroot>
</preferences>
<users group="root">❹
    <user name="root" pwd="$1$YjyhKEyu$WWqPoJ1HtqRIyKqcD1KRa." home="/root"
shell="/bin/bash"/>
</users>
<packages type="image" patternType="onlyRequired">❺
    <opensusePattern name="SLEPOS_Template_Graphical"/>
    <package name="haveged" bootinclude="true"/>
    <package name="posbios" bootinclude="true"/>
    ...
    <package name="java-1_7_0-ibm"/>
    <package name="aaa_base"/>
    <package name="bash"/>
    ...
    <archive name="bootsplash.tar" bootinclude="true"/>
    <archive name="gdm.tar"/>
    <!--begin wireless support❻
        <package name="kernel-firmware" bootinclude="true"/>
        <package name="wpa_supplicant" bootinclude="true"/>
        <package name="wireless-tools" bootinclude="true"/>
        <package name="libnl" bootinclude="true"/>
        <package name="grub" bootinclude="true"/>
        <archive name="wlan.tar.gz" bootinclude="true"/>
    end wireless support-->
    <!--begin SUSE Manager support❼
        <package name="suse_manager_client_registration" />
    end SUSE Manager support-->
</packages>
<packages type="bootstrap">
    <package name="filesystem"/>
    <package name="glibc-locale"/>
</packages>
<repository type="rpm-md">❽
    <source path="{SLEPOS 11 SP3 i386}"/>
</repository>
<repository type="rpm-md">
    <source path="{SLES 11 SP3 Updates i386}"/>
</repository>
<repository type="rpm-md">
    <source path="{SLEPOS 11 SP3 Updates i386}"/>
</repository>
<repository type="rpm-md">
    <source path="{SLES 11 SP3 i386}"/>
</repository>
<!--begin wireless support
        <drivers type="drivers">❾
```

Building SLEPOS Images   **135**

```
            <file name="drivers/net/wireless/*"/>
            <file name="drivers/net/wireless/*/*"/>
        </drivers>
    end wireless support-->
</image>
```

❶ The `image` element carries all basic information on the image description file. The `name` attribute provides the base name of the image, the `displayname` attribute allows setup of the boot menu title and `schemeversion` the current version of KIWI.

❷ The `description` element is used to provide some basic information on the creator of the image and a basic description of the image's purpose. The `author` element holds the image author's real name and the `contact` element a valid e-mail address. `specification` holds a short description of the image's purpose.

❸ The `preferences` element holds information needed to create the logical extend. The `type` element determines the type of image to be created. SUSE Linux Enterprise Point of Service supports the following values for `type`: `oem`, `pxe`, and `iso`. If your `config.xml` contains more than one `type` element, you either need to add the `primary` attribute (with its value set to `true`) to the `type` that should be used for the final image, or the first entry is used by default.

   `defaultdestination` and `defaultroot` are used if KIWI is not called with the `destdir` option or the `root` option, respectively.

❹ The `Users` element lists the users belonging to the group specified with the group attribute. At least one user child element must be specified as part of the users element. Multiple users elements may be specified.

   SLEPOS image templates contain the `root` user by default. The default root password is `linux`.

❺ The `packages` element serves as a container for all the `package` elements used to designate the packages to be handled by KIWI. There are several types of package sets supported by KIWI: `image` includes all the packages which make up the image and are used to finish the image installation, `boot` includes the list of packages needed to create a new operating system root tree, and `delete` includes all packages marked for deletion and which are not needed in the final image.

❻ The section, marked in `config.xml` by `begin/end wireless support`, contains configuration necessary for PXE booting via wireless networks. It is commented out in the default config file of the

minimal image. WPA configuration (`/etc/wpa_supplicant/`
`wpa_supplicant.conf`) is contained in the `wlan.tar.gz` tarball. WPA
configuration can be eventually adjusted there.

❼ The section, marked in `config.xml` by `begin/end SUSE Manager`
`support`, contains the package needed for SUSE Manager integration.

❽ The `repository` element references any package sources used in building
this image. Repositories are referenced using repository aliases, for example
`{SLES 11 SP3 i386}`. These aliases are mapped to repository urls via the
`/etc/kiwi/repoalias` file. You also need to specify the `type` of the
repository, in this case `rpm-md`.

❾ This section contains drivers needed for the wireless operation.

8.2.2 Preparing the Image Configuration

To prepare a new image configuration using one of the customized SUSE Linux
Enterprise Point of Service templates, proceed as follows:

1 Create the directory to hold the image description.

To create a system image of a graphical operating system without a desktop
environment, use the following command:

`mkdir /var/lib/SLEPOS/system/graphical-default`

2 Copy the template configuration to the image description directory:

```
cp -R /usr/share/kiwi/image/SLEPOS/graphical-3/* \
/var/lib/SLEPOS/system/graphical-default/
```

3 Create an empty directory to hold the final image:

`mkdir /var/lib/SLEPOS/system/image/graphical-default`

4 Adjust the image configuration file `config.xml` to match your purpose:

4a Check whether the value of `defaultroot` points to the proper directory
for the chroot environment needed to build the image. In this case: `/var/`
`lib/SLEPOS/system/chroot/graphical-default`.

4b Check whether the value of `defaultdestination` points to the
appropriate destination folder to hold the final image. In this case: `var/`
`lib/SLEPOS/system/images/graphical-default`.

4c Add the paths to the repositories needed to build your image. If you are building your image from the standard SUSE Linux Enterprise Point of Service package sources, specify `/var/lib/SLEPOS/` `dist/`*base_distribution*.

4d Add any optional configuration or scripts you need for your particular image as described under Section 8.2.1, "Understanding the KIWI Configuration" (page 133).

5 Check whether `config.xml` is still well-formed XML to avoid parser problems when running the actual image building commands:

```
xmllint --noout /var/lib/SLEPOS/system/graphical-default/config.xml
```

If this command does not return any messages at all, the XML is well-formed and you can proceed with creating the image. If it returns error messages, fix the errors it returned and retry until no more errors occur.

6 Perform the actual image preparation, but make sure the following requirements are met, before you execute the `kiwi` command:

- A `chroot` directory under `/var/lib/SLEPOS/system/chroot/` `graphical-default` must not exist before you start preparing the image. Remove any remainders of earlier image builds.

WARNING: Directories Mounted with the --bind Option

When removing `/var/lib/SLEPOS/system/chroot/` `graphical-default`, make sure that no bind mount is done in that directory. These may be left over by a previous preparing process aborted unexpectedly. To check for such leftovers, run the command:

```
mount | grep bind
```

If you have any bind mount result inside that directory, first unmount it with the command `umount <target-directory>`.

- Zypper or YaST must not run while you invoke the image preparation and build commands. These commands make use of Zypper and will be blocked by other processes requesting the same services.

```
cd /var/lib/SLEPOS/system/
```

```
kiwi --prepare ./graphical-default --root ./chroot/graphical-default
```

8.2.3 Creating the KIWI Image

After the image preparation has finished successfully, proceed with creating the image:

1 Run the imaging command:

```
kiwi --create ./chroot/graphical-default --destdir ./images/graphical-default
```

KIWI creates the system image as well as any additional files needed to deploy the image. Find the result of the imaging process under /var/lib/SLEPOS/ system/images/graphical-default.

2 Check whether the resulting image matches your needs. If not, you may modify the image configuration inside the prepared physical extend by either:

- editing the files under /var/lib/SLEPOS/system/chroot/ graphical-default, or

- entering the chroot environment with chroot /var/lib/SLEPOS/ system/chroot/graphical-default, using the utilities available in the image to edit the configuration and exiting the chroot environment with exit.

Re-run the imaging command:

```
kiwi --create ./chroot/graphical-default --destdir ./images/graphical-default
```

For more information on the KIWI command and the options available, run the kiwi --help command.

NOTE: Building SUSE Linux Enterprise 10 Images

For building SUSE Linux Enterprise 10 images, we recommend using a SUSE Linux Enterprise 10 build machine. However, you can also build SUSE Linux Enterprise 10 images with the KIWI version included in SUSE Linux Enterprise 11, if needed. In this case, make sure to add the following option when running the image command

```
--fs-inodesize 128
```

This is necessary because the file system tools in SUSE Linux Enterprise 11 use a different inode size than in SUSE Linux Enterprise 10.

8.2.4 Building Customized SUSE Linux Enterprise Point of Service Images

SUSE Linux Enterprise Point of Service supports building various different types of images suitable for different deployment scenarios. To complete some of these images, additional KIWI commands must be executed. The following sections introduce the different image types and their build process.

8.2.4.1 Building Network Boot Images

In environments where the available network infrastructure is suitable to boot SUSE Linux Enterprise Point of Service terminals over the LAN, you can use network boot images and boot clients using PXE. To build network boot images with KIWI, proceed as follows:

1 Select the `pxe` image type in `config.xml` as described in Section 8.2.1, "Understanding the KIWI Configuration" (page 133).

2 Run the `--prepare` and `--create` commands of KIWI as described in Section 8.2.3, "Creating the KIWI Image" (page 139).

8.2.4.2 Creating Images for Wireless Setup

Boot images used for the wireless setup must have wireless setup enabled. The following lines must be present in the `config.xml` file, in the `<packages type="image"...<` section:

```
<!-- begin wireless support -->
            <package name="kernel-firmware" bootinclude="true"/>
            <package name="wpa_supplicant" bootinclude="true"/>
            <package name="wireless-tools" bootinclude="true"/>
            <package name="libnl" bootinclude="true"/>
            <package name="grub" bootinclude="true"/>
            <archive name="wlan.tar.gz" bootinclude="true"/>
<!-- end wireless support -->
```

Also, the wireless drivers must be enabled in the drivers section of the `config.xml` file:

```
<!-- begin wireless support -->
        <drivers type="drivers">
                <file name="drivers/net/wireless/*"/>
                <file name="drivers/net/wireless/*/*"/>
        </drivers>
<!-- end wireless support -->
```

The necessary lines are already present in the provided configuration of the minimal image, they are just commented out. The wireless configuration is contained in the `/etc/wpa_supplicant/wpa_supplicant.conf` file present in the `wlan.tar.gz` tarball and can be adjusted there.

To create the initial boot image with KIWI, use the `kiwi --bootusb` *initrd* command. The image must be of the netboot type. The *initrd* must be an initrd file with wireless support enabled in the `config.xml` file. The kernel is expected to be in the same directory and follow the same naming convention. For example:

```
cd /var/lib/SLEPOS/system/images/minimal-3.4.0
kiwi --bootusb initrd-netboot-suse-SLES11.i686-2.1.1.splash.gz
```

The resulting image can be used for booting from an USB stick or it can be preloaded on the hard drive.

8.2.4.3 Building Bootable CD Images With a System Image

In environments where no suitable network infrastructure is available to boot SUSE Linux Enterprise Point of Service terminals over the LAN, you can use bootable CDs containing system images. To build such image CDs, proceed as follows:

1 Select the `isoboot` image type in `config.xml` as described in Section 8.2.1, "Understanding the KIWI Configuration" (page 133).

2 Run the `--prepare` and `--create` commands of KIWI as described in Section 8.2.3, "Creating the KIWI Image" (page 139).

3 Change to the directory containing your image data:

```
cd /var/lib/SLEPOS/system/images/image_name
```

4 Burn the ISO image to CD using a CD burning application of your choice (k3b or Nautilus, for example).

8.2.4.4 Building Bootable CD Images Without a System Image

If the terminals are not able to boot from network over PXE but network is present, CDs without a system image can be used for booting the client system. The system image is downloaded via the network after the boot. To build such images, proceed as follows:

1 Select the `pxe` image type in `config.xml` as described in Section 8.2.1, "Understanding the KIWI Configuration" (page 133).

2 Run the `--prepare` and `--create` commands of KIWI as described in Section 8.2.3, "Creating the KIWI Image" (page 139).

3 Change to the directory containing your image data:

```
cd /var/lib/SLEPOS/system/images/image_name
```

4 Build the ISO image using the following KIWI command:

```
kiwi --bootcd path_to_initrd
```

5 Burn the resulting ISO image to CD using a CD burning application of your choice (k3b or Nautilus, for example).

8.2.4.5 Booting Images from USB Stick

The image can be booted from an USB stick. In that case it initializes service partition on the hdd device identified by DISK variable in config. This way, it is possible to setup a shop faster without the need of having network connections upfront and without the initial PXE boot cycle to fill the system partitions. The resulting partition table should be identical to what would be the outcome of a regular PXE boot/install.

To create an offline USB image on Combo Server, proceed as follows:

1 Start with a built image. Only boot image is needed, so you can use both the minimal and the graphical image:

```
cd /var/lib/SLEPOS/system/images/graphical-3.4.0
```

2 Create the bootusb image:

```
kiwi --bootusb initrd-netboot-suse-SLES11.i686-2.1.1.splash.gz
```

3 Add 1 GB of free space to the image:

```
dd if=/dev/zero bs=1M count=1024 >> initrd-netboot-suse-
SLES11.i686-2.1.1.splash.raw
```

4 Resize the partition (using fdisk delete it and create a new one - it defaults to whole disk):

```
fdisk initrd-netboot-suse-SLES11.i686-2.1.1.splash.raw <<EOT
d
n
p
1


w
EOT
```

5 Set up the partition device:

```
DEV=/dev/mapper/`kpartx -s -v -a initrd-netboot-suse-
SLES11.i686-2.1.1.splash.raw |cut -f 3 -d ' '`
```

6 Resize the filesystem on the partition:

```
e2fsck -f $DEV
resize2fs $DEV
```

7 Set the partition label to SRV_SLEPOS_TMPL. This label marks the partition with newest offline configuration:

```
tune2fs -L SRV_SLEPOS_TMPL $DEV
```

8 Mount the filesystem:

```
mount $DEV /mnt
```

9 Install POS_Image-Tools (not part of the default admin.branch server pattern):

```
zypper -n in POS_Image-Tools
```

10 Use the existing config.mac as a template for offline installation. This creates config.default and the referenced files to the partition:

```
posSyncSrvPart --source-config config.00:00:90:FF:90:04 --dest-dir /mnt
```

11 Unmount everything:

```
umount /mnt
kpartx -d initrd-netboot-suse-SLES11.i686-2.1.1.splash.raw
```

12 The `initrd-netboot-suse-SLES11.i686-2.1.1.splash.raw` image is now ready.

Alternatively, the `KIWI/config.default` can be created manually. This is an example:

```
IMAGE=/dev/sda3;minimal.i686;3.4.0;192.168.124.254;8192
PART=3000;83;/srv/SLEPOS,1000;82;swap,3000;83;/
DISK=/dev/disk/by-id/pci-0000:00:1f.2-scsi-0:0:0:0
POS_KERNEL=linux
POS_INITRD=initrd.gz
POS_KERNEL_PARAMS= panic=60 ramdisk_size=710000 ramdisk_blocksize=4096
 vga=0x314 splash=silent console=tty0 console=ttyS0,115200 mac_separator=":"
  POS_KERNEL_PARAMS_HASH=db8571ae6dfacaf1
fd24053b74a07aa4
```

The partition must contain the referenced files, i.e.:

```
image/minimal.i686-3.4.0
image/minimal.i686-3.4.0.md5
boot/linux
boot/linux.md5
boot/initrd.gz
boot/initrd.md5
```

It is recommended to specify DISK device by `/dev/disk/by-path/` because it avoids problems with random ordering of sda, sdb. This is important especially for booting off usb stick. `/dev/disk/by-path` is however hardware dependent, so it can't be used for generic image.

8.2.5 Deploying KIWI Images

The deployment process of available KIWI images strongly depends on the type of image built. Detailed information about how each implementation works is provided in Section 1.4 "Activating an Image" in `/usr/share/doc/packages/kiwi/kiwi.pdf`.

There are also several real life examples available in this document which guide through the deployment details of all the respective image types. See also Section

1.6 "Real-Life Scenarios - A Tutorial" in `/usr/share/doc/packages/kiwi/`
`kiwi.pdf`.

9 SLEPOS Customization

9.1 Using Terminals with IDs

Terminals can be registered not only under automatically generated names (see `scEnumerationMask` and `scWorkstationBaseName`) but also under custom names. To enable this, a list of allowed IDs must be specified for the respective `scLocation` object. The `scIdPool` multivalue attribute is used to specify the list of allowed IDs. The IDs are entered sequentially via `posAdmin`:

```
posAdmin --DN cn=mybranch,ou=myorgunit,o=myorg,c=us --modify --multival
--scLocation --scIdPool '=>Id1'
posAdmin --DN cn=mybranch,ou=myorgunit,o=myorg,c=us --modify --multival
--scLocation --scIdPool '=>Id2'
```

Using `posAdmin` only, modifications to `scIdPool` can be cumbersome, especially when a large number of IDs is present. It is therefore preferable to use the `pos` script and its `id-list`, `id-add` and `id-delete` subcomands (for more information, see Section B.3.12, "pos" (page 279).

Using `posAdmin` only, modifications of `scIdPool` can be cumbersome, especially when a large number of IDs is present. This can be alleviated by taking advantage of `scIdPool` being a multivalued attribute.

When `scIdPool` is defined, the `posleases2ldap` script creates the `/srv/tftpboot/KIWI/idlist` file for terminals to allow ID selection from the pool of values.

Once the ID is selected for a given terminal, it is written under the respective `scWorkstation` object into the `scId` attribute.

9.2 Using Terminals with Roles

To set up the LDAP database for a role-based approach, the following is necessary:

NOTE: Creating Necessary Objects with `pos`

Necessary LDAP objects can be created with `posAdmin`. You can also use `pos`, which is easier to use but less general. For more information about `pos`, see Section B.3.12, "pos" (page 279).

9.2.1 Creating the `scRole` Object

Create the `scRole` object with the following attributes:

Table 9.1: *Attributes for scRole Elements*

Name	Role	Description
cn	Must	cn name.
scRoleName	Must	Name of the role displayed in the list on terminal.
scRoleDescription	May	Description of the role displayed in the list on terminal.
scAllowedHwTypes	May	Multi-value parameter, marks role to be used only with given hardware types.

The `scRole` object must be located under `scRefObjectContainer`, which can be located either under the `organization` or `scLocation` object. If the role object is located under `scLocation`, the role is considered local. If the role object is located above `scLocation`, it is global.

Assuming the `scLocation` DN is `cn=mybranch,ou=myorgunit,o=myorg,c=us`, the command to add `scRefObjectContainer rolecontainerA` under the location is:

```
posAdmin --base cn=mybranch,ou=myorgunit,o=myorg,c=us --add --
scRefObjectContainer --cn rolecontainerA
```

To add a role `roletest`, use:

```
posAdmin --base cn=rolecontainerA,cn=mybranch,ou=myorgunit,o=myorg,c=us
 --add --scRole --cn roletest --scRoleName 'Testing Role' --
scRoleDescription 'Testing description'
```

9.2.2 Adding Related Objects Under `scRole`

In the role-based approach, the role object contains `scCashRegister` objects, which are used in the same sense as the `scCashRegister` objects under global container (`cn=global,o=myorg,c=us` in our example) in the non-role-based (legacy) mode.

When a role is selected in a terminal, `posleases2ldap` tries to find the role in the LDAP database, finds the appropriate `scCashRegister` object (with `scCashRegisterName` equal to the `HWTYPE` of the terminal or default) and uses it to find the `scPosImage` and other releavant data. The `scCashRegister` under `scRole` has to contain an `scDevice` object as in the legacy case.

`scRole` can also contain configuration objects, the `scConfigFileTemplate`, `scConfigFileSyncTemplate` and `scPxeFileTemplate`. These configuration objects can be located under `scPosImage`, `scRole`, `scCashRegister`, `scWorkstation` objects, and linked by the `scConfigFileDn` attribute of the `scWorkstation` object with priority increasing from the former to the latter.

For terminals that should use a role, put a specific or a default `scCashRegister` under the `scRole` as in the legacy mode (see Section 4.6.2.1, "Adding an `scCashRegister` Object" (page 44).

9.2.3 Enabling Roles

To enable roles for a given `scLocation`, set appropriate values in the `scAllowRoles` and `scAllowGlobalRoles` attributes of the relevant `scLocation` object. The attributes have the following effects:

Table 9.2: *Effects of scAllowRoles and scAllowGlobalRoles Attributes*

scAllowRoles	scAllowGlobalRoles	Effect
TRUE	TRUE	Role-based mode, all roles enabled.
TRUE	FALSE	Role-based mode, only roles under `scLocation` are used.
FALSE	TRUE	Non-role-based legacy mode (SLEPOS10, NLPO9 like).
FALSE	FALSE	Non-role-based legacy mode (SLEPOS10, NLPO9 like).

To set the `scAllowRoles` attribute, use:

```
posAdmin --DN cn=mybranch,ou=myorgunit,o=myorg,c=us --modify --scLocation --
scAllowRoles FALSE
```

Proceed accordingly for other cases.

If roles are enabled, relevant role list files are created in the `/srv/tftpboot/KIWI` directory. The booting terminal uses these files to show the list of available roles. Then the booting terminal reports the selected role back to the Branch Server in the `hwtype.MAC.hash` file. The file is processed by the `posleases2ldap` command to create the `/srv/tftpboot/KIWI/config.MAC` according to the data specified in the `scRole` and update or create a new `scWorkstation` registration in the LDAP.

The terminal then reads the `config.MAC` file and continues the booting sequence accordingly.

Effectively, each `scRole` object behaves as a whole LDAP in the previous legacy mode, enabling different behavior for the same terminal type according to the role selected.

9.3 API Description

The API allows third-party terminal-based applications to perform operations on the Branch Server or Administration Server, such as getting lists of available roles and IDs or changing these.

All communication between the client and the server is performed via the tftp protocol. The terminal is identified by its MAC address to get information about the current terminal configuration. The client downloads the `KIWI/config.MAC` file.

9.3.1 The KIWI/config.*MAC* file

The `KIWI/config.MAC` file consists of *VARIABLE=value* pairs. It should contain at least these variables:

- `HWTYPE`

- `POS_ID`

- `POS_ROLE`

- `IMAGE`

9.3.2 Getting Lists of Available Roles and IDs

To get a list of available IDs, the `KIWI/idlist` file should be read. This file has a one ID per line format.

To get the list of available roles, the following files should be read in the presented order. The file found first should be used:

1. `KIWI/rolelist.`*`MAC`*

2. `KIWI/rolelist.`*`encoded hwtype`*

3. `KIWI/rolelist`

The encoded hwtype is the original hwtype string with all characters not matching the regular expression `[-_A-Za-z0-9]` changed to their hex values in the `%`*`xx`* format. For example `a b` is encoded as `a%20b`.

The format of the list of available roles is as follows:

`dn|scRoleName|scRoleDescription`

9.3.3 Changing ID and/or Role

1 The client uploads the `upload/hwtype.`*`MAC.`*`HASH` file. *`HASH`* is the MD5 checksum of the file content. The file consists of *`NAME`*`=`*`value`* pairs. It should use only values where a change is requested. Supported names are:

- `POS_ID`

- `POS_ROLE`

NOTE: Clearing the ID

There is a difference between `POS_ID=` (which clears the ID) and missing `POS_ID` (which keeps it unchanged).

---

2 The client waits until the uploaded file disappears, which the client checks by trying to download the file.

3 The client reads `KIWI/config.`*`MAC.`*`POS_HWTYPE_ERR_HASH == `*`HASH`* means that an arror occured. The `POS_ERR` variable contains information about the error. If there are no errors and the `POS_ID` variable contains the assigned ID, `POS_ROLE` contains the assigned role and `IMAGE` is not empty, the change has been successful.

9.4 Using Role Related Hooks

When booting an image for the first time, the KIWI boot code runs, where users can hook in custom shell script code in several places to extend the boot workflow according to their needs. The following Role-related hooks can be used for modifying the boot process of the terminal (for example to replace the role/ID selection dialog).

In general, a hook that only sets the variables to fixed values can be replaced by putting the variables in the kernel command line.

NOTE: Hooks Used by Netboot Images

Certain KIWI hooks are used by SLEPOS netboot images therefore they can't be used for customization. The following hooks are used by netboot:

```
init.sh
postLoadConfiguration.sh
postdownload.sh
postpartition.sh
preException.sh
preLoadConfiguration.sh
preNetworkRelease.sh
preswap.sh
```

9.4.1 hooks/roles.sh

This hook is called after downloading the role configuration. It can either take over the boot process completely (use the roles API and reboot at the end) or set variables that affect the boot process.

It takes the following inputs:

$IDLIST
   Path to a locally stored Id list file (the file may be empty or missing).

$ROLELIST
   Path to a locally stored role list file (the file may be empty).

$POS_ROLLBACK
   Path to a locally stored roll back file (the file may be empty).

`$CONFIG`
> Path to locally stored config file (the file may be empty).

The hook can overwrite the `$CONFIG` file with a new configuration. It can also set the following variables:

`POS_DISABLE_BOOT_HOTKEY`
> Disables the `Press C to change configuration` message if not empty.

`POS_FORCE_ROLE_SELECTION`
> If not empty, forces the role selection and new registration (instead of using the role from `$CONFIG`).

`POS_SELECTED_ID`
> Selected ID.

`POS_SELECTED_ID_TIMEOUT`
> Non-empty value indicates that the ID selection has been timed out and the value should be selected by the server.

`POS_SELECTED_ROLE`
> Selected role DN.

`POS_SELECTED_ROLE_TIMEOUT`
> Non-empty value indicates that the role selection has been timed out and the value should be selected by the server.

`POS_DISABLE_ROLE_DIALOG`
> If non-empty, do not show the role dialog. This should be selected if the hook itself sets the values of the `POS_SELECTED_*` variables.

9.4.2 hooks/selectRole.sh

This hook can replace the role selection dialog. It is only called when the machine is newly registered or when the role selection was forced. It is not called during normal boot with existing `config.MAC`. It can show an alternative role selection dialog and/or set the variables `POS_SELECTED_*` and `POS_DISABLE_ROLE_DIALOG`, which are described above.

9.5 Securing Your Setup

A SUSE® Linux Enterprise Point of Service setup includes various components that should be secured against intentional and unintentional tampering with the data and against software misbehavior. Securing your setup involves several different aspects:

Physical Server Security

First and foremost, every server component of the SUSE Linux Enterprise Point of Service setup must be secured against unauthorized access. Physically isolating the servers from other machines is just one aspect of providing physical security. For details, refer to Section 9.5.1, "Physical Server Security" (page 155).

Network Security

All servers connected with each other over potentially insecure networks, for example, Administration Server and Branch Server, need to be secured against unauthorized access via the networks they are connected to. For details, refer to Section 9.5.2, "Network Security" (page 156).

Data Security

Both the Administration Server and the Branch Servers contain vital data that need to be protected to maintain a fully functional and secure setup. The most important part is securing the LDAP directory on the Administration Server, which is used to maintain the system structure, configuration and deployment method for all Branch Servers and Point of Service terminals, and other important data. For details, refer to Section 9.5.3, "Data Security" (page 156).

Application Security

Once physical, network and data security are provided, tighten the security of your setup even further by using AppArmor. AppArmor profiles are used to confine applications and keep them from performing unnecessary file or directory accesses and this helps to make sure that every profiled application only does what it was designed to do and cannot become a security risk. For more details on AppArmor usage on SUSE Linux Enterprise Point of Service, refer to Section 9.5.4, "Application Security" (page 158).

9.5.1 Physical Server Security

Your instance of SUSE Linux Enterprise Point of Service is set up in a highly secure corporate environment using third-party security solutions and various other security measures, but you still need to make sure that nobody gains unauthorized physical access to your severs and can log in to tamper with your setups.

The following list provides a few basic security-related things you should bear in mind when creating your setup:

- Keep your severs in a separate server room that is only accessible to a few authorized people gaining access only via key cards, key codes, PIN numbers, finger print authentication, etc.

- Use BIOS and boot loader passwords to prevent anyone from manipulating the boot process of your servers.

9.5.2 Network Security

Even if your SUSE Linux Enterprise Point of Service network is secured against the Internet (using third-party security solutions and firewalls), secure your severs against unauthorized access from inside:

- All servers should only allow access from the `root` account.

- Create one single user account via YaST, namely the `root` account.

- Do not export or import any file systems on these servers, for example, do not allow NFS or Samba shares on your servers.

SUSE Linux Enterprise Point of Service provides some security against data manipulation via the network:

- LDAP-related network traffic can be configured via secure SSL/TLS channels.

- Image data is exchanged between servers via rsync and md5sums are calculated and checked to provide data integrity.

9.5.3 Data Security

The most vital data of your SUSE Linux Enterprise Point of Service setup is stored in the LDAP directory on the Administration Server. Whoever gains control over this setup data can manipulate the setup of any server or terminal in your setup. Therefore, limit the list of users with access to the LDAP directory to the bare minimum and make sure they obtain the least possible privileges only. Use LDAP

Access Control Lists (ACL) as part of the LDAP server configuration to restrict access to your LDAP data.

The configuration of your OpenLDAP server is located under `/etc/openldap/slapd.conf`. For more information on how this configuration file is generated and maintained, refer to Section B.3.3, "posInitAdminserver" (page 270).

ACLs allow you to specify separate access controls to different parts of the configuration. You can create different ACLs for user password data, server configuration data, and configuration of different locations, and so forth.

Before creating ACLs, perform an analysis of users and privileges needed to run your configuration. These may depend on the type of setup you have chosen and may vary. As an example, let us assume you run the following setup:

• A central Administration Server managed by the global administrator role.

• Independent Branch Servers managed by local administrators.

Thus, you need to make sure that both, your user configuration on the Administration Server and the ACLs in the LDAP server configuration reflect these roles and provide suitable privileges to these user roles without providing too many privileges.

The following example includes creating effective ACLs and a user setup as outlined above. Modify both the ACLs and the user configuration to match your own setup:

1 Create ACLs similar to the following and make sure you replace the example entries by the ones matching your setup. Ensure the more general rules are specified *after* the more specific ones. The first matching rule is evaluated and the following rules are ignored:

```
access to dn.base="" by * read ❶
access to * attrs=userPassword
    by anonymous auth
    by self write ❷
access to dn.regex="^.*(cn=.*,ou=.*,o=myorg,c=us)$"
    by dn.regex="^.*,$1$" write
    by users read ❸
access to *
    by self write
    by users read ❹
```

❶   Allow read access to the Root-DSE.

❷   Allow unauthenticated clients to use the `userPassword` attribute for authentication. Authenticated clients (users) are allowed to change their own password.

❸   Allow access to any DN matching the regular expression. Using the `$`, you limit the matches to just those strings that contain nothing beyond the last character. All DNs matching the regular expression are granted write access, and authenticated users may read the objects, but not write to them.

❹   Allow access to anything. Entries themselves may write to their entries, authenticated users may read them, but not modify the entries.

2 For each location, create a location user. For example, create a user for each branch location. This user is then granted (write) access to all LDAP data concerning his location, but cannot change the data of the other locations.

```
posAdmin --base cn=mybranch,ou=myorgunit,o=myorg,c=us --add --scPOSUser
 --cn mybranchuser --userPassword "locationPassword"
```

3 Now the `--user` option can be set to the following in all `posAdmin` commands concerning the `cn=mybranch,ou=myorgunit,o=myorg,c=us` location:
```
--user cn=mybranchuser,cn=mybranch,ou=myorgunit,o=myorg,c=us
```

The default LDAP user can now be replaced by this user, especially for the `posInitBranchserver` command.

```
Enter the DN of the LDAP user for administration tasks [default:
 cn=admin,o=myorg,c=us]
cn=mybranchuser,cn=mybranch,ou=myorgunit,o=myorg,c=us
```

TIP: For More Information

For more details on the syntax of the `slapd.conf` configuration file and the ACLs, refer to the manual pages of `slapd.conf(5)`, `slapd.access(5)`, and `slapacl(8)`. The `slapacl` command allows you to verify that your ACLs work as planned.

9.5.4 Application Security

Any piece of software used in your setup probably contains some inherent security vulnerabilities, which mostly slip by unnoticed as the respective functions may not be used routinely. To protect your setup from these vulnerabilities, SUSE Linux Enterprise Server and SUSE Linux Enterprise Point of Service come with the AppArmor protection framework. AppArmor provides profiles for some of the most important applications that specify which files these programs are allowed to read, write and execute. By using these profiles, you ensure that a program does what it is supposed to do and nothing else.

Use AppArmor to protect each of your servers. If you need additional profiles, use the YaST AppArmor tools to generate new profiles. To learn more about AppArmor, refer to the AppArmor documentation included in the Security Guide available at `http://www.novell.com/documentation/sles11/`.

9.5.5 Using Encrypted Partitions on Terminals

Image passwords can be defined for both system partition (partition containing system image) and data partition. Since the former is image- and version-related and the latter is data partition-related, the location differs in LDAP and setup.

There are two possible configurations, with passwords present on Branch Server only and with passwords stored also on a USB stick.

If passwords are stored on the Branch Server only, the configuration is more secure, but network connection to the Branch Server is needed to mount the encrypted partitions and the service partition cannot be encrypted. For the best security, do not use the service partition and related features (such as WiFi). If the service partition is used, kernel, initrd, WiFi credentials and other files stored on the service partition are unencrypted.

If the passwords are also stored on a USB disk, the setup is less secure, manual setup is needed, but booting without network access to the Branch Server is possible. For more information, see Section 9.5.5.1, "Storing Passwords on a USB Stick" (page 161)

To enable system partition encryption (to use an encrypted image), add a version of the respective `scPosImage` via the `scImageVersion` object, with the following attributes: `scVersion=X.Y.Z, scDisabled=FALSE, scPassword=password`

It is not possible to enter a password via the scPosImageVersion attribute of the scPosImage object. Password protected image versions must be added via scImageVersion objects. Image versions defined via scPosImageVersion and scPosVersion are used together. In case of conflict, the scPosVersion object takes precedence.

For example:

```
posAdmin --base cn=minimal,cn=default,cn=global,o=myorg,c=us --add --
scImageVersion --scDisabled FALSE --scVersion 2.1.5 --scPassword 'secret'
```

For more information about the scImageVersion object, see Section 10.5.19, "scImageVersion" (page 226).

To enable encryption for a data partition, define the partition via the scPartition object placed under the appropriate scHarddisk object with the following attributes: scPartNum=0, scPartType=83, scPartMount='/', scPassword=password. For an explanation of the scPartition parameters, see Section 10.5.20, "scPartition" (page 226).

It is not possible to enter a partition password using the scPartitionsTable attribute, and these two approaches are mutually exclusive. The partition table defined via scPartition object has higher priority than the definition via scPartitionsTable. If an scPartition object is present, scPartitionsTable is ignored.

A password for the root (scPartMount='/') partition supplied via this mechanism is ignored since for the root partition the image password is used.

For example:

```
posAdmin --base cn=sda,cn=cshr4152,cn=global,o=myorg,c=us --add --
scPartition --scPartNum 0 --scPartSize 2000 --scPartMount 'x' --
scPartType 82 --description 'swap'

posAdmin --base cn=sda,cn=cshr4152,cn=global,o=myorg,c=us --add --
scPartition --scPartNum 1 --scPartSize 4000 --scPartMount '/' --
scPartType 83 --description 'root partition'

posAdmin --base cn=sda,cn=cshr4152,cn=global,o=myorg,c=us --add --
scPartition --scPartNum 3 --scPartSize 12000 --scPartMount '/data' --
scPassword 'secret' --scPartType 83 --description 'data'
```

For more information about the scPartition object, see Section 10.5.20, "scPartition" (page 226).

NOTE: Using an Un-Encrypted Image Again

If you deploy an encrypted image to the terminal and then change the default image to a non-encrypted image and reboot the terminal, you will be asked for the luks password. Select No and the dialog disappears.

9.5.5.1 Storing Passwords on a USB Stick

It is recommended to create an USB disk to enable local boot with encrypted data partition without connection to the Branch Server. The disk should be kept in a secure place. To create the disk, follow these steps:

1 Insert a USB flash disk formatted with ext3 when the system is running.

2 Create a fstab entry for it:

```
mkdir /usb_key
echo "/dev/sdb1 /usb_key ext3 defaults,nofail 1 2" >> /etc/fstab
```

3 Mount it:

```
mount /usb_key
```

4 Create a keyfile:

```
dd if=/dev/random of=/usb_key/keyfile count=1 bs=512
```

5 Add the keyfile to the second slot of the luks container:

```
cryptsetup luksAddKey /dev/sda3 /usb_key/keyfile
```

And enter the first slot password (found in LDAP or config.mac). /dev/sda3 is the encrypted data partition.

6 Add the crypttab entry:

```
echo "luks_sda3 /dev/sda3 /usb_key/keyfile luks" >/etc/crypttab
```

After the local boot, the encrypted partition will be mounted automatically. For details, see `man crypttab` and `fstab`.

9.6 Specifying Kernel Command Line Options for Selected Terminals

To specify kernel command line options for selected terminals, the `scPxeFileTemplate` object must be added to the LDAP database. This object can be placed in the same position as `scConfigFileTemplate` and `scConfigFileSyncTemplate` (typically under the `scCashRegister` object).

For example, if the test terminal is registered via `scCashRegister` cn=cashreg1, cn=global, o=*myorg*, c=*us*, you can create `scPxeFileTemplate` pxetest under this `scCashRegister` with the command:

```
posAdmin
--base cn=cashreg1,cn=global,o=myorg,c=us
--add --scPxeFileTemplate --cn pxetest --scMust TRUE
--scKernelParameters 'vga=785, RELOAD_IMAGE=yes'
```

After `posleases2ldap` is run and the machine registered, there should be a specific pxe file in the `/srv/tftpboot/boot/pxelinux.cfg` directory. The name of the file is derived from the MAC address of the machine, prefixed with `01` and with digit pairs separated with `-`, for example: `01-00-11-25-a7-d6-1e`.

The file should contain the line `'append default parameters, vga=785, RELOAD_IMAGE=yes'`, where *default parameters* are the same parameters as those in the default pxe file in the same directory as well as any other kernel parameters specified in other `scPxeFileTemplate` objects or created via a specific kernel or initrd in the `scDistributionContainer`.

The order of parameters is determined by the objects under which they are specified. The linux and initrd are specified first, then parameters from `scPxeFileTemplate` objects located under `scPosImage`, `scRole`, `scCashRegister`, `scConfigFileDn` attributes of `scWorkstation` and under `scWorkstation` itself.

9.6.1 Specifying Kernel Parameters for All Terminals

To specify kernel paramters for all terminals on all branches at once, place the `scPxeFileTemplate` under the default distribution container (the `scDistributionContainer` with `cn=default`). To specify kernel parameters for all terminals on a single branch, place the `scPxeFileTemplate` under `scLocation` or under the tftp service object of this branch.

Such PXE objects will then be considered default and will be written into `/srv/tftpboot/boot/pxelinux.cfg/default` and used by all terminals on the given Branch Server. ata in this file are regenerated during each main cycle of `posleases2ldap` and also during the Branch Server initialization by `posInitBranchserver`.

SLEPOS uses some standard default pxe parameters (from the `TFTP_DEFAULT_KERNEL_PARAMETERS` line in the default configuration file), which are appended under `scLocation` during the initialization of the Branch Server by `posInitBranchserver` as an `scPxeFileTemplate` object named `posdefaults`.

If a terminal also uses a specific pxe parameter object and a specific pxe file (01-M-A-C..) is generated, the default parameters from the default pxe are also present there. However, they have lower priority (they are written before the specific parameters).

9.7 Configure KIWI to Use the FTP Protocol

KIWI needs atftp only for loading the kernel and initrd. For downloading the actual image the ftp protocol can be used.

To enable ftp, follow these steps:

1 Create a `scPxeFileTemplate` under the relevant object (used during registration of the terminal that needs this functionality) of `scRole` or `scCashRegister` or `scPosImage`. Default kernel parameters can also be used. For more information, see Section 9.6.1, "Specifying Kernel Parameters

for All Terminals" (page 163). Set the following parameters: `scMust TRUE`, `scKernelParameters kiwiservertype=ftp`.

2 Add the `scService` object under `scBranchserver` with `scServiceName ftp`, `scDnsName ftp` and `scServiceStatus TRUE`.

3 Make sure that the needed ports are open on the network interface, where terminals are connected. The ftp/21 port must be open. The open passive port range (default 30000:30400) must match the pure-ftp configuration in `/etc/SLEPOS/template/pure-ftpd.conf.template`.

4 Reinitialize the Branch Server if the pure-ftp server has not yet been initialized.

5 Boot the terminal.

9.8 Changing the Server Language

If you need to change the language that was defined during the initial installation of a SUSE® Linux Enterprise Point of Service Administration Server or Branch Server, you can do so by restarting YaST and selecting a different system language.

9.8.1 Changing the Language Selection

To change the language of your Administration or Branch Server:

1 Start YaST.

2 In the YaST Control Center, select *System > Choose Language*.

3 Select the desired language, then click *Accept*.

The language selected in YaST applies to the operating system, including YaST and the desktop environment. If your system needs additional packages to support the new language, you can install them with YaST.

9.8.2 Installing a Language RPMs

To install the RPMs required to support the selected language on the server:

1 In the YaST Control Center, select *Software Management.*

The YaST package manager dialog appears (see Figure 9.1, "YaST Package Manager" (page 165)).

Figure 9.1: *YaST Package Manager*

2 Use the *Filter > Languages* option to verify that the required language support for the Administration Server or Branch Server features is installed on your system.

- If the language is selected, it is already installed on your system and you do not need to select it.

- If the language is not selected, it is not installed on your system. Select the required language for installation.

3 Click *Accept* to install the selected language support.

4 Exit YaST.

The LDAP Directory on SUSE Linux Enterprise Point of Service

10

LDAP directory is a vital part of SUSE Linux Enterprise Point of Service, containing almost all configuration data, system structure description, user access rules, and more. Unlike LDAP directories in versions prior to SLEPOS 11, the LDAP architecture now consists of more partially redundant LDAP databases.

The SUSE Linux Enterprise Point of Service LDAP directory runs on OpenLDAP 2.4. LDAP entries are managed using the `posAdmin` tool. For more information on `posAdmin`, see Section 10.2, "Using posAdmin to Manage the LDAP Directory" (page 174).

NOTE: Using GQ to Browse LDAP Directory

The GQ LDAP browser may fail with a `Cannot find last-resort schema server 'local host'` alert message when used with the SLEPOS LDAP database. If you want to use GQ, disable anonymous access to rootDSE in the `/etc/openldap/slapd.conf` configuration file. To disable anonymous access, put a # under the `#enabling anonymous access to rootDSE for speeding up LDAP server start':` section:

```
#access to dn="" by * read
```

Alternatively, you can grant anonymous read access to the subschema subentry (cn=subschema). After the line `access to dn="" by *  read` in the `/etc/openldap/slapd.conf` file, add the following two lines:

```
access to dn.base="cn=Subschema"
        by * read
```

10.1 LDAP Architecture and Synchronization

The central database is located on the Administration Server and acts as the main LDAP database and LDAP replication provider. Since SLEPOS 11, each Branch Server has its own LDAP replica for independent use, thus saving network bandwidth and maintaining all functionality if the connection to Administration Server is lost.

For security and management reasons, only a part of the central LDAP database is replicated on each Branch Server: the section common to all Branch Servers (read-only access) and the organizational unit branch in which the current Branch Server is configured (read-write access).

10.1.1 Administration Server LDAP

In the Administration Server LDAP the SLEPOS 11 system is configured. The LDAP directory must be initialized before any Branch Server installation or deployment. Administration Server LDAP is managed by the posAdmin tool.

10.1.1.1 Administration Server Access Control List

SLEPOS11 introduces Access Control List (ACL) to:

- protect the Administration Server LDAP directory against unauthorized access (credentials no longer distributed to Branch Servers),

- grant write access for each Branch Server to its subtree and restrict other parts of the directory.

ACL is automatically managed by posAdmin when a new scLocation object is created or deleted. Default ACRs (Access Control Rules) restraining anonymous users are activated when Administration Server is initialized by the `posInitAdminServer` command.

ACL is stored in the LDAP dynamic `cn=config` database and also in the `/etc/openldap/acl.ldif` file. The file is used to preserve ACL during the OpenLDAP server restart. This file should be kept secure.

Each Branch Server has only access to its respective LDAP subtree. For example, if the `scLocation dn` of the Branch Server is `cn=mybranch,ou=myorgunit,o=myorg,c=us`, the Branch Server only has read and write access to the `cn=mybranch,ou=myorgunit,o=myorg,c=us` subtree.

In previous versions, the Branch Server had read and write access to the whole organizational unit (`ou`). LDAP replication is directly affected by this change. Now only the relevant subtree is replicated (replication of general readonly items is preserved (for example `cn=global,o=myorg,c=us` and `cn=standards,o=myorg,c=us`). Branch Server may see other organizational units but sees them empty.

Manual Configuration of ACL

The Access Control List `default` is automatically generated during `posInitAdminServer` execution. The rule definition starts with:

```
#STARTACL-default
```

The following lines grant read access to the LDAP subtree `cn=global,o=myorg,c=us` for any authenthicated user and blocks others:

```
access to dn.subtree="cn=global,o=myorg,c=us"
 by users read
 by anonymous none
```

This grants read access to any LDAP `scHardware` object class for any authenthicated user and blocks others:

```
access to filter="(objectClass=scHardware)"
 by users read
 by anonymous none
```

This grants read access to LDAP root for authenthicated users and blocks others:

```
access to dn.base="o=myorg,c=us"
 by users read
 by anonymous none
```

posAdmin ends the ACR named "default" with:

```
#ENDACL-default
```

When the Branch Server scLocation LDAP object is added by posAdmin, the following ACR is added, with the appropriate marker starting the ACR definition for Branch Server located in the organizational unit ou=*myorgunit*, o=*myorg*, c=*us*:

```
#STARTACL-ou=myorgunit,o=myorg,c=us
```

The following lines grant write access to the LDAP subtree ou=*myorgunit*, o=*myorg*, c=*us* for Branch Servers authenthicated against the scLocation object cn=*mybranch*, ou=*myorgunit*, o=*myorg*, c=*us* and no access for other users (except the Administration Server root user). It allows LDAP the compare method for anonymous users so they can authenticate themselves.

```
access to dn.subtree="ou=myorgunit,o=myorg,c=us"
 by dn.base="cn=mybranch,ou=myorgunit,o=myorg,c=us" write
 by users none
 by anonymous auth
```

The ACR ends with the marker corresponding with the Branch Server:

```
#ENDACL-ou=myorgunit,o=myorg,c=us
```

A typical problem with ACL is that despite wrong settings LDAP Bind is successful, LDAP filter is valid, but the LDAP search returns an empty result.

To identify the problematic ACL, search for the access to keyword followed by your search base DN or the DN under which your base DN is located. Remove that entry.

Remember to restart the LDAP server after modifying the /etc/openldap/ acl.ldif file.

WARNING: Non-Persistent Changes

If you are configuring LDAP server via the cn=config configuration interface, remember these changes are not persistent in current configuration.

10.1.1.2 Synchronization Provider

The Administration Server LDAP performs a crucial role in the SLEPOS central management. To support the Branch Server's independent opperation when a network connection to the Administration Server LDAP is unavailable, the

Administration Server provides LDAP synchronization. Administration Server LDAP provides each Branch Server LDAP with its respective content, according to the defined ACL, via the LDAP SyncProv protocol.

The synchronization provider is activated by the following statements in the `slapd.conf` file:

```
# sycnrepl provider configuration
overlay syncprov
syncprov-checkpoint 100 5
syncprov-sessionlog 100
```

Provider activation is done by the `overlay syncprov` statement.

`syncprov-checkpoint 100 5` forces the LDAP server to store the current contextCSN (value where the actual database state is stored) in the database after 100 operations or 5 minutes, whichever occurs first. This reduces the time and processing power needed to restart the LDAP server after a crash.

The `syncprov-sessionlog 100` statement tells the LDAP server to store up to 100 write operations in the dedicated log, which is then used to ease the determining LDAP control attributes. It is used primarily in `refreshOnly` synchronization mode, which is used while switching Branch Server from online to offline mode.

10.1.2 Branch Server LDAP

Branch Server LDAP is an exact replica of `cn=global` and Branch Server's organizational unit subtree. Its purpose is to lower the network bandwidth usage by LDAP search and read operations and to support Branch Server's ability to work without a network connection to the Administration Server.

10.1.2.1 Branch Server Access Control List

The Branch Server ACL is simple. It restricts access to the database to Branch Server root DN (as root DN can access everything anyway).

The Branch Server ACL is stored in OpenLDAP's `slapd.conf` (default path `/etc/openldap/slapd.conf`):

```
access to dn.subtree="o=myorg,c=us"
by dn.base="cn=mybranch,ou=myorgunit,o=myorg,c=us" write
by users none
by anonymous auth
```

This rule is applied to the main Branch Server database. There are two additional global rules to provide general compatibility with some LDAP browsers, mainly GQ, and speed up the start of the LDAP server:

```
access to dn="" by * read
access to dn.base="cn=Subschema" by * read
```

The Branch Server ACL should not require any maintenance and is only changed during Branch Server reinitialization.

NOTE: Modifying the Global LDAP Section on Branch Server

Using SLEPOS administrator user name and password on Branch Server is unsupported due to the nature of LDAP subsystem organization. The only way to modify the `cn=global` LDAP subtree from the Branch Server is to use remote ssh to Administration Server.

10.1.2.2 Branch Server Synchronization

Compared to the Administration Server synchronization controls, Branch Server synchronization settings are much more complex. Every synchronization issue should be solvable on the Branch Server side.

The Branch Server synchronization consists of two steps:

- SyncRepl consumer,

- LDAP chaining.

SyncRepl consumer

SyncRepl (Synchronized Replication) is the main database update mechanism. It continually asks Administration Server LDAP for changes and updates Branch Server LDAP accordingly as the "RefreshAndPersist" LDAP synchronization mode is used.

SyncRepl is usually controlled by the `posASWatch` script, but with the `pos` command, manual control is also possible: `pos status` displays current synchronization status, `pos start` starts synchronization, and `pos stop` stops synchronization.

For debugging purposes, the following command prints the current SyncRepl state:

```
ldapsearch -x -LLL -h localhost -D cn=admin,cn=config -w password -b
 cn=config '(objectClass=*)' 'olcSyncrepl'
```

The typical setup with SSL looks like this:

```
{0}rid=000 provider="ldaps://adminserver.mycompany.us"
    bindmethod=simple
    timeout=0
    network-timeout=0
    binddn="cn=mybranch,ou=myorgunit,o=myorg,c=us"
    credentials="secret"
    starttls=no
    tls_cacert=/etc/SLEPOS/keys/certs/ca.crt
    searchbase="o=myorg,c=us"
    scope=sub
    type=refreshAndPersist
    retry="2 +"
```

If SSL is not used, the `tls_cacert=/etc/SLEPOS/keys/certs/ca.crt` line is not present.

Chaining

Chaining with the updateRef directive is the second part of the Administration Server LDAP and Branch Server LDAP collaboration. It handles updates in the opposite direction to that of the SyncRepl consumer when Branch Server is in online mode.

When a write request arrives on Branch Server LDAP and the Branch Server is in online mode, the request is forwarded using LDAP updateRef and chaining the overlay to Administration Server LDAP, where the actual request is executed. The UpdateRef directive is set up and maintained by the `posASWatch` daemon together with SyncRepl. Chaining settings are persistent and stored in the Branch Server's `slapd.conf`:

```
overlay                 chain
chain-uri               "ldaps://adminserver.mycompany.us"
chain-idassert-bind     bindmethod="simple"
                        binddn="cn=mybranch,ou=myorgunit,o=myorg,c=us"
                        credentials="secret"
                        mode="self"
chain-return-error      TRUE
```

These settings reflect the typical SLEPOS chain overlay setup.

When Branch Server is in offline mode, updateRef and Syncrepl are deactivated by posASWatch.

10.2 Using posAdmin to Manage the LDAP Directory

In a SUSE® Linux Enterprise Point of Service system, `posAdmin` is a command line tool used to add, modify, remove, or query Branch Server and Point of Service terminal information in the LDAP directory. For an overview of the LDAP directory structure and a reference of all SUSE Linux Enterprise Point of Service elements represented in the LDAP directory, refer to Chapter 10, *The LDAP Directory on SUSE Linux Enterprise Point of Service* (page 167).

Starting with an overview of mandatory LDAP objects and general command line options for `posAdmin`, the following sections explain how to define objects for Branches and Point of Service terminals and how to manage image objects with `posAdmin`. Find out which `posAdmin` options to use for modifying, removing or querying LDAP entries and how to update hardware information for specific Point of Service terminals, if needed.

NOTE: Must and May Attributes for LDAP Objects

Each LDAP object has two types of attributes: must and may attributes. The must attributes are the minimum requirements for an object. The may attributes are optional. This table lists only those may attributes that are relevant to SUSE Linux Enterprise Point of Service.

10.2.1 Mandatory LDAP Objects

When you run the `posInitAdminserver` command to configure the LDAP directory on the Administration Server, the following objects are automatically created:

- Country,

- Organization,

- Locator Object (`scHardware`),

- Global Container (`scRefObjectContainer`),

- Default Distribution Container (`scDistributionContainer`),

- `scPosImage` object for the minimal image.

With these objects in place, you must then use posAdmin to create the following mandatory objects in the LDAP tree:

Branch Objects:

- One or more `organizationalUnit` objects to represent your organization's structure.

- An `scLocation` object for each site where a Branch Server is located.

- An `scServerContainer` to contain all the Branch Server objects for a given site.

- An `scBranchServer` object and its associated configuration objects for each Branch Server in your system.

`scPosImage` Objects:
  Point of Service image objects for the system image files which the Branch Server should distribute to Point of Service terminals.

Point of Service Terminal Objects
  For example, `scCashRegister` objects and their associated configuration objects for each type of Point of Service terminal in your system:

- `scHarddisk` or `scRamDisk`,

- `scPxeFileTemplate`,

- `scConfigFileTemplate` (optional),

- `scConfigFileSyncTemplate` (optional).

IMPORTANT: LDAP Objects and Branch Server/Point of Service Terminals

Some administrative tasks in your SUSE Linux Enterprise Point of Service system depend on the existence of certain LDAP objects:

- Before you can run `posInitBranchserver` and deploy the Branch Server, you must have created the `scBranchServer` object and its supporting organizational structure.

- Before you boot the Point of Service terminals, you must create the scPosImage objects in the LDAP database. The images must be activated before you boot the Point of Service terminals. Terminals require an activated scPosImage object before they can download the corresponding physical image from the Branch Server. Activate either by setting the scPosImageVersion attribute of the relevant the scPosImage object to active or by creating a non-disabled scImageVersion object. For more information on activating images, see Section 4.6.2.8, "Activating Images" (page 52).

When you boot the Point of Service terminals, posleases2ldap automatically creates a Workstation object (scWorkstation) in the LDAP directory for every Point of Service terminal that registers on the Branch Server. For information on this process, see Section 6.3.3, "The hwtype.*MAC.HASH* File" (page 90).

As soon as the scWorkstation objects exist in the directory, you can define attributes specific to particular workstations. For example, you can assign a specific system image (scPosImage) object to a workstation. For instructions on this procedure, see Section 4.6.2.9, "Assigning an Image to a Point of Service Terminal" (page 53).

10.2.2 General Command Options

Find an overview of general posAdmin command line options in Table 10.1, "posAdmin: General Command Line Options" (page 176).

Table 10.1: *posAdmin: General Command Line Options*

Option	Description
--user	Specifies a username. Options --user and --password are not mandatory. If not used, username and password are read from the configuration file.
--password	Specifies a password. Used primarily together with --user for user authentication. For example,

Option	Description
| | ```
posAdmin --user
 cn=admin,o=myorg,c=us --password
 secret
``` |
| | If you use the `--user` option on the command line without password, you are prompted for a password. |
| `--base` | Specifies a base context in the LDAP directory. When you add a new location (branch), you specify an organization or organizational unit as a base. For example, |
| | ```
--base o=myorg,c=us --base
 ou=myorgunit,o=myorg,c=us
``` |
| | In some cases, you can use an abbreviation or a common name for the base. This is only possible if the common name is a unique value in the directory. For example: |
| | ```
--base myorgunit
``` |
| | If posAdmin cannot determine the base (no base or more than one base is found), it exits with an error message. |
| `--help` | Displays the basic command options. |

10.2.3 Modifying LDAP Entries

The modify option enables you to modify, add, or delete attributes of existing LDAP objects. Only may attributes can be added or deleted.

To add or to modify attributes, specify the element, an attribute value pair, and a DN. The main difference between command arguments in add, remove, and modify operations is that the add operation specifies the base DN of the directory element
```

below which the new entry should be created with the `--base` option. The modify and remove operations identify the target element with the `--DN` option.

If an operation is not finished successfully, posAdmin returns an error message.

Table 10.2, "posAdmin Options for Modifying LDAP Objects" (page 178) summarizes the posAdmin command options for modifying LDAP objects.

Table 10.2: *posAdmin Options for Modifying LDAP Objects*

Attribute	Type	Explanation
`--DN`	must	Distinguished name of the element to modify.
`--object`	must	Object with must or may attributes to be modified, for example: `scWorkstation`.
`--attribute`	must	Attribute, for example: `scPosImageVersion`.
`--value`	may	If a value is given, the attribute is modified; otherwise, the attribute entry is deleted.

The following command removes an image reference in terminal `CR01` (`scPosImageDn` value under `scWorkstation` object):

```
posAdmin
--modify --scWorkstation --scPosImageDn --DN
 cn=CR01,cn=mybranch,ou=myorgunit,o=myorg,c=us
```

The following command removes both image reference and image version in terminal `CR01` (`scPosImageDn` and `scPosImageVersion` values under `scWorkstation` object):

```
posAdmin
--modify --scWorkstation --scPosImageDn --scPosImageVersion
--DN cn=CR01,cn=mybranch,ou=myorgunit,o=myorg,c=us
```

The following command adds a new or modifies an existing image reference:

```
posAdmin
--modify --scWorkstation --scPosImageDn
 cn=myMinimal,cn=myTestImages,cn=global,o=myorg,c=us
--DN cn=CR01,cn=mybranch,ou=myorgunit,o=myorg,c=us
```

The following command adds a new or modifies an existing image reference and image version:

```
posAdmin
--modify --scWorkstation --scPosImageDn
 cn=myMinimal,cn=myTestImages,cn=global,o=myorg,c=us
--scPosImageVersion 2.1.0;active --DN
 cn=CR01,cn=mybranch,ou=myorgunit,o=myorg,c=us
```

The option `--multival` is used to add, remove, or modify values of attributes with multiple subvalues. Only one such subvalue can be be modified by a single `posAdmin` command. Other subvalues are preserved.

The following command adds image version `2.1.1;active` to the image `myMinimal` (`scPosImageVersion` value under `scPosImage` object):

```
posAdmin
--modify --multival --scPosImage --scPosImageVersion '=>2.1.1;active'
--DN cn=myMinimal,cn=myTestImages,cn=global,o=myorg,c=us
```

The following command removes image version `2.0.4;active` (if it exists):

```
posAdmin
--modify --multival --scPosImage --scPosImageVersion '2.0.4;active=>'
--DN cn=myMinimal,cn=myTestImages,cn=global,o=myorg,c=us
```

The following command modifies image version `2.0.4;active` to `2.0.4;passive` (assuming it exists):

```
posAdmin
--modify --multival --scPosImage --scPosImageVersion
 '2.0.4;active=>2.0.4;passive'
--DN cn=myMinimal,cn=myTestImages,cn=global,o=myorg,c=us
```

The following commands manipulate `scIdPool` values. For example, to add `priId0` to a new subvalue, use:

```
posAdmin --DN cn=mybranch,ou=myorgunit,o=myorg,c=us --modify --multival
--scLocation --scIdPool '=>priId0'
```

To add `secId1` and `secId2` together to one new subvalue, use:

```
posAdmin --DN cn=mybranch,ou=myorgunit,o=myorg,c=us --modify --multival
--scLocation --scIdPool '=>secId1;secId2'
```

The `scIdPool` should then be represented as:

```
priId0
secId1;secId2
```

To remove `secId1` and `secId2`, use:

```
posAdmin --DN cn=mybranch,ou=myorgunit,o=myorg,c=us --modify --multival
--scLocation --scIdPool 'secId1;secId2=>'
```

Because of the nature of multivalue attributes, it is not possible to manipulate IDs within the same subvalue separately. To only remove `secId1`, use:

```
posAdmin --DN cn=mybranch,ou=myorgunit,o=myorg,c=us --modify --multival
--scLocation --scIdPool 'secId1;secId2=>secId2'
```

To see what IDs are present and how they are inserted, use `posAdmin`:

```
 posAdmin --base ou=myorgunit,o=myorg,c=us \
--query --scLocation --scIdPool
```

10.2.4 Removing LDAP Entries

To remove an object from the LDAP directory, use the `--remove` option and the `--DN` attribute with the unique name of the object to delete. If the referred object has subentries, you must add the `--recursive` option.

Table 10.3, "posAdmin Options for Deleting LDAP Objects" (page 180) summarizes the posAdmin command options for deleting LDAP objects.

Table 10.3: *posAdmin Options for Deleting LDAP Objects*

Option	Type	Description
--DN	must	Distinguished name of the object to delete.

Option	Type	Description
--recursive	may	Option to delete an object with all sub-objects.

The following command removes all images in the distribution container (scDistributionContainer object) myTestImages including the container itself:

```
posAdmin
--remove --recursive  --DN cn=myTestImages,cn=global,o=myorg,c=us
```

The following command removes the image (scPosImage object) myMinimal in the distribution container myTestImages:

```
posAdmin
--remove --DN cn=myMinimal,cn=myTestImages,cn=global,o=myorg,c=us
```

The following command removes registered terminal (scWorkstation object) CR01:

```
posAdmin
--remove --DN cn=CR01,cn=mybranch,ou=myorgunit,o=myorg,c=us
```

Terminals can be also removed according to the time of their last boot, which is stored in the scLastBootTime of the scWorkstation object. To delete workstations that were not booted in last T seconds, use: pos ws-remove --no-boot-in-last T. To delete workstations that were not booted since specified date, use: pos ws-remove --no-boot-since datetime, where datetime is a date/time string compatible with linux date, for example 2013-08-13 15:21:14. If scLastBootTime is empty, the workstaton will never be deleted.

Under normal conditions, workstations are additionaly checked whether they are online or not, and deleted only if offline and older than specified. To override this check, use --force parameter. On the other hand, if you only want to test which workstations will be removed, use --dry-run parameter.

10.2.5 Querying LDAP Objects

To query LDAP, use the --query option, --DN path option, an object option such as --scLocation or --scBranchServer, and, if desired, an attribute value pair(s). Also, there are the `--list` and `--full` switches that control how and what data are displayed, with treeview and queried attributes only as default.

Table 10.4, "posAdmin Options for Querying the LDAP Database" (page 182) summarizes the posAdmin command options for querying the LDAP database.

Table 10.4: *posAdmin Options for Querying the LDAP Database*

Option	Type	Description
`--base` *base*	may	The base option sets the base in which to search for objects. The default base is the organization (o=*myorg*,c=*us*).
`--DN` *regexp*	may	Regular expression for distinguished name of the queried element.
`--object`	may	Object to be queried, e.g., `--scLocation`.
`--attribute` *regexp*	may	Show only objects whose attribute value conforms to the regular expression. The `--attribute` options can also be used without specified values. In such a case, all objects are shown, but only the specified attributes are printed in the output (other attributes are ommited).

Option	Type	Description
--list	may	Displays the result as a list, not as a tree (useful for script processing).
--full	may	Displays all attributes and all their values (--attribute --value filtering still takes place). Also enables display of DN for each object.
--showDN	may	Displays all DNs of found objects also in the tree view.

For example, to list all locations in the ou=*myorgunit*,o=*myorg*,c=*us* organizational unit showing all data, use:

```
posAdmin --base ou=myorgunit,o=myorg,c=us \
--query --scLocation
```

To list all locations in the ou=*myorgunit*,o=*myorg*,c=*us* organizational unit showing only ipNetworkNumber, use:

```
posAdmin --base ou=myorgunit,o=myorg,c=us \
--query --scLocation --ipNetworkNumber
```

To list all locations in the ou=*myorgunit*,o=*myorg*,c=*us* organizational unit with the ipNetworkNumber 192.168.1.0, use:

```
posAdmin --base ou=myorgunit,o=myorg,c=us \
--query --scLocation --ipNetworkNumber 192.168.1.0
```

To list all IDs in all locations in the ou=*myorgunit*,o=*myorg*,c=*us* organizational unit, use:

```
posAdmin --base ou=myorgunit,o=myorg,c=us \
--query --scLocation --scIdPool
```

To find out if there is a workstation registered with ID equal to `terminal1`, use:

```
posAdmin --query --scWorkstation --cn terminal1
```

To find if there is any workstation registered with ID containing the `terminal` substring and ending with two or three digits and having mac address composed of digits only, use:

```
posAdmin --query --scWorkstation --cn '.*terminal.*\D*\d{2,3}' --macAddress
 '(\d\d:){5}\d\d'
```

To find all roles under role containers `roles1` or `roles2` and show all their attributes, use:

```
posAdmin --query --DN '.*,cn=(roles1|roles2),.*' --scRole --full
```

To get a plain list consisting only of DNs of all cash registers using a raid scheme, use:

```
posAdmin --query --scCashRegister --scRaidScheme '.*'  --list | grep DN: |
 cut -d ' ' -f2
```

10.2.6 posAdmin XML Interface

Adding SLEPOS LDAP objects via `posAdmin` can be a time consuming and confusing process prone to errors. To address this inconvenience, SLEPOS is introducing a new XML interface for `posAdmin`. With the XML interface, it is possible to export LDAP data to an XML file and import data from an XML file into the LDAP database.

The XML approach has the following advanges:

• Ability to define more than one LDAP object at a time.

• Improved readability of object definitions for human administrators and scripts.

• Implementation of precise validation checks performed before actually writing to the LDAP database.

10.2.6.1 Exporting LDAP Database to XML

To export the complete LDAP database to an XML file, use:

```
posAdmin --export --type XML --file filename
```

You can also export a database subtree by using the `--base` option with the appropriate baseDN parameter:

```
posAdmin --export --type XML --file filename --base baseDN
```

10.2.6.2 Importing XML to LDAP Database

To import the SLEPOS XML file into the LDAP database use:

```
posAdmin --import --type XML --file filename
```

The XML import is performed in three steps:

1. Validation of the XML file (see Section 10.2.6.5, "SLEPOS XML validation" (page 188)).

2. Validation of SLEPOS data with imported data applied (see Section 10.3, "LDAP Validation and Checking" (page 194)).

3. If both checks are succesful, the LDAP database is updated. In case of any error, the import is interrupted and an explanatory message displayed.

10.2.6.3 Using XML to Modify LDAP Data

SLEPOS XML supports four types of modification of LDAP data:

insert
> Use to add new data if the existing LDAP data should not be modified.
>
> If data being added already exist in the LDAP database, they are skipped and the import continues. This is the default modification type.

replace
> Use to add new data or to replace existing LDAP data.
>
> If data being added already exist in the LDAP database, LDAP data are overwritten. XML must specify all required attributes. If an element uses `replace modifyType`, all its children must also use `replace modifyType`.

update

Use update to modify existing LDAP data.

XML does not need to specify all required attributes. Attributes with nonempty tags are replaced in LDAP data. Attributes with empty tags are deleted from LDAP data. Unspecified attributes will not be changed.

delete

Use to delete LDAP data.

If data do not exist in the LDAP database, the operation is skipped. If an element uses `delete modifyType`, all its children must use `delete modifyType`.

The following example adds a new global role `role2`, deletes the description of `role1`, changes the global image name `graphical` to `graphical-updated` and deletes the global image `testImage`, all using one XML file:

```
<?xml version="1.0" encoding="utf-8" standalone="no"?>
<slepos xmlversion="0.2" xmlns="http://www.suse.com/SLEPOS"
 xmlns:xi="http://www.w3.org/2001/XInclude">
    <!-- add scRole role2 as global role. Not specified modifyType defaults
 to insert -->
    <scRole dn="cn=role2,cn=global,o=myorg,c=us">
        <attributes>
            <scRoleName>ramdisk role</scRoleName>
            <scRoleDescription>use ramdisk</scRoleDescription>
        </attributes>
    </scRole>

    <!-- delete description of role1 -->
    <scRole dn="cn=role1,cn=global,o=myorg,c=us" modifyType="update">
        <attributes>
            <scRoleDescription />
        </attributes>
    </scRole>

    <!-- update image name graphical to graphical-updated -->
    <scPosImage dn="cn=graphical,cn=default,cn=global,o=myorg,c=us"
 modifyType="update">
        <attributes>
            <scImageName>graphical-updated</scImageName>
        </attributes>
    </scPosImage>

    <!-- delete testImage -->
    <scPosImage dn="cn=testImage,cn=default,cn=global,o=myorg,c=us"
 modifyType="delete">
        <attributes />
```

```
        </scPosImage>
</slepos>
```

10.2.6.4 SLEPOS XML Format

Example of scLocation object in SLEPOS XML:

```
<?xml version="1.0" encoding="utf-8" standalone="no"?>

<slepos xmlversion="0.2" xmlns:slepos="http://www.suse.com/SLEPOS"
xmlns:xi="http://www.w3.org/2001/XInclude">
    <organization dn="o=myorg,c=us">
        <attributes />
      <organizationalUnit dn="ou=myorgunit">
        <attributes>
          <description>My organizational unit</description>
        </attributes>
        <scLocation dn="cn=mybranch">
          <attributes>
            <ipNetworkNumber>192.168.125.0</ipNetworkNumber>
            <ipNetmaskNumber>255.255.255.0</ipNetmaskNumber>
            <scDhcpRange>192.168.125.10,192.168.125.50</scDhcpRange>
            <scDhcpFixedRange>192.168.125.51,192.168.125.151</
scDhcpFixedRange>
            <scDefaultGw>192.168.125.253</scDefaultGw>
            <scDynamicIp>TRUE</scDynamicIp>
            <scWorkstationBaseName>CR</scWorkstationBaseName>
            <scEnumerationMask>00</scEnumerationMask>
            <scDhcpExtern>FALSE</scDhcpExtern>
            <userPassword>password</userPassword>
            <scDnsMapFunc>direct</scDnsMapFunc>
            <scIpMapFunc>transform:([0-9.]+)</scIpMapFunc>
          </attributes>
        </scLocation>
      </organizationalUnit>
    </organization>
  </slepos>
```

SLEPOS XML data are always encapsulated by the <slepos></slepos> tags
specifying SLEPOS and XInclude namespaces.

The <attributes> element must always be present even if it defines no
attributes.

Each objectClass element (for example <scLocation>) has an optional parameter
modifyType with the following possible values: insert, replace, update,
and delete. If not specified, modifyType defaults to insert.

You can find an example of SLEPOS XML configuration for a combined server (Administration Server and Branch Server on a single machine) in `/usr/share/doc/packages/POS_Contrib/SLEPOS-XML/`.

Specifying LDAP Distinguished Names (DNs)

In SLEPOS XML, each element representing a LDAP object class has a mandatory attribute DN. The content of the DN attribute depends on the position of the element:

* If the element is directly under the `<slepos:slepos>` element, the DN attribute must contain the full DN of the entry this element is representing. The only exception is when the `<slepos:slepos>` element specifies its `baseDN` attribute. In such a case, the DN attribute is specified in relation to the `baseDN` attribute.

* In all other cases, the DN attribute must be specified relative to its parent.

In the provided example, the DN of organization is `o=myorg,c=us` and because it is the direct child of `<slepos:slepos>`, the complete DN is specified. In comparison, the `scLocation`'s complete DN is `cn=mybranch,ou=myorgunit,o=myorg,c=us`, but we specify only the first part of its DN, so attribute dn is `cn=mybranch`.

Handling `scConfigFileTemplate` objects

The `scConfigFileTemplate` objects in LDAP contain actual data of given configuration files. SLEPOS XML files do not include this data directly. The respective configuration files are created during the export in the same directory as the SLEPOS XML file. Their filenames are in the following format: `xml_file_name-entry_dn`.`conf` and are written as `scConfigFileData` attribute to XML.

During import, it is checked if the `scConfigFileData` attributes link to existing files. If yes, the given files are loaded and inserted as `scConfigFileData` objects, otherwise `scConfigFileData` are left intact.

10.2.6.5 SLEPOS XML validation

Validation of SLEPOS XML is done via the command:

```
posAdmin --validateXML --file filename [--schema <filename>]
```

It performs XML validation against SLEPOS XML RelaxNG schema. If the --schema parameter is not specified, the validation schema is generated from the SLEPOS LDAP schema.

10.2.6.6 Evaluation of Modifications and Limitations

Modifications are evaluated in the order of the elements in the XML file. This is important when the same data are modified multiple times in one XML file. The same rules apply as for adding to LDAP. For example, it is allowed to insert and delete the very same data in one XML file, which results in no change in LDAP. Inserting two or more elements with the same DN means that the first element is written to LDAP but others are skipped. Because of this way of evaluation, it is not possible to change the `delete` or `replace` modification types in children elements.

SLEPOS XML modification currently does not allow moving or renaming of entries (the moddn/modrdn LDAP operation).

10.2.6.7 Compatibility and Converting of Different XML Versions

In SLEPOS both versions 0.1 and 0.2 of SLEPOS XML are supported. Note that `posAdmin` XML export produces SLEPOS XML version 0.2. SLEPOS ships with XSL template for converting SLEPOS XML 0.1 to 0.2. This template is stored in /etc/SLEPOS/template/XML/SLEPOSxml0.1to0.2.xslt.

Use the following command to convert the XML file:

```
xsltproc -o newXMLFile /etc/SLEPOS/template/XML/
SLEPOSxml0.1to0.2.xslt oldXMLFile
```

10.2.7 SLEPOS posAdmin Graphical User Interface

SLEPOS posAdmin-GUI is graphical tool to ease configuration of branch servers, images and cash registers. posAdmin-GUI utilizes the YaST graphical library to provide a familiar look and feel. posAdmin GUI is included in the additional SLEPOS package `POS_Server-AdminGUI`.

The `posAdmin-GUI` command can be started if the `POS_Server-AdminGUI` package and its requirements are installed. The initialized SLEPOS environment is not a requirement. GUI is started by the `posAdmin-GUI` command (specifically `/usr/sbin/posAdmin-GUI.pl`). The `posAdmin-GUI` command accepts one optional parameter containing the filename of the XML file generated by posAdmin-GUI or the XML file exported from LDAP. However, posAdmin-GUI works only with one BranchServer (scLocation) object, using exported XML file with more scLocations results in no BranchServer (scLocation) data loaded. Only global images (scPosImage), cash registers (scCashRegister) and roles (scRole) are loaded.

The posAdmin GUI work flow is divided into 4 stages: BranchServer specific configuration, Images, Cash Registers and Final stage.

10.2.7.1 BranchServer configuration

The first stage covers the Branch Server (`scLocation`, `scNetworkcard`, `scService`, ...) and roles configuration. This stage is further divided into several parts:

Company details and its organizational structure
Organization, country, organizational units and location details together create LDAP Distinguished Name (DN) for the Branch Server's `scLocation` object. Additional organizational units can be added by clicking on *Add nested OU*. DN is created by concatenating entered data "from the bottom" — location as the first up to the organization and the country.

Enablement of the external DHCP, local and global roles
The *External DHCP* check box sets `scDhcpExtern` attribute to `TRUE` to disable the SLEPOS managed DHCP service.

To enable the role-based approach, *Use roles* must be checked. Checking only *Use global roles* does not enable roles at all. If *Use global roles* and *Use roles* are checked, the role-based mode and all roles (defined under global and location) are enabled. If *Use roles* is checked and *Use global roles* is not checked, the role-based mode is enabled, but only the roles defined under the location are used. If *Use roles* is not checked, roles are not enabled at all.

Roles configuration

Individual roles can be configured in the roles configuration window accessible after clicking on the *Roles configuration* button. The roles configuration window presents option to configure the ID pool (the `scIdPool` attribute). Individual IDs are separated by semi-colon ';'. Then you can add, edit or remove roles.

To add a role ensure you have selected *<add new role>* in the list of roles, select local or global role, enter the role name and click *Add role*.

To modify a role, select the role in the role list, update any role attributes and click *Update role*.

To remove a role, select the role in the role list and click *Remove role*.

For each role, the file templates can be managed by clicking *Manage file templates*. When done editing, click *Return to BS configuration* to return.

File templates configuration

Static file templates (`scConfigFileTemplate`), dynamic file templates (`scConfigFileSyncTemplate`) and PXE file templates (`scPxeFileTemplate`) can be configured here.

To add a template, ensure you have selected *<add new template>* in list of templates, then select the type of template and fill in required information. The *Source file* points to the file on the server to load, the *Target file* is the path where to put the loaded file in the deployed workstation.

To modify a template, select the template in template list, update any attributes and click *Update template*.

To remove a template, select the template in the template list and click *Remove template*.

When you are done, click *Return* to return back to the previous configuration window.

Configuration of the Branch Server services and network

Branch Server services configuration usually needs little adjusting. It preloads services default configurations which should suit almost all use cases. Note: service specific parameters cannot contain arbitrary settings. They refer to

LDAP attributes, so only attributes present in the SLEPOS LDAP schema can be entered. Usage model is similar to the Roles and File templates configuration.

The Branch Server network configuration covers configuration of the network to which workstations are connected (branch internal network). There is no need to define network cards facing WAN, VPN, etc. The Branch Server hostname refers to the common name (cn) attribute of the `scBranchServer` object in LDAP and means the hostname of the Branch Server in the branch internal network. The Branch Server network address refers to `ipNetworkNumber`, the network mask refers to `ipNetmaskNumber`, the default gateway refers to `scDefaultGw`, the DHCP fixed IP range refers to `scDhcpFixedRange`, the DHCP dynamic IP range refers to `scDhcpRange`attribute of the `scLocation` object class.

Advanced options after enabling "Advanced mode"
The advanced mode is enabled by checking the *Advanced mode* checkbox. The following attributes are available in the advanced mode: the IP mapping function (`scIpMapFunc`), the DNS mapping function (`scDnsMapFunc`), the associated domain (`associatedDomain`), the enumeration mask (`scEnumerationMask`), the workstation base name (`scWorkstationBaseName`) and the server container (the common name of the `scServerContainer` object).

All values are either imported from the provided XML or filled with SLEPOS defaults.

10.2.7.2 Images configuration

Images configuration lists all registered local and global images. To add a new image, make sure *<add new image>* is selected in the image list.

All fields corresponds to LDAP attributes of the *scPosImage* LDAP object: the image name (`scImageName`), the image version (`scImageVersion`), the image file (`scImageFile`). The password for encrypted images can be entered after enabling the advanced mode, which also reveals DHCP options for the remote boot (`scDhcpOptionsRemote`), the DHCP options for local boot (`scDhcpOptionsLocal`) and block size (`scBsize`). The configuration of file templates is also available for every image.

10.2.7.3 Cash register configuration

Cash register configuration lists all registered local, global and role based (if enabled) cash registers. To add a new cash register, make sure that *<add new image>* is selected in the list of cash registers.

In the default mode, there is only one editable field, the *CashRegister name*, which corresponds to the `scCashRegisterName` attribute of the `scCashRegister` LDAP object. The associated image field is dynamically filled from the list of registered images.

An important part of the cash register configuration is disk management, which is done in the *Manage disks* window. The disk configuration differs for hard disks and ram disks. The posAdmin-GUI adapts itself according to the disk type. The ram disk configuration is simple by filling the device ID (`scDevice` attribute of `scRamDisk` object). The hard disk configuration needs partitioning to be set up. The needed partitioning related fields are the partition number (`scPartNum`), the partition type (`scPartType`), the partition mountpoint (`scPartMount`), the partition size (`scPartSize`) and the partition password (`scPassword`). After filling these information (see Section 4.6.2.3, "Adding an `scHarddisk` Object" (page 46)) click on *Add partition*. After all partitions are added, click *Add disk* or *Update disk*.

10.2.7.4 Finalize

If posAdmin-GUI is running on a configured Administration Server, the *Update LDAP database* button is enabled together with the *Create Offline Initialization File after LDAP is updated* checkbox. Using this you can directly update the SLEPOS LDAP with the new configured data and also create the package for offline/automated Branch Server configuration. If posAdmin-GUI is not running on Administration Server or you don't want to update LDAP immediately, you can export the configured data as a SLEPOS XML file by using the *Create XML configuration* button. This XML file can be edited and imported to SLEPOS LDAP using the `posAdmin --import --type XML --file <filename>` command and/or used as a base for another Branch Server and provided as a start argument to posAdmin-GUI.

10.2.8 Editing LDAP Database Using External Tools

SUSE Linux Enterprise Point of Service LDAP database entries are variously interconnected and sometimes contain automatically computed values. The posAdmin tool is aware of that and it updates all related parts of the database when necessary. However, when other tools are used, for example LDAP editors like GQ or JXplorer, they are not aware of such dependencies. posAdmin provides LDAP refresh feature which recomputes and updates all dependencies for every entry in the LDAP tree:

```
posAdmin --refresh
```

The `posAdmin --refresh` command should be called after each modification of the LDAP database using 3rd party tools. This feature can be safely called on a regular basis e.g. by using cron daemon.

10.3 LDAP Validation and Checking

SLEPOS contains LDAP validation and checking tools. Simple validation and checking is automatically performed during each `posAdmin` addition or modification call. Full validation is performed during SLEPOS XML import or on demand via the following command:

```
posAdmin --validate
```

There is an important difference between LDAP validation during XML import and validation invoked by the `posAdmin --validate` command. If important LDAP objects are found missing during the XML import, the missing objects are reported, but the import continues without a failure. In contrast, calling `posAdmin --validate` returns an error the first time a file is missing and stops validation.

Additionally, XML and LDIF files can be validated against the SLEPOS database. LDIF files can be validated using the following command:

```
posAdmin --validateLDIF --file filename
```

XML can be validated using the following command:

```
posAdmin --validateXML --file filename
```

10.4 Logical Structure of the LDAP Directory

The LDAP directory is designed with multiple, hierarchical object classes so it can accommodate large corporate structures. The following list describes the standard object classes represented in the SUSE Linux Enterprise Point of Service LDAP directory tree. For a complete listing of SUSE Linux Enterprise Point of Service object classes and their attributes, see Section 10.5, "LDAP Objects Reference" (page 201) or refer to the OpenLDAP schemata specific to SUSE Linux Enterprise Point of Service that are located under `/etc/openldap/schema/sc-pos-attr.schema` and `/etc/openldap/schema/sc-pos-pos-obj.schema`, respectively.

Root

   The top level in the LDAP tree. The root represents the world. The next level is represented by Country.

Country

   The country in which the organization is located. The next level is represented by Organization.

Organization (`organization`)

   The name of the organization represented in the LDAP tree. The next level is represented by:

   - Locator Object,

   - Global,

   - Organizational Units.

Locator Object (`scHardware`)

   posInitAdminserver initially creates an object of the type `scHardware`, for example `cn=standards, o=`*`myorg,`* `c=`*`us`*. The purpose of this object is to contain the default PXE boot filename (in the `scDhcpOptionsRemote`, being `/boot/pxelinux.0`, by default).

Global (`scRefObjectContainer`)

   This initial reference object container is created automatically.

All globally valid information for a chain or company—that is server hardware, Point of Service hardware, or client images—is stored in the global container in the form of reference objects. These reference objects are linked to the actual entries for the Point of Service terminals and servers in the branches using distinguished names.

The initial LDAP structure after installation includes only one `scRefObjectContainer` named global under the directory root. Other `scRefObjectContainer` objects can be added as needed. However, the `scRefObjectContainer` container objects should always have `cn=global` and also appear only once per directory level. This provides great flexibility. For example, each server can be assigned its own reference objects and therefore its own hardware types. On the other hand, if all servers have the same hardware, a unified standard can be defined in the global container on the regional or organizational level. The next level is represented by:

- Distribution Container ,

- Hardware Reference Object,

- Role.

Distribution Container (`scDistributionContainer`)
A container for the distribution of sets of images.

A distribution set is a collection of images designed for Point of Service terminals on a given version of the Linux kernel. The Default distribution container references the current kernel version included in SUSE Linux Enterprise Point of Service. The next level is represented by Image Reference Object.

Image Reference Object (`scPosImage`)
The Image Reference object stores information about an image stored on the Administration Server.

By default, an Image Reference object is created for the minimal client image. For information on adding this object class to the LDAP directory, see Section 4.6.2.6, "Adding an `scPosImage` Object" (page 51). The next level is represented by:

- File-Based Configuration Template,

- LDAP-Based Configuration Template.

File-Based Configuration Template (`scConfigFileSyncTemplate`)
`scConfigFileSyncTemplate` objects are used when running services, such as X Windows, which require hardware-dependent configuration files. The `scConfigFileSyncTemplate` object points to the configuration file that a Point of Service terminal needs to run a given service. This object differs from `scConfigFileTemplate` objects because the configuration data is not stored in the object; rather, the object points to a configuration file outside the LDAP directory.

This element can also exist under `scCashRegister` objects.

For information on adding this object class to the LDAP directory, see Section 4.6.2.5, "Adding an `scConfigFileSyncTemplate` Object" (page 49).

LDAP-Based Configuration Template (`scConfigFileTemplate`)
`scConfigFileTemplate` objects are used when running services, such as the X Window service, which require hardware-dependent configuration files. An `scConfigFileTemplate` object contains the configuration file data that a Point of Service terminal needs to run a given service.

This element can also exist under `scCashRegister` objects.

For information on adding this object class to the LDAP directory, see Section 4.6.2.4, "Adding an `scConfigFileTemplate` Object" (page 48).

Hardware Reference Object (`scCashRegister`)
The Hardware Reference object stores information about Point of Service hardware.

Typically, you should define an `scCashRegister` object for each type of terminal used on the SUSE Linux Enterprise Point of Service system; however, if a Point of Service terminal does not have an `scCashRegister` object for its specific hardware type, it will use the configuration defined in the default `scCashRegister` object. For information on adding this object class to the LDAP directory, see Section 4.6.2.1, "Adding an `scCashRegister` Object" (page 44). The next level is represented by:

- Hard Disk,

- RAM Disk,

- File-Based Configuration Template,

- LDAP-Based Configuration Template.

Hard Disk (`scHarddisk`)

The configuration for a Point of Service terminal hard disk.

For information on adding this object class to the LDAP directory, see Section 4.6.2.3, "Adding an `scHarddisk` Object" (page 46).

RAM Disk (`scRamDisk`)

The configuration for a Point of Service terminal RAM disk.

For information on adding this object class to the LDAP directory, see Section 4.6.2.2, "Adding an `scRamDisk` Object" (page 46).

Organizational Units (`organizationalUnit`)

Organizational units were introduced to improve organizational coherence. They typically represent organizational structures such as regions, branches or divisions.

For information on adding this object class to the LDAP directory, see Section 4.6.1.1, "Creating organizationalUnit Objects" (page 39). The next level is represented by Location.

Location (`scLocation`)

A branch office; this is a site where a Branch Server and Point of Service terminals are located. Location containers are used to store information about the deployed Point of Service terminals and the Branch Servers. This and all other information that can be modified at the Branch Server should be stored or referenced in the Location containers to limit the need to grant write privileges to subtrees.

For information on adding this object class to the LDAP directory, see Section 4.6.1.2, "Adding an `scLocation` Object" (page 39). The next level is represented by:

- Workstation,

- Server Container.

Workstation (`scWorkstation`)

The Workstation object stores information for a specific Point of Service terminal. Using information from the Hardware Reference object (`scCashRegister`) and Image Reference object (`scPosImage`), `posleases2ldap` automatically creates a Workstation object in the LDAP directory for every Point of Service terminal that registers on the Branch Server. For information on this process, see Section 6.3.3, "The hwtype.*MAC.HASH* File" (page 90).

Server Container (`scServerContainer`)
A container for all the Branch Server objects for a given site. The information pertaining to the Branch Servers is stored in the Server container.

To provide system redundancy and failover, there can be multiple Branch Servers for each site.

For information on adding this object class to the LDAP directory, see Section 4.6.1.3, "Adding an `scServerContainer` and `scBranchServer` Objects" (page 40). The next level is represented by: Branch Server.

Branch Server (`scBranchServer`)
The Branch Server object stores configuration information that is specific to each Branch Server. There must be a Branch Server object for every Branch Server in the SUSE Linux Enterprise Point of Service system.

IMPORTANT: Defining the Branch Server Hostname

The location of the `scBranchServer` object in the LDAP directory must correspond to the hostname defined for the Admin/Branch Server during installation. For example, if the hostname is `bs.mybranch.myorgunit.myorg.us`, the DN of the `scBranchServer` object has to be `cn=bs,cn=server,cn=mybranch,ou=myorgunit,o=myorg,c=us`. You must create the `scBranchServer` object and its supporting organizational structure before you can run `posInitBranchserver` and deploy the Branch Server. For information on creating the Branch Server objects, see Section 4.6.1, "Creating Branch Server Objects in LDAP" (page 38).

The Administration Server does not have an associated object in the LDAP tree structure.

For information on adding this object class to the LDAP directory, see Section 4.6.1.3, "Adding an `scServerContainer` and `scBranchServer` Objects" (page 40). The next level is represented by:

- Service,

- Network Card,

- Hard Disk.

Service (`scService`)
:   The configuration for Branch Server services like DNS, TFTP, or DHCP.

    For information on adding this object class to the LDAP directory, see Section 4.6.1.3, "Adding an `scServerContainer` and `scBranchServer` Objects" (page 40).

Network Card (`scNetworkcard`)
:   The configuration for a Branch Server network interface card.

    For information on adding this object class to the LDAP directory, see Step 3 (page 41).

Hard Disk (`scHarddisk`)
:   The configuration for the Branch Server's boot hard disk.

    For information on adding this object class to the LDAP directory, see Section 4.6.2.3, "Adding an `scHarddisk` Object" (page 46).

Role (`scRole`)
:   The definition of a role.

    For information on adding this object class to the LDAP directory, see Section 9.2, "Using Terminals with Roles" (page 148).

To illustrate how the directory structure is used, here is a sample query procedure using objects from the example LDAP structure described above.

1. A search is performed for an object of object class `scLocation` with `cn=eastbay`.

NOTE: Search Scope of the Core Scripts

The core scripts only search for the names of the object classes. The common name for an entry is not used.

---

2. Below `scLocation` a search for an object of object class `scServerContainer` (server) is carried out.

3. Below this `scServerContainer`, we search for an an object of object class `scBranchServer` with `cn=bs`.

4. Data specific to this server is located below this `scBranchServer` object, such as objects of object class `scNetworkcard`, in which the IP addresses are indicated.

5. All the data that generally applies to this hardware type, such as partitioning, is read from a reference object of object class `scRefServer` in which this hardware is described. These reference objects are always organized as containers of an object of object class `scRefObjectContainer`.

6. Next, the reference objects that are valid for this Branch Server are located. First the attribute `scRefServerDn` in the `scBranchServer` object that represents this server is read. If a DN is included here, the target is used as the reference object for the Branch Server.

7. If the entry is empty, the search for an object of the object class `scHardware` moves upward in the directory structure, one level at a time. If the attribute `scRefServerDn` is set for this type of object, this DN is taken as the target; if not, the search continues upward in the directory structure. If no appropriate object with this attribute is found all the way up to the root level, the process aborts with an error.

The procedure is similar for Point of Service terminal hardware. In this example, in addition to the referenced hardware type (through attribute `scRefPcDn` to a `scCashRegister` object), `scPosImageDn` points to the reference image `scPosImage` object.

10.5 LDAP Objects Reference

This section provides an alphabetical list of all SUSE Linux Enterprise Point of Service elements represented in the LDAP directory. The must attributes for each element must be defined when creating the element with posAdmin. The may attributes are optional. All elements are structural.

10.5.1 organizationalUnit

Organizational Unit (`organizationalUnit`) objects are containers that typically represent regions, divisions, or branches within a company. These objects can be nested to visually represent the structure and organization of your company. Branch location objects are created in `organizationalUnit` containers within the LDAP directory.

Table 10.5: *organizationalUnit*

Name	Type	Description
`ou`	must	name of organizational unit
`description`	may	`description` of the organizational unit

10.5.2 scBranchServer

The Branch Server object stores configuration information that is specific to each Branch Server. There must be a Branch Server object for every Branch Server in the SUSE Linux Enterprise Point of Service system. Note that the Administration Server does not have an associated object in the LDAP tree structure.

IMPORTANT: Defining the Branch Server Hostname

The location of the `scBranchServer` object in the LDAP directory must correspond to the hostname defined for the Branch Server during installation. For example, if the hostname is `bs.mybranch.myorgunit.myorg.us`, the `dn` of the `scBranchServer` object is `cn=bs,cn=server,cn=mybranch,ou=myorgunit,o=myorg,c=us`. You must create the `scBranchServer` object and its supporting organizational structure before you can run `posInitBranchserver` and deploy the Branch Server. For information on creating the Branch Server objects, see Section 4.6.1, "Creating Branch Server Objects in LDAP" (page 38).

For information on adding this object class to the LDAP directory, see Section 4.6.1.3, "Adding an `scServerContainer` and `scBranchServer` Objects" (page 40).

Table 10.6: *scBranchServer*

Name	Type	Description
cn	must	hostname of the server
scPubKey	may,singlevalue	Public key stored at server for the SSH client
scRefServerDn	may,singlevalue	DN of a scRefServer

10.5.3 scCashRegister

The scCashRegister objects (also called hardware reference objects) store information about specific Point of Service hardware.

Typically, you should define an scCashRegister object for each type of terminal used on the SLEPOS system. However, if a Point of Service terminal does not have a specific scCashRegister object for its specific hardware type, it will use the configuration defined in the default scCashRegister object. For information on adding this object class to the LDAP directory, see Section 4.6.2.1, "Adding an scCashRegister Object" (page 44).

Table 10.7: *scCashRegister*

Name	Type	Description
cn	must	Common name of this object, from first part of DN
scCashRegisterName	must,multivalue	The model type of the Point of Service terminal. If this field is set to "default", the current scCashRegister object is used as the default Point of

Name	Type	Description
		Service configuration. If a Point of Service terminal does not have an `scCashRegister` object for its specific hardware type, it will use the configuration defined in the default `scCashRegister` object
`scDiskJournal`	may,singlevalue	Turn on disk journaling. This will only occur on diskfull systems. (`TRUE` or `FALSE`)
`scPosDeltaImageDn`	may,multivalue,deprecated	DN of delta image for a Point Of Service terminal
`scPosImageDn`	may,singlevalue	The DN of the default system image defined for this Point of Service terminal type
`scRaidScheme`	may,singlevalue	Definition of RAID. Only RAID type 1 is supported. The format of the entry is: 1 disk1 disk2. The disks can be specified by name (`/dev/sda`) or by id (`/dev/disk/by-id/ata-ST3160815AS_Z4A1ATWL`).

Name	Type	Description
		The values are separated by spaces

10.5.4 scConfigFileSyncTemplate

scConfigFileSyncTemplate objects are used when running services, such as X Windows, which require hardware-dependent configuration files. The scConfigFileSyncTemplate object points to the configuration file that a Point of Service terminal needs to run a given service. This object differs from scConfigFileTemplate objects, because the configuration data is not stored in the object; rather, the object points to a configuration file outside the LDAP directory.

This element exists under Image Reference objects (class scPosImage), but it can also exist under scCashRegister objects.

For information on adding this object class to the LDAP directory, see Section 4.6.2.5, "Adding an scConfigFileSyncTemplate Object" (page 49).

Table 10.8: *scConfigFileSyncTemplate*

Name	Type	Description
cn	must	Name of configuration file
scBsize	must,singlevalue	Block size for the TFTP download of the system image. Minimum 4096 for image size up to 128MB, maximum 65464 for image size up to 2GB
scConfigFile	must,multivalue	File name of configuration file

Name	Type	Description
scConfigFileLocalPath	must,singlevalue	The local source path of the configuration file on the Administration Server. For example, `/srv/SLEPOS/config/X11/xorg.conf.mydata`. This path must be located in the rsync directory
scMust	must,singlevalue	Enable or disable the configuration file. (TRUE or FALSE)
description	may	
scConfigMd5	may,singlevalue	The MD5 checksum value of the configuration file, automatically generated by posAdmin

10.5.5 scConfigFileTemplate

scConfigFileTemplate objects are used when running services, such as the X Window service, that require hardware-dependent configuration files. An scConfigFileTemplate object contains the configuration file data that a Point of Service terminal needs to run a given service. This element can also exist under scCashRegister objects.

For information on adding this object class to the LDAP directory, see Section 4.6.2.4, "Adding an scConfigFileTemplate Object" (page 48).

Table 10.9: *scConfigFileTemplate*

Name	Type	Description
cn	must	Name of configuration file
scBsize	must,singlevalue	Block size for the TFTP download of the system image. Minimum 4096 for image size up to 128MB, maximum 65464 for image size up to 2GB
scConfigFile	must,multivalue	File name of configuration file
scConfigFileData	must,singlevalue	Content of the configuration file, automatically filled by posAdmin
scMust	must,singlevalue	Enable or disable the configuration file. (TRUE or FALSE)
description	may	
scConfigFileParser	may,singlevalue	Name of parserFunction to apply
scConfigMd5	may,singlevalue	The MD5 checksum value of the configuration file, automatically generated by posAdmin

10.5.6 scPxeFileTemplate

The `scPxeFileTemplate` object is used to specify command line options for selected terminals. This object can be placed in the same position as `scConfigFileTemplate` and `scConfigFileSyncTemplate` (typically under the `scCashRegister` object). It has the following attributes:

Table 10.10: *scPxeFileTemplate*

Name	Type	Description
cn	must	Name of pxe template
scKernelParameters	must,singlevalue	Kernel parameters to append, to use in a custom pxe boot file
scMust	must,singlevalue	Enable or disable the configuration file. (TRUE or FALSE)
description	may	

10.5.7 scDistributionContainer

An `scDistributionContainer` is a container for the distribution of sets of images. A distribution set is a collection of images designed for Point of Service terminals on a given version of the Linux kernel. The Default distribution container references the current version of the kernel included in SUSE Linux Enterprise Point of Service.

Table 10.11: *scDistributionContainer*

Name	Type	Description
cn	must	Common name of this object, from first part of DN

Name	Type	Description
scInitrdName	must,singlevalue	Filename of the initrd.gz placed in the /boot directory
scKernelName	must,singlevalue	Filename of the kernel placed in the /boot directory
scKernelExpression	may,singlevalue	Expression used to match the scKernelVersion string against uname
scKernelMatch	may,singlevalue	Rule for matching scKernelVersion with the uname result. Valid are MATCH_VERSION, MATCH_ALL, MATCH_EXPRESSION
scKernelVersion	may,singlevalue	Version string written to config file to indicate the version of this kernel

The default scDistributionContainer has scKernelName=linux and scInitrdName=initrd.gz. If a distribution container is created with either one of those two names different, a specific pxe file is then created under /srv/tftpboot/boot/pxelinux.cfg when a terminal registers. (See also Section 9.6, "Specifying Kernel Command Line Options for Selected Terminals" (page 162).) This ensures that the specific kernel and initrd get properly loaded.

10.5.8 scHarddisk

An scHarddisk object describes the configuration of the hard disk of a Point of Service terminal. For information on adding this object class, refer to Section 4.6.2.3, "Adding an scHarddisk Object" (page 46).

Table 10.12: *scHarddisk*

Name	Type	Description
cn	must	Common Name
scDevice	must,multivalue	The name of the device. E.g. eth0 / dev/hda /dev/ hda1 ...
scHdSize	may,singlevalue	Size of the hard disk in MB
scPartitionsTable	may,singlevalue,deprecated in favor of scPartition	A semicolon-separated (;) list of partition entries. Each entry consists of three space-separated parameters: the size in megabytes, the partition type ID (82 or S for swap, 83 or L for a Linux partition), and the mount point. If the mountpoint equals /, the partition is assumed to be the root partition, and x means no mountpoint (for example for swap). For the last partition, size can be specified as x which results in

Name	Type	Description
		all remaining available space to be used.

10.5.9 scHardware

Reference standard PC hardware type and server hardware.

Table 10.13: *scHardware*

Name	Type	Description
cn	must	Common name of this object, first part of DN
scDhcpOptionsRemote	may,singlevalue	The boot option of the Point of Service terminal. The mandatory value is `/boot/pxelinux.0`
scPosDeltaImageDn	may,multivalue,deprecated	DN of delta image for a Point Of Service terminal
scPosImageDn	may,singlevalue	The DN of the default system image defined for this Point of Service terminal type
scRefMonitorDn	may,singlevalue	DN of monitor type
scRefPcDn	may,singlevalue	DN to PC hardware type
scRefServerDn	may,singlevalue	DN of a scRefServer

Name	Type	Description
scSUSEManager	may,singlevalue	SUSE Manager address (FQDN/ip address)

10.5.10 scLocation

An scLocation object represents a branch office, which is a site where a Branch Server and Point of Service terminals are located. Location containers are used to store information about the deployed Point of Service terminals and the Branch Servers. This and all other information that can be modified at the Branch Server should be stored or referenced in the Location containers to limit the need to grant write privileges to subtrees.

For information on adding this object class to the LDAP directory, see Section 4.6.1.2, "Adding an scLocation Object" (page 39).

Table 10.14: *scLocation*

Name	Type	Description
cn	must	Name of the Location or Branch
ipNetmaskNumber	must	Local network mask
ipNetworkNumber	must	Local network number
scDefaultGw	must,multivalue	IP address of default gateway for location. This is normally a router to the corporate wide area network.
scDhcpExtern	must,singlevalue	Allow an external DHCP server to be used instead of setting up own on the Branch Server (TRUE

Name	Type	Description
		or `FALSE`, default `FALSE`)
`scDhcpFixedRange`	must,singlevalue	The fixed IP address range of the DHCP server reserved for the Point of Service terminals. Comma-separated value pair, e.g. 192.168.1.55, 192.168.1.88.
`scDhcpRange`	must,singlevalue	The dynamic IP address range of the DHCP server. This is needed to register the Point of Service terminals. Comma-separated value pair, e.g. 192.168.1.10, 192.168.1.54.
`scDynamicIp`	must,singlevalue	Enable or disable registration of new terminals on the Branch Server when `scDhcpExtern` is set to `FALSE`. (`TRUE` or `FALSE`, default `TRUE`)
`scEnumerationMask`	must,singlevalue	Enumaration mask for Point Of Service terminals and printers, e.g. 000 or 00 (default 000)
`scWorkstationBaseName`	must,singlevalue	The base name of the Point of Service

Name	Type	Description
		terminals to create a unique name for each terminal. Used in combination with the `scDhcpFixedRange` attribute and `scEnumerationMask` (default CR)
userPassword	must	Branch access password to central LDAP database and/or SUSE Manager
associatedDomain	may	DNS domain name
scAllowGlobalRoles	may,singlevalue	Allow roles outside of this branch. (TRUE or FALSE, default FALSE)
scAllowRoles	may,singlevalue	If TRUE and scAllowGlobalRoles is TRUE, the role-based mode and all roles are enabled. If TRUE and scAllowGlobalRoles is FALSE, the role-based mode is enabled, but only roles under this branch are used. If FALSE, roles are not enabled. (TRUE or FALSE, FALSE)
scDnsDn	may,multivalue	DN of a scRefServer

Name	Type	Description
scDnsMapFunc	may,multivalue	DNS mapping function (NONE | DIRECT | TRANSFORM:*regexp*)
scIdPool	may,multivalue	Set of possible Point Of Service terminal IDs
scIpMapFunc	may,multivalue	IP mapping function (NONE | DIRECT | TRANSFORM:*regexp*)
scLdapDn	may,multivalue	DN of a scRefServer
scLocked	may,singlevalue,deprecated	0 or time when DB was locked, is set by SLEPOS tools, DO NOT set manually
scPrinterBaseName	may,singlevalue,deprecated	The base name of the Point of Service printers to create a unique name for each printer. It is used in combination with the scDhcpFixedRange attribute and scEnumerationMask.
scSynchronizedImageDn	may,multivalue	Images and CashRegister DN to be automatically synchronized from the Administration Server

10.5.11 scNetworkcard

An `scNetworkcard` object stores the configuration for a Branch Server network interface card.

Table 10.15: *scNetworkcard*

Name	Type	Description
ipHostNumber	must	IP-Address
scDevice	must,multivalue	The name of the device. E.g. `eth0` / `dev/hda` `/dev/hda1` ...
ipNetmaskNumber	may	Netmask
macAddress	may,multivalue	MAC address in maximal, colon separated hex notation, eg. 00:00:92:90:EE:F2
scModul	may,singlevalue,deprecated	The name of the Linux kernel module for the network interface card.
scModulOption	may,singlevalue,deprecated	The module options for the network interface card to be passed to the kernel

10.5.12 scPosImage

The Image Reference object stores information about an image stored on the Administration Server. By default, an Image Reference object is created for the Minimal client image. For information on adding this object class to the LDAP directory, see Section 4.6.2.6, "Adding an `scPosImage` Object" (page 51).

Table 10.16: *scPosImage*

Name	Type	Description
cn	must	Common name of this object, from first part of DN
scBsize	must,singlevalue	Block size for the TFTP download of the system image. Minimum 4096 for image size up to 128MB, maximum 65464 for image size up to 2GB
scDhcpOptionsLocal	must,singlevalue	Additional DHCP options for local boot
scDhcpOptionsRemote	must,singlevalue	The boot option of the Point of Service terminal. The mandatory value is /boot/pxelinux.0
scImageFile	must,singlevalue	File name of the image. e.g. mydesktop.arch
scImageName	must,singlevalue	The name of the system image; for example, mydesktop
scConfigFile	may,multivalue	File name of configuration file
scPosImageVersion	may,multivalue,deprecated in favor of scImageVersion	The version number of the system image, followed by the flag passive or active; i.e.,

Name	Type	Description
		2.0.4; active. The version number and the flag are semicolon-separated (;)

10.5.13 scRamDisk

An scRamDisk object represents the configuration of a Point of Service terminal RAM disk.

For information on adding this object class to the LDAP directory, see Section 4.6.2.2, "Adding an `scRamDisk` Object" (page 46).

Table 10.17: *scRamDisk*

Name	Type	Description
cn	must	Common Name
scDevice	must,multivalue	The name of the device. E.g. `eth0 / dev/hda /dev/ hda1` ...

10.5.14 scRefObjectContainer

`Global` (scRefObjectContainer, cn=global): All globally valid information for a chain or company—that is server hardware, Point of Service hardware, or client images—is stored in the Global container of the class `scRefObjectContainer` in the form of reference objects. These reference objects are linked to the actual entries for the Point of Service terminals and servers in the branches using unique names.

The initial LDAP structure after installation includes only one `scRefObjectContainer` named `global` under the directory root. Other scRefObjectContainer objects can be added as needed. However, the scRefObjectContainer container objects should always have cn=global and appear only once per directory level. This provides great flexibility. For example, each server can be assigned by its own reference objects and therefore by its own hardware types. On the other hand, if all the servers have the same hardware, a unified standard can be defined in the global container on the regional or organizational level.

Table 10.18: *scRefObjectContainer*

Name	Type	Description
cn	must	Name for scRefObjectContainer
description	may	container description

10.5.15 scServerContainer

Server Container (scServerContainer): A container for all the Branch Server objects for a given site. The information pertaining to the Branch Servers is stored in the Server container.

To provide system redundancy and failover, there can be multiple Branch Servers for each site.

For information on adding this object class to the LDAP directory, see Section 4.6.1.3, "Adding an scServerContainer and scBranchServer Objects" (page 40).

Table 10.19: *scServerContainer*

Name	Type	Description
cn	must	name of server container

10.5.16 scService

`scService` contains the configuration for Branch Server services like DNS, TFTP, or DHCP.

For information on adding this object class to the LDAP directory, see Section 4.6.1.3, "Adding an `scServerContainer` and `scBranchServer` Objects" (page 40).

Table 10.20: *scService*

Name	Type	Description
cn	must	name of the service
scDnsName	must,multivalue	The name of entry in the DNS table under which the service is available.
scServiceName	must,multivalue	Name of the service. Supported services are dns, dhcp, tftp, ftp and posleases.
scServiceStartScript	must,singlevalue	Filename of the init script in /etc/init.d
scServiceStatus	must,singlevalue	Enable service (TRUE or FALSE, default TRUE)
ipHostNumber	may	listening IP address for the service
scDhcpDynLeaseTime	may,singlevalue	DHCP service specific. Lease time for dynamic leases (first boot) (default 300)

Name	Type	Description
scDhcpFixedLeaseTime	may,singlevalue	DHCP service specific. Lease time for fixed leases (final registration) (default 14400)
scPosleasesChecktime	may,singlevalue	posleases service specific. For how long should posleases2ldap pause before checking uploads. (seconds)
scPosleasesMaxNotify	may,singlevalue	posleases service specific. Maximum number of booted image notifications (maximum of scNotifiedImage entries)
scPosleasesTimeout	may,singlevalue	posleases service specific. How often should posleases2ldap update internal cache. (seconds)
scServiceEmail	may,multivalue	Where should the service send an e-mail to

NOTE: IP address of TFTP service

During Branch Server initialization, the tftp configuration file (`/etc/sysconfig/atftpd`) correctly assumes IP address of the TFTP service from the `ipHostNumber` of the tftp `scService` object), and not simply the IP address of the Branch Server.

10.5.17 scWorkstation

The Workstation object stores information for a specific Point of Service terminal.
Using information from the Hardware Reference object (scCashRegister) and
Image Reference object (scPosImage), posleases2ldap automatically creates
a Workstation object in the LDAP directory for every Point of Service terminal that
registers on the Branch Server. For information on this process, see Section 6.3.3,
"The hwtype.*MAC.HASH* File" (page 90).

Table 10.21: *scWorkstation*

Name	Type	Description
cn	must	name of the workstation
ipHostNumber	may	assigned IP address
macAddress	may,multivalue	MAC address in maximal, colon separated hex notation, eg. 00:00:92:90:EE:F2
scAllowedRolesDn	may,multivalue	DNs of allowed roles. If empty, all roles are permitted
scConfigFileDn	may,multivalue	Reference for a configuration type object (scConfigFileTemplate, scConfigFileSyncTemplate, scPxeFileTemplate)
scConfigUpdate	may,singlevalue	Indicate configuration files should be updated on the next boot. (TRUE or FALSE)

Name	Type	Description
scDiskJournal	may,singlevalue	Turn on disk journaling. This will only occur on diskfull systems. (TRUE or FALSE)
scId	may,multivalue	Contains ID assigned to the Point Of Service terminal
scImageVersion	may,singlevalue	Image version in format *yyyymmddserial*
scLastBootTime	may,singlevalue	Linux time of last time when terminal boot was detected by Branch Server
scNotifiedImage	may,multivalue	Contains image and version, the time of notification, and md5sum of the associated config.MAC file separated by semicolons
scPosDeltaImageDn	may,multivalue,deprecated	DN of delta image for a Point Of Service terminal
scPosGroupDn	may,multivalue,deprecated	DN of a CR group.
scPosImageDn	may,singlevalue	The DN of the default system image defined

Name	Type	Description
		for this Point of Service terminal type
scPosImageVersion	may,multivalue,deprecated in favor of scImageVersion	The version number of the system image, followed by the flag passive or active; i.e., 2.0.4; active. The version number and the flag are semicolon-separated (;)
scPosRegisterBiosVersion	may,singlevalue	BIOS version of a Point Of Service terminal
scPosRegisterType	may,singlevalue	Cash Register type associated with Point Of Service terminal
scRefPcDn	may,singlevalue	DN to PC hardware type
scRoleBased	may,singlevalue	The Point Of Service terminal use roles. (TRUE or FALSE)
scRoleDn	may,multivalue	DN of the role assigned to the Point Of Service terminal
scSerialNumber	may,singlevalue,deprecated	Serial number of the used workstation
scStandardPrinter	may,multivalue,deprecated	Name of the standard printer

Name	Type	Description
scStandardPrinterDn	may,singlevalue,deprecated	DN of the standard printer for a location or workstation
userPassword	may	

10.5.18 scRole

The `scRole` object stores information about specific roles.

Table 10.22:   *scRole*

Name	Type	Description
cn	must	Common name of this object, from first part of DN
scRoleName	must,singlevalue	Name of the role. Displayed in the list on the Point Of Service terminal
scAllowedHwTypes	may,multivalue	Allow role to be used only with given hardware types
scDiskJournal	may,singlevalue	Turn on disk journaling. This will only occur on diskfull systems. (TRUE or FALSE)
scRoleDescription	may,multivalue	Description of the role. Displayed in the list on

Name	Type	Description
		the Point Of Service terminal

10.5.19 scImageVersion

The `scImageVersion` object replaces the `scPosImageVersion` attribute of the `scPosImage` object. The `scImageVersion` supports more features, such as encrypted images.

Table 10.23:   *scImageVersion*

Name	Type	Description
scVersion	must,singlevalue	Image version number ($x.y.z$ format)
scDisabled	may,singlevalue	Enables or disables this version for registration. (TRUE or FALSE)
scPassword	may,singlevalue	Image or partition password. In case of partition password * means random password will be generated each boot. Userful for swap partitions

10.5.20 scPartition

The `scPartition` replaces the `scPartitionsTable` attribute of the `scHarddisk` object. The `scPartition` supports more features, such as encrypted partitions.

Table 10.24: *scPartition*

Name	Type	Description
scPartNum	must,singlevalue	Defines the order of partitions (not the partition number shown by fdisk, the real partiton number is determined by KIWI during terminal boot)
scPartType	must,singlevalue	The type of partition (82 or S for swap, 83 or L for a Linux partition)
description	may	partition `description`
scPartMount	may,singlevalue	The mount point of the partition. Use / for the root partition. Use x for a partition without a mountpoint (for example a swap partition)
scPartSize	may,singlevalue	Size of partition in (binary) megabytes. For the last partition, size can be specified as x, which results in all remaining available space to be used
scPassword	may,singlevalue	Image or partition password. In case of partition password * means random

Name	Type	Description
		password will be generated each boot. Userful for swap partitions

Migration from Older Versions

11

This section covers migration from NLPOS9 and SLEPOS10 systems to SLEPOS11.

11.1 Migration from NLPOS9 to SLEPOS11

Migrating from NLPOS9 to SLEPOS11 consists of two steps. The first step is performed by using the `nlpos9_backup_data.sh` script to collect all the NLPOS9 configuration data, including the LDAP database and images. The second step is the installation of a new SLES11 system with the SLEPOS11 Add-On and the migration of the collected NLPOS9 data.

11.1.1 NLPOS9 Migration Script

The migration script `nlpos9_backup_data.sh` is needed for preparing migration data. This script is distributed with SUSE Linux Enterprise Point of Service 11 CD in the `migration/` directory on the product CD.

Table 11.1: *nlpos9_backup_data.sh Options*

Option	Description
`--cn`	must

Option	Description
--scCashRegisterName	must

Options: -f, --file=<FILE.tar.gz|bzip2> save migration data to file
(supported .tar, .tgz, .tar.gz, .tar.bz2); -d, --directory=<DIRECTORY> save
migration data to existing directory; --force force product version checking; -q, --
quiet provide less detailed output; -v, --verbose provide more detailed output; -V, --
version print the version of script being used; -h, --help show this help message --
usage display brief usage message.

11.1.2 Migration Procedure

1   Install a new SLES11 system. The SLEPOS11 Add-On can either be installed
    during the SLES11 installation or afterward using the YaST Add-On Installer.

2   When installing SLEPOS11 Add-On, you will be asked for the migration file.
    Provide the path to the backup file you have created. The migration will be
    performed.

NOTE: Network Interfaces

During the installation of SLES11, set up your network interfaces as
specified in the SLEPOS10 LDAP database.

---

3   Installation will ask for a confirmation of detected installations (Administration
    Server, Branch Server, Image Server) and will perform a new configuration of
    SLEPOS11 based on your NLPOS9 configuration.

4   If the Branch Server migration fails because of a wrong configuration of the DNS
    or IP address or unavailibility of the Administration Server, migration can be
    completed manually after the SLES11 installation with the command:

```
posInitBranchserver --noninteractive --reinitialize=/etc/SLEPOS/
branchserver.conf
```

11.1.3 Post-Migration Procedures

11.1.3.1 Firewall Configuration

Firewall settings are not migrated by SLES11 upgrade. The firewall has to be manually configured after the installation and the migration process are completed.

On the Administration Server SLEPOS11 SP2 uses:

- ldap/389 or ldaps/636 (tcp),

- rsync/873 (tcp).

On the Branch Server (on the network interface where terminals are connected), SLEPOS11 SP2 uses:

- tftp/69 (udp),

- dns/53 (udp,tcp),

- dhcp/67 (udp).

On the Branch Server (on the network interface where terminals are connected), SLEPOS11 SP2 optionally uses (if FTP is configured):

- ftp/21,

- ftp passive port range (default 30000:30400) must match the pure-ftp configuration in `/etc/SLEPOS/template/pure-ftpd.conf.template`.

11.1.3.2 ScHarddisk LDAP Entry

Many disk drives available in `/dev/hd`X in SLEPOS10 are available in `/dev/sd`X in SLEPOS11. This can cause problems after migration.

For example, if there is a `scCashRegister` object with `scHarddisk /dev/hda` in the SLEPOS10 LDAP database, migrating to SLEPOS11 with old images and an old kernel works correctly. The old images contain an old kernel with the naming scheme used in SLEPOS10. But when you assign newly-built SLEPOS11 images to the `scCashRegister` object, you have to change `scHarddisk` accordingly.

11.1.3.3 Using NLPOS9 Images Under SLEPOS11

After migrating the Administration Server and rebuilding the boot image (initrd file `initrd.gz` and kernel file `linux`), the NLPOS9 images requiring the NLPOS9 kernel will fail to boot.

You have to manually create a new `scDistributionContainer`, rename the old NLPOS9 `initrd.gz` and `linux` file to something else and insert their new names as `scInitrdName` and `scKernelName`. Also ensure that these files are located in the `/srv/tftpboot/boot` directory, and that those transferred images are properly referenced in all relevant `scCashRegister` or `scWorkstation` objects.

The `posleases2ldap` command will create a correct, terminal-specific configuration during registration (or the `pos dump-all` command will create this configuration for already registered terminals).

Please note, that during the first boot when the registration takes place, the terminal using the NLPOS9 image will freeze after the image upload since the NLPOS9 image will be deployed to the default SLEPOS11 boot kernel. After reboot however, everything will work correctly since from that time on, the above mentioned specific configuration will be used during each start-up process.

11.2 Migration from SLEPOS10 to SLEPOS11

Migrating SLEPOS10 to SLEPOS11 is done during SLES10 upgrade to SLES11. No pre-migration actions are required, but backing up of the SLEPOS10 system is recommended.

11.2.1 Pre-Requisites

• Installed and configured SLEPOS10 system,

• SLES11 media,

• SLEPOS11 Add-On product.

11.2.2 Pre-Migration Backup

It is highly recommended to back up your SLEPOS10 configuration before upgrading. On the Administration Server, backup configuration files are stored in the `/etc/SLEPOS` directory and the LDAP database. The LDAP database can be backed up by saving output of the `slapcat` command or the content of the `/var/lib/ldap` directory.

On the Branch Server, only the `branchserver.conf` configuration file is affected by the migration procedure.

11.2.3 Migration Procedure

1 Start the installation of SLES11 as an upgrade from your current SLES10 and SLEPOS10 system. When asked for the installation add-on, provide the path to your SLEPOS11 add-on.

NOTE: Network Interfaces

During the installation of SLES11, set up your network interfaces as specified in the SLEPOS10 LDAP database.

---

2 During the installation of the SLEPOS11 add-on, the previous SLEPOS10 installation is detected automatically. You will be asked to confirm the detected components or to make adjustments.

3 After confirming the installation, SLEPOS11 will be installed and configured according to the existing SLEPOS10 installation.

4 If the Branch Server migration fails because of a wrong configuration of DNS or the IP address or unavailibility of the Administration Server, migration can be completed manually after the SLES11 installation with the command:

```
posInitBranchserver --noninteractive --reinitialize=/etc/SLEPOS/
branchserver.conf
```

NOTE: Log Files Related to Migration

In case of any problems during migration, please see `/var/log/YaST2/y2log` and the `/var/log/messages` log files.

11.2.4 Post-Migration Procedures

11.2.4.1 Firewall Configuration

Firewall settings are migrated by the SLES11 upgrade. In case some firewall problems occur, consult the Post-migration procedures chapter under NLPOS9 migration.

11.2.4.2 ScHarddisk LDAP Entry

Many disk drives available in `/dev/hd`*X* in SLEPOS9 are available in `/dev/sd`*X* in SLEPOS11. This can cause problems after migration.

For example, if there is a `scCashRegister` object with `scHarddisk /dev/hda` in the SLEPOS10 LDAP database, migrating to SLEPOS11 with old images and an old kernel works correctly. The old images contain an old kernel with the naming scheme used in SLEPOS10. But when you assign newly-built SLEPOS11 images to the `scCashRegister` object, you have to change `scHarddisk` accordingly.

11.3 Manual Conversion of Image Configurations for SLEPOS 11 SP2

Image configurations created in SLEPOS 11 or SLEPOS 11 SP1 must be converted for use in SLEPOS 11 SP2. This conversion is done automatically in Image Creator. If you want to use old configurations directly in KIWI, convert the configurations using `xsltproc` and the stylesheet provided in `/usr/share/kiwi/xsl/convertSleposSp1toSp2.xsl`.

The following example assumes default paths and overwrites the old configuration file with the new one. To keep the old configuration and save the output to a different file, change the `-o` parameter:

```
xsltproc -o /var/lib/SLEPOS/system/image_name/config.xml \
         /usr/share/kiwi/xsl/convertSleposSp1toSp2.xsl \
         /var/lib/SLEPOS/system/image_name/config.xml
```

11.4 Migration from SLEPOS11 SP1 to SLEPOS11 SP2

No pre-migration actions are required.

11.4.1 Pre-Requisites

- Installed and configured SLEPOS11 SP2 system with latest updates,

- available SMT service.

11.4.2 Migration Procedure

1 Save the content of the LDAP database on the SLEPOS11 SP1 Administration Server to an ldif file:

```
slapcat >sp1.ldif
```

2 On the SLEPOS11 SP1 Administration Server, save system and boot images excluding pxe and kiwi files:

```
find /srv/SLEPOS/boot /srv/SLEPOS/image  \! -type d \! -path
 "*pxelinux*"  \
-print |tar czf sp1-images.tar.gz -T-
```

3 Move the `sp1.ldif` and `sp1-images.tar.gz` to a freshly installed SLEPOS11 SP2 FP2 Administration Server. Make sure the fix for bnc#775040 is installed.

4 Unpack the `sp1-images.tar.gz` file to the root directory (`/`).

5 Run `posInitAdminserver`. The organisation and country must be the same as on the original installation. It is possible to change password or encryption.

6 Delete the preconfigured image, which might conflict with the migrated one:

```
posAdmin --remove --recursive --DN cn=default,cn=global,o=myorg,c=us
```

7 Import the ldif file:

```
posAdmin --import --type LDIF --file sp1.ldif
```

There will be warnings that the organisation objects already exist. It is normal.

8 Validate the LDAP database:

```
posAdmin -v info --validate
```

9 Reinstall Branch Servers.

10 Run `posInitBranchserver` on every Branch Server.

Append `--enable-pos-services` option to `posInitBranchserver` call if you had `posleases2ldap` and `posASWatch` running on the Branch Server.

11 Regenerate `config.MAC` and other files on every Branch Server:

```
pos dump-all
```

12 Boot the terminals.

11.5 Migration from SLEPOS11 SP2 to SLEPOS11 SP3

The migration consist of three steps:

1 Collect the old data from the Administration Server.

Use the SLEPOS backup tool `slepos_backup_data.sh` to collect the old configuration, LDAP and images. To use this tool, make sure you have installed the `POS_Migration` package from SLEPOS11 SP3 on your old system:

```
/usr/lib/SLEPOS/migration/slepos_backup_data.sh -f backup_file_name.tgz
```

2 Migrate the data to SLEPOS11 SP3 Administration Server

Transfer the collected backup to your SLEPOS11 SP3 server (make sure the `POS_Migration` package is installed) and call `slepos_migrate.sh` tool:

```
 /usr/lib/SLEPOS/migration/slepos_migrate.sh --deploy_type=AS -
f backup_file_name.tgz
```

After the migration is completed, call `posAdmin --validate` to make sure the LDAP database was correctly imported.

3 Reinitialize Branch Servers

Branch Servers are not migrated, they are always initialized as new. After a Branch Server is (re)initialized, call `pos dump-all` to regenerate configuration files for cash registers.

Note, that it is possible to use SLEPOS11 SP2 images with SLEPOS11 SP3 servers.

Troubleshooting

12

This section describes the analysis and correction of some specific error situations in a SUSE® Linux Enterprise Point of Service system.

12.1 Debugging SLEPOS Commands

You can set the verbosity level for console output and log files of all SLEPOS commands and tools in the same way, with the POS_FORCE_VERBOSITY environment variable.

The verbosity level for the console output can be specified with --verbose=*level* or -v *level*. The verbosity level for the log files can be specified with --syslog=*level*. The *level* can have the following values: emerg (panic conditions), alert (conditions needing immediate correction), crit (critical conditions), err (errors), warn (warnings), notice (conditions requiring special handling), info (informational messages), or debug (debugging messages).

12.2 Collecting SLEPOS Data for Bug Reporting

For easy collection of SLEPOS log files, configuration files and LDAP directory content for bug reporting, the `save_poslogs` tool is provided. For more information, see Section B.3.13, "save_poslogs" (page 283).

12.3 Server Infrastructure

The setup and operating procedures for SUSE Linux Enterprise Point of Service servers are easy in most circumstances. However, the distributed nature of the system might provide some challenges. The following section describes frequently encountered difficulties with name resolution.

12.3.1 Name Resolution

Care must be taken to ensure that the system can resolve its own name to its IP address on the branch network, especially when configuring the Branch Servers with `posInitBranchserver`.

If the system has only one network interface or if the eth0 interface is the branch network interface, the correct resolution is done through the `/etc/hosts` file, where YaST adds the correct entries. Otherwise, add the corresponding line to `/etc/hosts` manually or make sure that DNS is able to resolve the hostname.

12.3.1.1 Symptoms

If the DHCP server configuration file `/etc/dhcpd.conf` is not created properly, `poscheckip` returns the following error code:

```
# poscheckip
# echo $?
1
```

If the `dhcpd.conf` file is created properly, `poscheckip` returns the correct hostname, address, netmask and domain as follows:

```
# poscheckip
```

```
bs      192.168.150.1   255.255.255.0   Lab.HQ.myorg.us
# echo $?
0
```

12.3.1.2 Tips

- Make sure that `/etc/named.conf` lists the right parent. Configure the DNS servers as forwarders.

- Add the hostname to `/etc/hosts`.

- When using DHCP to configure the external (WAN) network interface of the Branch Server, set the DHCP client on the Branch Server to modify `named.conf` instead of `resolv.conf` in `/etc/sysconfig/network/config`. The variables are *MODIFY_RESOLV_CONF_DYNAMICALLY* and *MODIFY_NAMED_CONF_DYNAMICALLY*. The template file is prepared for this.

12.3.2 Problems with Terminals after Branch Server Change

When a Branch Server is changed or reinstalled, but some terminals are still registered in the LDAP (for example, there are some `scWorkstation` objects under a respective `scLocation`), these terminals will not boot correctly. You have to recreate their `config.<MAC>` files manually.

To do this, run `pos dump-all` on the Branch Server. The command will create the needed files for all the affected terminals.

12.3.3 Problems with Changing the Branch Server Password

If it is not possible to change the Branch Server password using the `posInitBranchServer -p` command, you can change it manually:

On the *Admin server*, change the password in the LDAP database. Enter the following command in the command line (replace the mybranch, myorgunit, myorg and us variables with your configured values):

```
ldappasswd -x -d localhost -D "cn=admin,o=myorg,c=us" -
w "admin_password" "cn=mybranch,ou=myorg,o=myorg,c=us" -s
"new_branch_password"
```

On a *Branch Server*, follow the same procedures as in Section 4.1.1, "Changing the Administration Server Password" (page 31), but with a new Branch Server password and configuration file /etc/SLEPOS/branchserver.conf.

12.4 Operation

The following sections describe frequently encountered difficulties with system operation.

12.4.1 Image Building

Image Creator or KIWI cannot determine which user groups (GIDs) are to be created in post-installation scripts by the selected packages. If there is a conflict between GIDs added in the user configuration and GIDs added by post-installation scripts, image building will fail.

12.4.1.1 Symptoms

Image building fails with a message like groupadd: GID 100 is not unique or similar.

12.4.1.2 Tip

When configuring users to be created on the target system, avoid conflicting GIDs.

12.4.2 Image Distribution

The possyncimages tool distributes the boot and client images from the Administration Server to the Branch Server. It uses the rsync service to let the Branch Servers only download the files that need to be updated.

Enough space should be configured to keep at least two generations of image files. This redundancy ensures that there is a valid image available at all times.

rsync updates existing files, creates new files, and even deletes files that do not exist in the original download directory on the Administration Server.

12.4.2.1 Symptoms

The error message `rsync: error writing 4 unbuffered bytes - exiting: Broken Pipe` indicates that the Branch Server does not have enough disk space left to download all the images. Adequate space is required for both the staging area in `/srv/SLEPOS/` and the service area in `/srv/tftpboot`.

12.4.2.2 Tips

- Make sure that `config.MAC` files are regenerated (via the `pos dump-all` command on the Branch Server or via the `scConfigUpdate` attribute under the relevant `scWorkstation` set to `TRUE`) after new images have been distributed and especially after old images have been deleted.

- Make sure that there is enough space for new images even before old images have been deleted or delete old images before uploading new ones.

12.4.3 Point of Service Terminal Configuration

The process of registering new Point of Service terminals and updating the configuration information usually works without administrator intervention; however, it is a complex process. To facilitate this process, you must ensure the Administration Server always has a valid image configuration. In LDAP, the image versions must be entered and made active (see Section 4.6.2.6, "Adding an `scPosImage` Object" (page 51) for details), and the image files must be made available with the right filename (*image_name-version*) and with the right permissions (world-readable).

12.4.3.1 Symptoms

The error message `No Imageversion is available` from `posleases2ldap` or `pos dump-all` means that no valid image file for the active version exists. Make sure that the image has been transferred to the Branch Server and that the version in LDAP has an active flag attached.

12.4.3.2 Tip

Keep at least two generations of image files available and active in LDAP at all times. The Point of Service downloads the latest client image version available on the Branch Server.

12.4.3.3 Troubleshooting Terminal Bootup Problems

If the Point of Service terminal does not successfully boot, check the following:

- Verify that an `scCashRegister` object exists for the Point of Service terminal. For more information, see Section 4.6.2.1, "Adding an `scCashRegister` Object" (page 44).

- Verify the configuration of the `scCashRegister` object for the Point of Service terminal. There must either be an scCashRegister object that corresponds to the HWTYPE attribute in the Point of Service terminal's `hwtype.MAC.HASH` file in the `/srv/tftpboot/upload/hwtype` directory or a default `scCashRegister` object that will work for the Point of Service terminal.

- Verify that the Point of Service image configured in the `scPosImageDn` attribute of the `scCashRegister` object is available in the `/srv/tftpboot/image/` directory on the Branch Server.

- Do not delete any of the default LDAP objects that are created when you install SUSE Linux Enterprise Point of Service. In particular, do not delete the global default minimal `scPosImage` object that is created in the default Distribution Container, even if you do not plan to use the minimal image.

- Each type of Point of Service terminal hardware must have a unique model name defined in the `scCashRegisterName` attribute of the `scCashRegister` object in LDAP.

  If two terminals have the same hardware name defined in their scPosImage objects, neither of them boots successfully, but a HWtype error is displayed on the Branch Server. To resolve the problem, change the `scCashRegisterName` value for one of the Point of Service terminals.

- Check the `boot.kiwi` log file of the terminal which failed to boot. This log file is uploaded to the Branch Server when the terminal fails to boot. The file is located in `upload/boot.kiwi.`*MAC*. If kiwidebug is enabled, the log file is always uploaded before starting the system image.

12.4.4 Loading CDBoot Images

If there are multiple CD drives in the Point of Service terminal, there is no way to designate a CD drive to use; the system chooses the first one it finds.

12.4.4.1 Symptoms

If the Point of Service terminal does not find the drive with the boot CD, it returns BIOS errors.

12.4.4.2 Solution

To solve the problem, insert the CD in the bootable CD drive.

12.5 Known Issues

This section describes known issues of the SUSE® Linux Enterprise Point of Service 11 system.

12.5.1 Image Creator Does Not Verify Group Name Validity

Image creator does not verify group name validity, therefore the administrator must make sure to only use group names beginning with a letter.

12.5.2 Roles Are Not Safely Escaped

The role name and description must not contain | and \n characters. Safe characters for `cn` in LDAP are `[-_a-zA-Z0-9]`.

Recent Documentation Changes

13

This section describes recent and important changes in the SUSE® Linux Enterprise Point of Service documentation.

- A new chapter describes the migration procedure from SLEPOS11 SP1 to SLEPOS11 SP2. See Section 11.4, "Migration from SLEPOS11 SP1 to SLEPOS11 SP2" (page 235). (2012-10-02)

- The description of the SLEPOS XML format has been updated. See Section 10.2.6.4, "SLEPOS XML Format" (page 187). (2012-10-02)

- The chapter describing the posAdmin XML interface has been updated. Modification of the existing LDAP data using XML is now possible. See Section 10.2.6, "posAdmin XML Interface" (page 184) and Section 10.2.6.3, "Using XML to Modify LDAP Data" (page 185). (2012-12-05)

- The section on querying LDAP objects has been updated. See Section 10.2.5, "Querying LDAP Objects" (page 181). (2012-12-05)

- The section on initializing LDAP database has been updated. SLEPOS can now coexist with existing LDAP databases. AdminServer now uses YaST CA Management interface for issuing and managing SSL See Section 4.2, "Initializing the LDAP Directory with `posInitAdminserver`" (page 32). (2013-05-07)

- A description of a new script for creating directory structure on service partition for offline boot was added. See Section B.3.14, "posSyncSrvPart" (page 284). (2013-05-07)

- A new section on booting special images (for example for BIOS update) was added. See Section 7.3, "Booting Special Images on Terminals" (page 114). (2013-05-07)

- A new section on creating images for booting and offline installation from USB sticks was added. See Section 8.2.4.5, "Booting Images from USB Stick" (page 142). (2013-05-07)

- A new section about using external tools for LDAP database modification and the new `posAdmin --refresh` feature was added. See Section 10.2.8, "Editing LDAP Database Using External Tools" (page 194). (2013-05-10)

- Dmraid fake raid controllers are now supported. See Section 6.3.1, "The config.*MAC* File" (page 83). (2013-08-1)

- The attribute `scLastBootTime` of `scWorkstation` object is used to store time of last boot. It is now possible to delete workstations according to the time and date of the last boot. See Section 10.2.4, "Removing LDAP Entries" (page 180). (2013-08-1)

- The Section 4.2, "Initializing the LDAP Directory with `posInitAdminserver`" (page 32) section has been updated. (2013-08-1)

- The Section 7.2, "SLEPOS High-Availabilty Installation Workflow" (page 112) section has been added. (2013-08-1)

- The `posLDIFReport` script has been added. See Section B.3.16, "posLDIFReport" (page 285). (2013-08-1)

- The Section B.3.5, "posldap2dhcp" (page 272) section has been updated. (2013-08-1)

- The Section 9.5.5, "Using Encrypted Partitions on Terminals" (page 159) section has been updated. (2013-08-1)

- The Section B.3.12, "pos" (page 279) section has been updated. (2013-08-1)

- The Section 3.2, "Preparing Source Repositories" (page 25) section has been updated. (2013-08-1)

- The Section 11.5, "Migration from SLEPOS11 SP2 to SLEPOS11 SP3" (page 236) section has been added. (2013-08-1)

- The Section 3.1, "Types of Images" (page 21) section has been updated. (2013-08-1)

- The Section 4.6.2.2, "Adding an `scRamDisk` Object" (page 46) section has been updated. (2013-08-20)

- The Section 6.2.3, "Using a Terminal with Multiple Network Interfaces" (page 83) section has been updated. (2013-08-20)

- The Section 4.2, "Initializing the LDAP Directory with `posInitAdminserver`" (page 32) section has been updated. (2013-08-20)

- The Section 8.1.5, "Building Server Images in Image Creator" (page 130) section was added. (2013-09-09)

SUSE Linux Enterprise Point of Service Files and Directory Structure

This section provides a quick reference for the directory structure.

A.1 Administration Server Directory Structure

`/etc/openldap/slapd.d`

The `LDAP` directory contains the LDAP server configuration database files which should not be edited directly. For modification, use the `ldapmodify` with DN `cn=admin,cn=config` and your SLEPOS administration password.

`/etc/SLEPOS/adminserver.conf`

The Administration Server directory contains the standard configuration file for the Administration Server. On the Combo Server, both `/etc/SLEPOS/adminserver.conf` and `/etc/SLEPOS/branchserver.conf` are used.

`/etc/SLEPOS/keys/`

The `keys` directory contains the keys and certificates required to secure LDAP communication between Administration Server and Branch Server.

During installation of the Administration Server, SLEPOS may automatically create and install custom SLEPOS CA and generate self-signed certificates to secure communication between Administration Server and Branch Server. For more information on setting up LDAP SSL, see Section 4.2, "Initializing the LDAP Directory with `posInitAdminserver`" (page 32).

`/etc/SLEPOS/keys/ca/`
This directory contains the CA certificate, keys, and all related data. This directory is managed by YaST CA Management module, use the `yast2 ca-mgm` command for management.

`/etc/SLEPOS/keys/ca/ca.crt`
This file contains the public key for the CA that signed the server certificate. This is only copied to the `rsync` directory if you enable LDAP SSL during installation of the Administration Server. The public key for the CA allows the Branch Servers to trust the Administration Server.

`/etc/SLEPOS/keys/ca/ca.key`
This files contains the CA's private key.

`/etc/SLEPOS/keys/certs/`
This directory contains the Administration Server certificate and keys.

`/etc/SLEPOS/keys/certs/server.crt`
This file contains the Administration Server certificate public key. This certificate is used to secure LDAP communication between Administration and Branch Server.

`/etc/SLEPOS/keys/certs/server.key`
This file contains the private key for the server certificate.

`/etc/SLEPOS/rsync/`
The `rsync` directory contains the configuration files for the rsync service.

`/etc/SLEPOS/rsync/rsyncd.conf`
This file contains the `rsync` configuration data for the Administration Server.

`/etc/SLEPOS/template/`
The `template` directory contains the template files required for the Administration and Branch Server services.

`/etc/SLEPOS/template/adminserver.conf.template`
This file contains the template for the Administration Server configuration file.

`/etc/SLEPOS/template/branchserver.conf.template`
This file contains the template for the Branch Server configuration file.

`/etc/SLEPOS/template/branchslapd.conf.template`
This file contains the template for Branch Server's local LDAP configuration. The `posInitBranchServer` script uses this template to create the openLDAP server configuration file, `/etc/openldap/slapd.conf`.

`/etc/SLEPOS/template/dhcpd.conf.header.template`
This file contains the template for the DHCP services.

`/etc/SLEPOS/template/dns-zonefile.header.template`
This file contains the template for the DNS services.

`/etc/SLEPOS/template/ldif.pos`
This file contains initial `LDAP` data for eDirectory. `posInitEdir` imports this file into the Administration Server's eDirectory server. This file uses the structure of the `ldap.pos.template`, but is populated with the names provided during installation.

`/etc/SLEPOS/template/ldif.pos.template`
This file contains the template for the `ldif.pos` file.

`/etc/SLEPOS/template/slapd.conf.template`
This file contains the template for `slapd` configuration. `posInitAdminserver` uses this template to create the openLDAP server configuration file `/etc/openldap/slapd.conf`.

`/etc/SLEPOS/template/XML/LDAPschema.xsl`
This is the XSL template for visualizing SLEPOS validation template in a web browser.

`/etc/SLEPOS/template/XML/basic.xml`
This file contains initial LDAP data for openLDAP database. The `posInitAdminserver` script imports this file into the Administration Server's openLDAP server.

`/etc/SLEPOS/template/XML/validateSLEPOSXMLv0.1.rng`
This is the validation template for SLEPOS XML v0.1.

`/srv/SLEPOS/certs/ca.crt`
This file contains the public key for the CA that signed the server certificate. This is only copied to the `rsync` directory if you enable LDAP SSL during installation of the Administration Server. The CA's public key allows the Branch Server to trust the Administration Server.

`/srv/SLEPOS/config/`
> The `config` directory contains hardware configuration files that are distributed by the Administration Server over rsync. Ultimately, these configuration files are distributed by the Branch Server to the Point of Service terminals over tftp.

NOTE: Referenced Configuration Files

Any configuration files referenced in the `scConfigFileSyncTemplate` object must be located in `/srv/SLEPOS/rsync/config/`.

`/srv/SLEPOS/image/`
> The `image` directory contains active client images that are distributed by the Administration Server over rsync. Ultimately, these images are distributed by the Branch Server to Point of Service terminals over tftp.

A.2 Branch Server Directory Structure

`/etc/SLEPOS/branchserver.conf`
> This file contains the LDAP base configuration. It is used on Branch Server and Combo Server.

`/etc/SLEPOS/dhcpd/`
> The `dhcpd` directory contains DHCP configuration header and DHCP configuration file.

`/etc/SLEPOS/dhcpd/dhcpd.conf`
> Contains the current slepos DHCP configuration for registered terminals (with fixed ip).

`/etc/SLEPOS/dhcpd/dhcpd.conf.header`
> The header of the `dhcp.conf` file to which `posleases2ldap` appends terminal specific data.

`/etc/SLEPOS/dhcpd/dhcpd.conf.old`
> The back up of the last used DHCP configuration.

`/etc/SLEPOS/keys/`
The `keys` directory contains the keys and certificates required to secure LDAP communication between Administration and Branch Servers.

`/etc/SLEPOS/keys/certs/`
The `certs` directory contains the Administration Server certificate and keys.

`/etc/SLEPOS/keys/certs/ca.crt`
This file contains the public key for the CA that signed the Administration Server's server certificate. This file is only distributed to Branch Servers if you enable LDAP SSL during installation of the Administration Server. The CA's public key allows the Branch Servers to trust the Administration Server.

`/etc/SLEPOS/salt.key`
This file contains a randomly generated key used for password obfuscation in SLEPOS configuration files.

`/etc/SLEPOS/template/pxelinux.cfg.template`
This file contains the template for `pxelinux.cfg` files. The `pxelinux.cfg` files are stored on the Branch Server. They indicate which kernel and RAM disk to load for the POS terminal. These files enable the Branch Server to distribute SLEPOS images.

SLEPOS automatically creates the `pxelinux.cfg` files based on the distribution container configurations in the LDAP directory.

`/etc/named.d/ldap_generated`
The directory contains generated dns configuration file (`named.conf`) for the DNS service provided by Branch Server for POS terminals.

`/srv/tftpboot/`
The `tftpboot` directory contains data for the TFTP and/or FTP services.

`/srv/tftpboot/KIWI/` or `/srv/tftpboot/CR`
Contains configuration files for all registered Point of Service terminals on the current Branch Server. Also contains `rollback.MAC` files indexing rollback information for given MAC addresses and, in the role-based case, rolelists and idlists. `/srv/tftpboot/CR` is a symlink to `/srv/tftpboot/KIWI` for backward compatibility.

`/srv/tftpboot/KIWI/MAC/`
Contains system configuration files for the individual Point of Service terminals, such as `xorg.conf`.

`/srv/tftpboot/KIWI/backup/`
Contains backups of all previously used configuration files.

`/srv/tftpboot/KIWI/rollback/`
Contains `config.MAC.hash` files used for restoring older configurations.

`/srv/tftpboot/boot/`
The `boot` directory contains the boot images and configuration files required to boot Point of Service terminals. On the Branch Server, this directory can also contain boot images used for rolled back configurations.

`/srv/tftpboot/boot/linux`
This file contains the default Linux kernel used to boot the Point of Service terminals via PXE.

IMPORTANT: Preparations on the Branch Server

The kernel image must be copied to the `/srv/SLEPOS/rsync/boot/` directory before running `posSyncImages` on the Branch Server.

`/srv/tftpboot/boot/linux.md5`
The md5 sum of the `linux` file.

`/srv/tftpboot/boot/initrd.gz`
The `initrd.gz` links the initrd image, which provides the second bootstrap used to PXE boot the Point of Service terminals.

IMPORTANT: Preparations on the Branch Server

The initrd image must be copied to the `/srv/SLEPOS/boot/` directory before running `posSyncImages` on the Branch Server. For more information on this process, see Chapter 4, *Setting Up the Administration Server* (page 29).

`/srv/tftpboot/boot/initrd.md5`
The md5 sum of the `initrd.gz` file.

`/srv/tftpboot/boot/menu.c32`
This file is a link to `/usr/share/syslinux/menu.c32` to allow presenting a pxe boot menu for selection of a specific boot images.

`/srv/tftpboot/boot/memdisk`

This file is a link to `/usr/share/syslinux/memdisk` to allow booting of specific images (e.g for BIOS update).

`/srv/tftpboot/boot/pxelinux.0`

This file is a link to `/usr/share/syslinux/pxelinux.0`, which is the first boostrap image used to PXE boot the Point of Service terminals.

`/srv/tftpboot/boot/pxelinux.cfg/`

This directory contains the configuration files required to pxe boot the Point of Service terminals. The file `pxelinux.cfg` indicates which kernel and initrd image to load for the Point of Service terminal. These files enable Branch Servers to distribute SLES images.

Branch Server automatically creates the `pxelinux.cfg` files based on the distribution container configurations and pxe objects in the LDAP directory. For more information, see Chapter 10, *The LDAP Directory on SUSE Linux Enterprise Point of Service* (page 167).

`/srv/tftpboot/boot/pxelinux.cfg/default`

This file contains the default configuration data for Point of Service terminal's PXE boot. This configuration file is used by all Point of Service terminals except those with specific kernel or initrd, or with a specific pxe configuration (see Section 9.6, "Specifying Kernel Command Line Options for Selected Terminals" (page 162)), or terminals that have been rolled back.

This file is created and modified by `posInitBranchserver`, `pos dump-lists`, `pos dump-all` and in every `posleases2ldap` loop.

`/srv/tftpboot/boot/pxelinux.config/01-`*`dash_separated_MAC`*

These are specific pxelinux files with custom configuration data. If you have a custom distribution container, a machine using specific kernel parameters, or a rolled back machine, the Branch Server generates custom pxelinux configuration files containing the kernel or kernel parameters associated with the relevant machine. The filename for custom pxelinux configuration files is the lowercase, '-' separated MAC address of the booting client, with `01` prefix.

For example, if the client MAC address is `00:11:25:A7:D6:1E`, the filename of the corresponding pxelinux configuration file is `01-00-11-25-a7-d6-1e`. If the machine has registered with more MAC addresses, specific pxe's are created for all those MAC addresses (one as a file and the rest of them as links).

`/srv/tftpboot/image/`
> The `image` directory contains the client images that are distributed to Point of Service terminals and their associated checksums.

`/srv/tftpboot/upload/`
> Serves as the destination directory to upload `hwtype.MAC.HASH` files for newly registered Point of Service terminals. These files are used to create the Point of Service terminal's workstation object in LDAP.
>
> This directory also stores the `bootversion.MAC` files that the `posleases2ldap` daemon uses to provide image install notification. When an image is successfully installed on a Point of Service terminal, the `linuxrc` script creates a `bootversion.MAC` file in the `/tftpboot/upload` directory on the Branch Server. `posleases2ldap` then transfers the information to the `scNotifiedImage` attribute in the `scWorkstation` object in LDAP and deletes the `bootversion.MAC` file.

`/srv/tftpboot/upload/backup/`
> Contains backup of all previously used hwtype and bootversion files.

A.3 Image Building Server Files and Directory Structure

The `template-version` part of the following paths should be replaced with the actual names of the image template directories in `/usr/share/kiwi/image/SLEPOS/`. For example, for the graphical image version 4.0.0, the `template-version` should be replaced with `graphical-4.0.0` or `graphical-4` (a symlink).

`/usr/share/kiwi/images/SLEPOS`
> This directory contains SLEPOS image templates, which are used for creating customized image configurations. They are stored in single subdirectories `template_name-version`. Symlinks from `template_name-majorname` to `template_name-version` are present (for example a link from `graphical-4` to `graphical-4.0.0`. Image Creator shows these templates in the *Base on Template* list.

`/usr/share/kiwi/image/SLEPOS/`*`template-version`*`/config.xml`
>   This file is the main configuration file. It is used to define base names, image
>   types, profiles, options, and the package/pattern list.

`/usr/share/kiwi/image/SLEPOS/`*`template-version`*`/config/`
>   The `config` directory contains optional shell scripts. These are executed after
>   all packages are installed. For example, you can include scripts here that remove
>   parts of a package. The name of the bash script must match the package name
>   listed in the `config.xml` file.

`/usr/share/kiwi/image/SLEPOS/`*`template-version`*`/config.sh`
>   `config.sh` contains an optional configuration script, executed at the end of the
>   installation.

`/usr/share/kiwi/image/SLEPOS/`*`template-version`*`/images.sh`
>   The `images.sh` file contains an optional configuration script, executed at
>   the beginning of the image creation process. It is still supported, but not used
>   in SLEPOS images version 4 and later. It is now recommended to use `usr/`
>   `share/kiwi/image/SLEPOS/`*`template-version`*`/root/build-`
>   `custom` for this purpose.

`/usr/share/kiwi/image/SLEPOS/`*`template-version`*`/config-`
`yast.xml`
>   The `config-yast.xml` file contains optional AutoYaST configuration data.
>   The file creates a profile `/root/autoinst.xml`, which can be used to create
>   a clone of an installation.

`/usr/share/kiwi/image/SLEPOS/`*`template-version`*`/root/`
>   The `root` directory contains files, directories, and scripts. It is used to adapt the
>   image environment after the installation of all package and lets you customize
>   your image with data that is not available as a package.

`/usr/share/kiwi/image/SLEPOS/`*`template-version`*`/repo/`
>   This directory was used as the repository containing RPM packages directly
>   accessible in Image Creator. It is no longer used in SLEPOS images version 4
>   and later. The functionality can be however restored by creating the directory
>   and adding the following to the `config.xml`:

```
<repository type="rpm-dir">
  <source path="this://repo"/>
</repository>
```

It is however recommended to consider other possibilities, like creating one central repository for pos packages and use this repository in all images.

`/var/lib/SLEPOS/dist/`
> This directory holds SLES and SLEPOS repositories; it contains RPM packages selectable in Image Creator. It is now deprecated and used only in cases when SMT is not used for repository management.

`/var/lib/SLEPOS/system/`
> This directory contains the `chroot` directory used for KIWI/Image Creator building of images, the `images` subdirectory containing built images and *image_name* subdirectories with all KIWI configuration files.

`/var/lib/SLEPOS/system/chroot/`*image_name*
> This directory is used by KIWI/Image Creator for building of the *image_name* image.

`/var/lib/SLEPOS/system/images/`*image_name*
> This directory contains the build image *image_name*. For example:

```
initrd-netboot-suse-SLES11.i686-2.1.1.gz
initrd-netboot-suse-SLES11.i686-2.1.1.kernel -> initrd-netboot-suse-
SLES11.i686-2.1.1.kernel.3.0.82-0.7-default
initrd-netboot-suse-SLES11.i686-2.1.1.kernel.3.0.82-0.7-default
initrd-netboot-suse-SLES11.i686-2.1.1.kernel.3.0.82-0.7-default.md5
initrd-netboot-suse-SLES11.i686-2.1.1.md5
initrd-netboot-suse-SLES11.i686-2.1.1.packages
initrd-netboot-suse-SLES11.i686-2.1.1.splash.gz
initrd-netboot-suse-SLES11.i686-2.1.1.splash.md5
initrd-netboot-suse-SLES11.i686-2.1.1.verified
image_name.i686-1.0.0
image_name.i686-1.0.0.config
image_name.i686-1.0.0.ext3 -> image_name.i686-1.0.0
image_name.i686-1.0.0.gz
image_name.i686-1.0.0.md5
image_name.i686-1.0.0.packages
image_name.i686-1.0.0.verified
```

`/var/lib/SLEPOS/system/`*image_name*
> This directory contains all KIWI configuration files for *image_name*. For example:

```
bootsplash.tar
config.sh
config.xml
config.xml.POSsave
```

```
root
wlan.tar.gz
```

SUSE Linux Enterprise Point of Service Files and Directory Structure

Point of Service Commands

In a SUSE® Linux Enterprise Point of Service system, a number of commands are provided to initialize and maintain Administration and Branch Servers. This section describes these commands and their usage.

B.1 Overview

All the programs required to manage the system and to generate configuration files are implemented in Perl and as shell scripts. All the filenames contain the prefix pos, so a quick overview of the available programs can be displayed using tab completion.

It is recommended to use the /usr/sbin directory as the storage location for SUSE Linux Enterprise Point of Service scripts. All the scripts can be controlled transparently using the posAdmin meta script, as long as they are not run by cron. The posAdmin script is designed to operate in the same way on the Administration Server as on the Branch Servers.

The basic mechanism for all actions (image transfer to a Branch Server, data readout from the directory) is a pull mechanism from the Branch Servers that is run directly on the Branch Servers. One important element is the central logging of all actions with success or failure flags on the Administration Server. For all actions, the rule must be transaction security or atomic execution to avoid inconsistent configuration files, for example.

B.2 Core Script Process

When Point of Service terminals are being set up in a branch or subsidiary, the `posleases2ldap` script must be started as a daemon on the Branch Server for the relevant branch. All other scripts are controlled by this script.

The interplay of scripts on the Branch Server works as follows:

1 `posleases2ldap` is started directly on the Branch Server. If the `scDynamicIp` attribute is not set to `TRUE` in the relevant `scLocation`, the script immediately terminates.

2 `posleases2ldap` is running as a daemon process and monitors the `/var/lib/dhcp/db/dhcpd.leases` file for changes. The script detects in which `scLocation` (branch) it is running, reading the IP address of the server.

3 If role mode is enabled or `scIdPool` is not empty, `posleases2ldap` periodically updates `rolelist` and `idlists` according to the LDAP database.

4 If `posleases2ldap` finds MAC addresses in the leases that are not yet entered in the directory, it generates new entries for the `scWorkstation` object class under the relevant `scLocation` object. The first items filled out are the required attributes `macAddress`, `ipHostNumber`, and the `cn` for the entry. The terminal's IP address and name are automatically generated, and the MAC address is taken from the `leases` file. These entries are like an outline.

5 The upload directory on the TFTP server is searched for files of the pattern *hwtype.MAC* or *hwtype.MAC.hash* that are being uploaded by Point of Service terminals registered from the DiskNetboot system. The Point of Service hardware type is specified in these files. For more information, see Section 6.4, "Booting the Point of Service Terminal" (page 92). If any files of this type are found, the following process runs:

- Using the MAC address, the relevant `scWorkstation` entry is looked up in the LDAP directory. With the content of the *hwtype.MAC* file, the corresponding `scRefPc` (the reference hardware type in the global container) is searched. In the `scRefPc` object (named after the hardware type), the image type for this hardware type is specified as a reference to a `scPosImage` object in the attribute `scPosImageDn`, which points to the reference image in the global container. The information about the reference hardware and image are then added to the `scWorkstation` object as distinguished names (DN) and the attributes are named `scRefPcDn` and `scPosImageDn`.

- All information is collected to generate the `/srv/tftpboot/KIWI/config.`*MAC* configuration file. It is possible to specify hardware type or image type dependent configuration files, such as `xorg.conf`, which is hardware type dependent. These files are generated in the `/srv/tftpboot/KIWI/`*MAC* directory. For this purpose, an object of the class `scConfigFileTemplate` can be added to the relevant `scRefPc` or `scPosImage` object in the global container.

  At this point, the `scConfigFileData` attribute of the `scConfigFileTemplate` object contains the required file. Hardware or image dependent configuration files are always looked up by the hardware order image.

  All newly generated files are initially named with the prefix `TMP_`.

- The configuration files are renamed from `TMP_*` to their final names. The `/srv/tftpboot/upload/hwtype.`*MAC*`.`*HASH* file is deleted. The registration of a newly detected Point of Service terminal is complete.

6 `posleases2ldap` starts `posldap2dns`. The zone files for the DNS server are regenerated from the directory data as a temporary file and renamed. The DNS service is restarted if there are any changes.

7 `posleases2ldap` starts `posldap2dhcp`. The `dhcpd.conf` file is regenerated from the directory data as a temporary file and renamed. The DHCP service is restarted if there are any changes.

8 `posleases2ldap` runs in a loop starting at Step 2 (page 264) until it is terminated or the `scDynamicIp` attribute in the `scLocation` object for the branch is set to `FALSE`.

9 `posleases2ldap` starts the ImageNotify daemon, which monitors `/srv/tftpboot/upload` for boot version, MAC address files, and transfers image notification data to LDAP.

B.3 Command Quick Reference

The remainder of this section provides a brief explanation of each SUSE Linux Enterprise Point of Service command, its function, and usage.

B.3.1 posNetworkInit

`posNetworkInit` is a helper script that finds the Branch Server network configuration in LDAP, and depending on the situation, updates either the Branch Server network configuration or the LDAP database. If successful, `posNetworkInit` prints the Branch Server's network details.

B.3.1.1 Function

`posNetworkInit` is used mainly within `posInitBranchServer` to determine the Branch Server network configuration and to update the network configuration and resolver (`/etc/resolv.conf`).

B.3.1.2 Usage

```
posNetworkInit [--ldapDev device] [--force] [device]
```

Table B.1: *posNetworkInit Options*

Option	Description
`device`	If more NICs are present on the Branch Server, choose the NIC with a name equal to the device.
`--force`	Forces reconfiguration of the NIC if the NIC is configured differently than in LDAP.
`--ldapDev device`	If more than one scNetworkcard object is defined in LDAP, choose the scNetworkcard with scDevice equal to the device.

B.3.2 posInitBranchserver

The purpose of `posInitBranchserver` is to generate the central configuration file for all other SUSE Linux Enterprise Point of Service commands. It is used on a Branch Server to configure the internal network, to generate configuration files for the DNS, DHCP and TFTP services, to activate the DNS, DHCP, TFTP and posLeases services at boot time, and to start the services if specified in LDAP.

B.3.2.1 Function

When running this command, you are prompted to enter the organization/company name, country abbreviation, IP address, and the LDAP administrator password of the Administration Server. The `/etc/SLEPOS/branchserver.conf` configuration file is generated by filling in the LDAP base, LDAP administrator password, and the FQDN of the Administration Server. The `/etc/SLEPOS/template/branchserver.conf.template` file is used as a template.

The `posInitBranchserver` command uses `posNetworkInit` to find internal network details in LDAP and update `/etc/resolv.conf` with basic DNS information. The `posNetworkInit` command also yields the domain name for this branch, which is used to generate proper configuration header files for the DHCP and DNS services, which in turn are needed for `posldap2dns` and `posldap2dhcp` scripts.

Branch Server services are then configured based on settings in LDAP. The Branch Server service is run and set to start at boot time only when attribute `scServiceStatus` is `TRUE` under its respective `scService` entry in LDAP.

For compatibility reasons, Branch Server checks LDAP if a `posLeases` service configuration is present. If not, the service is added to LDAP based on default values (`scPosleasesChecktime` set to 5 seconds, `scPosleasesTimeout` set to 60 seconds, and `scPosleasesMaxNotify` maximum of 6 boot notifications). Also, the `scServiceStatus` is set to `FALSE`.

DNS is only configured when the appropriate service is present in LDAP. The zone file header for posldap2dns is generated from `/etc/SLEPOS/template/dns-zonefile.header.template` and written to `/etc/named.d/ldap_generated/dns-zonefile.header`. The posldap2dns script then configures the rest of the DNS system. Proper DNS forwarder mode is set in Netconfig and the DNS service is started if enabled in LDAP.

DHCP service is only configured when the appropriate service is present in LDAP. After preparing `dhcp.conf.header` file, posldap2dhcp configures the rest of the DHCP service. Sysconfig is used to set the DHCP listening interface and chroot settings. Then the DHCP service is started if enabled in LDAP.

A multicast route is persistently set up. Sysconfig is used to set the TFTP listening address, directory and user. The rest is configured by the posldap2pxe script. Then the TFTP service is started if enabled in LDAP.

FTP service is available on the Branch Server. If enabled in LDAP, the service is configured based on the supplied template and started.

The rsync service is the only service which does not have an LDAP entry and is always configured and started.

NOTE: Registration of Terminals After Branch Server Change

When the Branch Server is changed (for example reinstalled) and terminals are still registered in LDAP, but no longer have the associated `/srv/tftpboot/KIWI/config.MAC` files present, these terminals will be reregistered by `posleases2ldap` when they upload the `hwtype.MAC.hash` file. Alternatively, you can use `posldap2crconfig --dumpall` to recreate all `config.MAC` files for all registered workstations. The only difference is that in case of a non-role-based approach (legacy), the `--dumpall` method will honor a customized scRefPcDn cash register reference (even if the referred cash register is not associated to the workstation's scPosRegisterBiosVersion). On the contrary, during the registration update via the uploaded hwtype.MAC file, the standard registration workflow is used. This means that scRefPcDn will be set to a cash register conforming to the workstation's scPosRegisterBiosVersion, or to a default one if not found.

---

posInitBranchserver only works correctly if the Branch Server data in LDAP has been created properly in advance using the posAdmin tool after the installation of the Administration Server. For further information, refer to Section 4.6.2, "Creating Point of Service Terminal Objects in LDAP" (page 43).

B.3.2.2 Usage

Run `posInitBranchserver` on a Branch Server.

Table B.2: *posInitBranchserver Options*

Option	Description
-r or --reinitialize [=*FILE*]	Reinitializes the Branch Server, default values are loaded from an existing Branch Server configuration file or from a file specified by *FILE*.
-f or --file =*FILE*	Specifies the path to SLEPOS offline installation file for offline initialization.
-n or --noninteractive	Performs unattended installation (-f or -r options are needed to specify source of information).
-p or --chpasswd	Change Branch Server LDAP password, Branch Server must be already initialized.
-V or --version	Displays the version of the script being used.
-h or --help	Displays available options and their description.
--usage	Displays basic usage information.

B.3.2.3 Files

```
/etc/SLEPOS/named/named.conf
/etc/SLEPOS/template/dhcpd.conf.header.template
/etc/SLEPOS/template/dns-zonefile.header.template
/etc/named.d/ldap_generated/dns-zonefile.header
/etc/SLEPOS/dhcpd/dhcpd.conf.header
/etc/SLEPOS/template/resolv.conf.template
/etc/resolv.conf
/etc/sysconfig/network/routes
/etc/sysconfig/network/config
/etc/sysconfig/dhcpd
/etc/sysconfig/atftpd
```

B.3.3 posInitAdminserver

The purpose of `posInitAdminserver` is to configure the OpenLDAP directory server software and to create the initial data in the LDAP directory. You are prompted to enter the organization/company name, country abbreviation, and the LDAP administration password. You can also enable or disable SSL communication. Company name and country abbreviation are used to compose the LDAP base DN in the form `o=myorg,c=us`.

NOTE: `posInitLdap.sh`

In previous SLEPOS versions, `posInitAdminserver` was called `posInitLdap.sh`, which is now a symbolic link to the `posInitAdminserver` command.

B.3.3.1 Function

`posInitAdminserver` uses `/etc/SLEPOS/template/slapd.conf.template` to create the OpenLDAP configuration file `/etc/openldap/slapd.conf`. The LDAP base DN and password are replaced from the `posInitAdminserver` command with the corresponding user entries. After generating the configuration file, the OpenLDAP service is started.

`posInitAdminserver` then uses the template file `/etc/SLEPOS/template/ldif.pos.template` to create an LDAP data file `/etc/SLEPOS/template/ldif.pos`, which it then imports into the LDAP directory. Now the initial LDAP directory structure is available on the Administration Server.

`posInitAdminserver` uses `posReadPassword.pl` when the password is entered to hide the password characters.

B.3.3.2 Usage

Run `posInitAdminserver` on an Administration Server.

Table B.3: *posInitAdminserver Options*

Option	Description
--regenerate	Forces regeneration of SSL certificates. Old certificates are deleted. This option should only be used for SSL. Default is not to regenerate.
-r or --reconfigure =*FILE*	Reconfigures the Administration Server with the provided configuration file.
-n or --noninteractive	Performs unattended installation (-f or -r options are needed).
-V or --version	Displays the version of the script being used.
-h or --help	Displays available options and their description.
--usage	Displays basic usage information.

WARNING

Running this command destroys any existing data in LDAP.

B.3.3.3 Files

```
/etc/openldap/ldap.conf
/etc/openldap/slapd.conf
/etc/SLEPOS/template/slapd.conf.template
/etc/init.d/ldap
/etc/SLEPOS/template/openldap.template
/etc/SLEPOS/template/ldif.pos.template
```

B.3.4 posldap2crconfig

`posldap2crconfig` is now a link to provide backward compatibility. It triggers `pos`. If used with `--dumpall`, it is equivalent to the `pos dump-all` command. If used alone, a single registration cycle is executed by calling `posleases2ldap -o -d`.

B.3.4.1 Function

See Section B.2, "Core Script Process" (page 264) for a detailed description of `posleases2ldap`.

B.3.4.2 Usage

`posldap2crconfig [--dumpall]`

B.3.4.3 Files

`/etc/SLEPOS/branchserver.conf`

B.3.5 posldap2dhcp

`posldap2dhcp` generates the DHCP daemon configuration file from LDAP.

B.3.5.1 Function

`posldap2dhcp` is called by `posleases2ldap` at regular intervals. First, all scLocation objects are looked up in LDAP. Each of these objects defines a subnet and for each of them a subnet declaration in the `dhcpd.conf` is generated.

The header zone file is taken from the file specified in the configuration file directive `LDAP2DHCP_TEMPLATEFILE`, which is `/etc/SLEPOS/dhcpd/dhcpd.conf.header` by default. The content of the header file is adapted to the installation by `posInitBranchserver` (see Section B.3.2, "posInitBranchserver" (page 267)).

The value of the `scDhcpRange` attribute in an `scLocation` object is translated into a range statement in the subnet declaration.

In addition, the options for tftpboot are written into each subnet declaration. For each scCashRegister, a fixed address declaration is generated.

The new dhcpd.conf file is first generated in a temporary directory. If it differs from the working version, dhcpc is run with the temporary file in check mode. If it passes the check, it is copied over the working file and the command to restart the DHCP daemon is returned to be executed by posleases2ldap.

The dhcp.conf file now allows persistent customizations. During the Branch Server initialization and when posldap2dhcp is run, the dhcp.conf file is rewriten from templates. However during normal operations, when a workstation is registered by posleases2ldap or its configuration is dumped by pos dump-* commands, the dhcp.conf file is only modified by adding or removing host entries. These are confined within a SLEPOS area marked by '##_POS_group_start' and '###_POS_group_end#' comments. These should not be altered, as well as the structure within them, or SLEPOS registration will not work. However all other data in the dhcp.conf can be freely modified or extended and customized, provided the whole file still forms a valid configuration.

B.3.5.2 Usage

posldap2dhcp is called by posleases2ldap.

B.3.5.3 Files

```
/etc/SLEPOS/branchserver.conf
/etc/dhcpd.conf -> /etc/SLEPOS/dhcpd/dhcpd.conf
/etc/SLEPOS/dhcpd/dhcpd.conf.header
```

B.3.6 posldap2dns

posldap2dns generates DNS configuration and zone files from LDAP.

B.3.6.1 Function

posldap2dns is called by posleases2ldap at regular intervals. First, all scLocation objects are looked up in LDAP. Each of these objects defines a subnet and for each of them a zone file is created.

The header of each zone file is taken from the file specified in the configuration file directive `POS_LDAP2DNS_ZONETEMPLATE`, which is `/etc/named.d/ldap_generated/dns-zonefile.header` by default. The content of the zone file header is adapted to the installation by `posInitBranchserver` (see Section B.3.2, "posInitBranchserver" (page 267)).

The value of the `scDhcpRange` attribute in an `scLocation` object is translated into a `\$GENERATE` directive. For each `scService` or `scHAService`, an A record is created or, if multiple objects of that kind point to the same IP address, a CNAME record. After that, an A record for each Point of Service terminal is generated.

Finally, the `/etc/named.d/ldap_generated/named.zones` file containing the definitions of all generated zones is created. It is included from within `/etc/named.conf`. If zones were changed, `posldap2dns` returns the appropriate commands to restart the DNS service. The commands are executed by `posleases2ldap`.

B.3.6.2 Usage

`posldap2dns` is called by `posleases2ldap`.

B.3.6.3 Files

```
/etc/SLEPOS/branchserver.conf
/etc/named.d/ldap_generated/
/etc/named.d/ldap_generated/dns-zonefile.header
/etc/named.d/ldap_generated/named.zones
/etc/named.conf
```

B.3.7 posleases2ldap

`posleases2ldap` registers new Point of Service terminals in LDAP and transfers image install notification data to LDAP. It also triggers `posldap2crconfig`.

B.3.7.1 Function

See Section B.2, "Core Script Process" (page 264) for a detailed description of `posleases2ldap`.

Figure B.1: *Overview of the posleases2ldap Workflow*

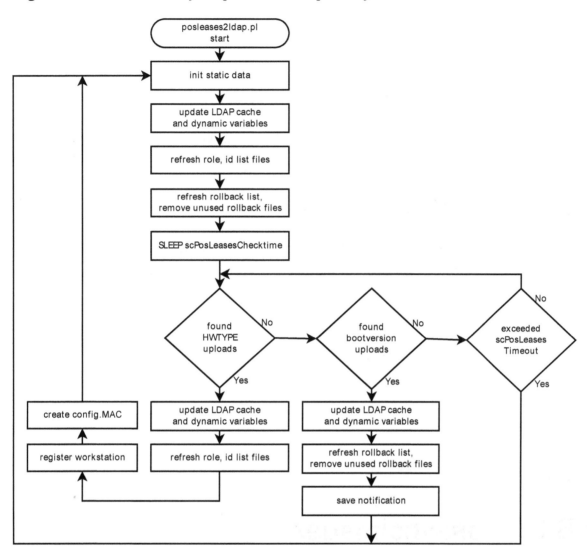

B.3.7.2 Usage

In normal operation, `posleases2ldap` is run as a daemon. It can be started by using the `/etc/init.d/posleases2ldap` init script, which is also used to start the daemon at boot time. To enable this, use `chkconfig posleases2ldap on`.

If `posleases2ldap` is started manually, it immediately runs in the background. To avoid this, use the optional parameter `-d`. If started this way, `posleases2ldap` stops when the shell is closed.

B.3.7.3 Files

```
/etc/SLEPOS/branchserver.conf
/srv/tftpboot/upload/hwtype.MAC.HASH
```

B.3.8 posReadPassword.pl

`posReadPassword.pl` is a helper script for the password entry that does not show the entered password.

B.3.8.1 Functions

`posReadPassword.pl` is called by `posInitAdminserver`, `posInitEdir`, and `posInitBranchserver` for password entry purposes.

B.3.8.2 Usage

In shell scripts, use a line such as

```
PASSWORD=`/usr/lib/SLEPOS/posReadPassword.pl`
```

B.3.8.3 Files

None.

B.3.9 possyncimages

The `possyncimages` command must be run on a Branch Server to download or update images from the Administration Server. It uses rsync and requires that the rsync service is properly configured and running on the Administration Server. This command can be run manually, but depending on your system requirements, you can create a cron job that runs the command every night to keep the images up to date.

B.3.9.1 Function

The `possyncimages --remote` command transfers the images from `/srv/SLEPOS` (images prepared by central administrator) on the Administration Server to `/srv/SLEPOS` on the Branch Server. It first downloads all available md5 files, then decides which images should be downloaded (as whole files or as deltas), then it runs `rsync` command for each image.

The `possyncimages --local` command transfers the images from `/srv/SLEPOS` on the Branch Server to `/srv/tftpboot` (images in production).

The `possyncimages` command without arguments performs both `--remote` and `--local`.

The list of downloaded images can be adjusted using the `scSynchronizedImagesDn` attribute. For more information, see Section 5.3.1, "Controlling the List of Images Downloaded by Branch Server" (page 72)

B.3.9.2 Usage

Run `possyncimages` on a Branch Server or set up a cron job. It may be useful to handle `possyncimages --remote` with cron but perform `possyncimages --local` manually when necessary. A crontab line to run nightly at 1 AM might look like this:

```
0 1 * * * /usr/sbin/possyncimages  --remote
```

B.3.9.3 Files

```
/etc/SLEPOS/branchserver.conf
```

B.3.10 registerImages

The `registerImages` command is used to copy the Point of Service images to the rsync directory on the Administration Server.

B.3.10.1 Function

The `registerImages` command copies the system image files to the rsync directory on the Administration Server (`/srv/SLEPOS`). It also provides functions for compressing the images, adding them to LDAP and installing boot images.

The `registerImages` command only works properly when the Administration Server and Image Building Server are installed on the same machine. If this is not the case, the images must be copied to the Administration Server manually first. For more information, see Section 4.7.3, "Manually Copying Images to the Administration Server's rsync Directory" (page 56).

B.3.10.2 Usage

The `registerImages` command uses the following options:

`-h` or `--help`
    Displays help.

`--gzip`
    Compress the image.

`--delta` *base_name-ver*
    Install also a delta (containing only necessary changes) image created against the given base.

`--move`
    Delete the source after successful installation.

`--no-hardlings`
    Do not use hardlinks, always copy files.

`--ldap`
    The corresponding LDAP entry.

`--image_cn` *cn*
    The `scPosImage` cn. The default value is taken from the filename.

`--container_cn` *cn*
    The `scDistributionContainer` cn. The default value is `default`.

`--kernel` *path*
    The path to the kernel part of the boot image to install.

`--initrd` *path*
    The path to the initrd part of the boot image to install.

`-v` *level* or `--verbose=`*level*
    Set the stderr verbosity level. The verbosity level can be specified by a number or as one of the following values: `emerg`, `alert`, `crit`, `err`, `warn`, `notice`, `info`, `debug`.

`--syslog=level`
> Set the syslog verbosity level. The verbosity level can be specified by a number or as one of the following values: `emerg`, `alert`, `crit`, `err`, `warn`, `notice`, `info`, `debug`.

B.3.11 posASwatch

The `posASwatch` service is used on Branch Servers to determine whether and when synchronization between Administration Server and Branch Server should be started. It is not needed when the Administration Server and Branch Server are configured on the same machine.

B.3.11.1 Function

The `posASwatch` service checks the availability of the Administration Server, the LDAP synchronization and replication, and the `posleases2ldap` core service.

B.3.11.2 Usage

On a Branch Server, run `rcposASWatch start` to start and `rcposASWatch stop` to stop the `posASwatch` service. To check the service status, use the `rcposASWatch status` command.

To ensure that the Branch Server starts the `posASWatch` command automatically at boot time, execute the `insserv posASWatch` command.

B.3.12 pos

Necessary LDAP objects can be created with `posAdmin`. You can also use `pos`, which is easier to use but less general.

B.3.12.1 Function

The `pos` command, depending on the subcommand used, easily creates necessary LDAP objects or reads improtant data from them.

B.3.12.2 Usage

The following commands are available:

```
pos help
```
Prints help.

```
pos id-list
```
Prints the ID list, one ID per line.

```
pos cr-list
```
Lists the registered cash register types.

```
pos image-list
```
Lists the registered images.

```
pos ws-list
```
Lists the registered workstations.

```
pos role-list
```
Lists roles. Can be used with `--hide-local` and `--hide-global` options to hide local or global roles.

```
pos id-add --id id
```
Adds a new ID *id*.

```
pos id-delete --id id
```
Deletes the ID *id*. If the `--force` option is used (`pos id-delete --force --id id`), the ID is deleted even if it is in use.

```
pos id-set --id id --workstation name or MAC
```
Assigns the ID *id* to the workstation specified by its LDAP name or MAC address.

```
pos role-create --cn cn --role name --description
description
```
Creates a new role. The `--cn` option specifies the LDAP CN of the new role. The `--role` specifies the role name that is shown to users. The `--description` specifies the role description that is shown to users.

```
pos role-add --cash-register cn or hwtype --image image
--role cn or name
```
Copies the global cash register configuration to the given role and assigns the image to it. The `--cash-register` option identifies the source cash register by its CN or hardware type. The `--image` option specifies the image CN or name. The `--role` option specifies the role CN or name.

If used with the `--force` option, the target cash register is replaced if it exists.

`pos role-cr-remove --role` *cn or name* `--cash-register` *cn or hwtype*

Removes a copy of the given cash register from the given role. The `--role` option specifies the role by its CN or name. The `--cash-register` option identifies the source cash register by its CN or hardware type.

`pos role-delete --role` *role cn or name*

Deletes a role.

`pos role-for-ws --roles` *role1[, role2, ...]* `[--workstation]` *name or MAC[,name or MAC,...]*

Sets the list of allowed roles for a given workstation. The workstation is specified by its LDAP name or MAC address.

`pos role-set --role` *role* `[--workstation]` *name or MAC[, name or MAC, ...]*

Assigns the given role to the given workstation. The `--workstation` option specifies the workstation by its name or MAC address. The `--role` option specifies the role by its cn or name.

`pos dump-ws [--workstation]` *name or MAC[, name or MAC...]*

Writes config.*MAC* for the given workstation. The `--workstation` option specifies the workstation by its name or MAC address.

`pos dump-lists`

Writes the role and ID lists, and refreshes the default pxe file.

`pos dump-all`

Writes the role, ID lists, default pxe and config.*MAC*, with specific pxe if needed, for all the workstations.

`pos remap-all`

Updates LDAP registration (ID to DNS and IP mapping) for all workstations. Should be used if `scDnsMapFunc` or `scIpMapFunc` was changed.

`pos sync [start|stop|status]`

Starts, stops, or checks LDAP synchronization between Administration Server and Branch Server.

```
pos pxe-bootmenu set [--imagespath <custom boot image
directory>] [--force]
```
Installs PXE menu. The `--imagespath` option contains the path to the
directory containing files to add into menu, they will be copied into the `boot/`
`ext` subdirectory. If this option is not supplied, only bios boot images currently
existing in `boot/ext` will be used.

The `--force` option allows to overwrite existing backup files.

In order for the pxe menu to not be reverted back, `posleases2ldap` must
be stopped, and no `pos dump` command can be run. Rebooting of the Branch
Server should also be avoided for pxe menu to stay intact, since the Branch
Server automatically starts the `posleases2ldap` service.

```
pos pxe-bootmenu undo [--force]
```
Restores the previous default and specific pxe files. The `--force` option allows
to overwrite the current file by backups (for specific pxe, default is always
overwritten). The images copied into `boot/ext` directory are not removed by
undo command, should be deleted manually if no more needed.

```
pos ws-remove [[--workstation] name or MAC[,name or
MAC...]|--no-boot-since date|--no-boot-in-last time] [--
force] [--dry-run]
```
Used to delete workstations not booted since specified date (according to
`scLastBootTime`). To delete workstations that were not booted in last T
seconds, use: `pos ws-remove --no-boot-in-last T`. To delete
workstations that were not booted since specified date, use: `pos ws-remove`
`--no-boot-since date`, where `date` is a date/time string compatible with
linux `date`, for example `2013-08-13 15:21:14`.

```
pos role-mode [--branch] [--enable|--disable|--allow-
global|--disallow-global|--status]
```
Sets role mode. The `--branch` option specifies the branch on which to
act, assuming local branch if not set and run on Branch Server. The `--`
`enable` option enables the rolebased mode. The `--disable` option disables
the rolebased mode. The `--allow-global` option allows and the `--`
`disallow-global` option disallows global roles. The `--status` option
prints the current role mode setting.

```
pos cfg-md5 [--branch] [--role|--cash-register|--
workstation] --cfgname or pos cfg-md5 --dn
```
   Sets configuration md5 sum. The `--branch` option specifies the branch on
   which to act, assuming local branch if not set and run on Branch Server. The
   `--role` option specifies the local role name or DN to use. The `--cash-
   register` option specifies the terminal to use, must be used together with the
   `--role` option. The `--workstation` option specifies the workstation to use.
   The `--cn` option specifies the name of `scConfigFileTemplate` to act on.
   The `--dn` option specifies the direct name of `scConfigFileTemplate` to
   act on.

The global option `--branch scLocation DN` specifies the branch for use on
the Administration Server.

B.3.13 save_poslogs

The `save_poslogs` is a tool for collecting log files, configuration files, and LDAP
directory content for easier error reporting.

B.3.13.1 Function

The `save_poslogs filename` command collects all SLEPOS relevant
configuration files (except `salt.key`, so that stored passwords remain encrypted),
all SLEPOS log files, and the whole LDAP database. It creates an archive containing
the collected items and log files with a complete list of collected items. The produced
archive is compressed according to `filename` extension. Recognized extensions
are `.tar`, `.tgz`, `.tar.gz`, and `.tar.bz2`.

B.3.13.2 Usage

The behavior of `save_poslogs` can be altered by the following options (in any
combination):

`--noldap`
   No LDAP database content is collected.

`--nolog`
   No log files are collected.

```
--noconfig
```
No configuration files are collected.

B.3.14 posSyncSrvPart

Creates a directory structure for offline boot on SLEPOS service partition.

B.3.14.1 Usage

posSyncSrvPart is started with the following command:
```
posSyncSrvPart [--server host/path] [--server-type tftp/ftp/local]
    [--source-config config] [--dest-config config]
    [--cleanup] [--dest-dir dir]
```

The following otions are available:

```
--source-config
```
Name of the configuration file on Branch Server. Default: `config.mac` with fallback to `config.default`.

```
--dest-config
```
Name of the configuration file on the service partition. Default: `config.default`.

```
--server
```
Branch Server hostname. The default value is `tftp`.

```
--server-type
```
`tftp` or `ftp` or `local`. The default value is `tftp`.

```
--dest-dir
```
The path to the service partition. Default: `/srv/SLEPOS` if it is mounted.

```
--cleanup
```
Delete all files on service partition that are not referenced from the configuration file.

B.3.15 posAdmin-GUI

posAdmin-GUI is a graphical tool for creating new Branch Server, Image, and CashRegister objects.

B.3.15.1 Usage

posAdmin-GUI is started with the following command:

```
posAdmin-GUI [YaST2_parameters] [SLEPOS_XML_file]
```

where *YaST2_parameters* is the path to the optional SLEPOS XML file and *YaST2_parameters* are optional YaST parameters. The following YaST2 options can be used with posAdmin-GUI (in any combination):

--fullscreen
  Fullscreen mode is used for `opt(`defaultsize) dialogs.

--noborder
  No window manager border is used for `opt(`defaultsize) dialogs.

--auto-fonts
  Picks fonts automatically, disregarding Qt settings.

--help
  Displays YaST2 help text.

B.3.16 posLDIFReport

The posLDIFReport script generates a report with a list of all Branch Servers and terminals in the SLEPOS environment. The report can be limited to terminals booted since a specified date. The report is generated from the LDIF file, which can be obtained suing slapcat or from the save_poslogs tarball.

B.3.16.1 Usage

posLDIFReport is started with the following command:

```
posLDIFReport [-w|--workstations] [-l|--locations] [-s|--statistics] [--since date] [file]
```

where *file* is the path to the LDIF file. If the file is not specified, the standard input is used. The following options can be used with posLDIFReport:

--workstations
  Create workstations report.

`--locations`
> Create branches/locations report.

`--statistics`
> Create overall statistics report.

`--since` *date*
> Consider only workstations booted since the specified date.

`--help`
> Displays the help.

Deprecated Elements

This section lists deprecated scripts and LDAP structures that are being superseded and may become unsupported in the future.

C.1 Deprecated Scripts

`posldap2crconfig`
> The functions of this script are superseded by `posleases2ldap` and `pos` calls. For more information, see Section B.3.4, "posldap2crconfig" (page 272).

C.2 Deprecated LDAP Structures

`scIdPool`
> It was possible to use this attribute to enter location's IDs by either new multivalue or separated by semicolons (or both). Now, only the first approach is supported, which means that there is only one ID per each subvalue of the multivalued `scIdPool` attribute.

`scPartitionsTable`
> This attribute is superseded by the `scPartition` object, which additionaly allows to specify a password for data (non-system) partition encryption. For more information, see Section 9.5.5, "Using Encrypted Partitions on Terminals" (page 159).

`scPosImageVersion`
> Similar to `scPartitionsTable`, this attribute is superseded by the `scImageVersion` object, which additionally allows to specify a password for the system partition encryption.

D

GNU Licenses

This appendix contains the GNU General Public License version 2 and the GNU Free Documentation License version 1.2.

GNU Free Documentation License

0. PREAMBLE

The purpose of this License is to make a manual, textbook, or other functional and useful document "free" in the sense of freedom: to assure everyone the effective freedom to copy and redistribute it, with or without modifying it, either commercially or noncommercially. Secondarily, this License preserves for the author and publisher a way to get credit for their work, while not being considered responsible for modifications made by others.

This License is a kind of "copyleft", which means that derivative works of the document must themselves be free in the same sense. It complements the GNU General Public License, which is a copyleft license designed for free software.

We have designed this License in order to use it for manuals for free software, because free software needs free documentation: a free program should come with manuals providing the same freedoms that the software does. But this License is not limited to software manuals; it can be used for any textual work, regardless of subject matter or whether it is published as a printed book. We recommend this License principally for works whose purpose is instruction or reference.

1. APPLICABILITY AND DEFINITIONS

This License applies to any manual or other work, in any medium, that contains a notice placed by the copyright holder saying it can be distributed under the terms of this License. Such a notice grants a world-wide, royalty-free license, unlimited in duration, to use that work under the conditions stated herein. The "Document", below, refers to any such manual or work. Any member of the public is a licensee, and is addressed as "you". You accept the license if you copy, modify or distribute the work in a way requiring permission under copyright law.

A "Modified Version" of the Document means any work containing the Document or a portion of it, either copied verbatim, or with modifications and/or translated into another language.

A "Secondary Section" is a named appendix or a front-matter section of the Document that deals exclusively with the relationship of the publishers or authors of the Document to the Document's overall subject (or to related matters) and contains nothing that could fall directly within that overall subject. (Thus, if the Document is in part a textbook of mathematics, a Secondary Section may not explain any mathematics.) The relationship could be a matter of historical connection with the subject or with related matters, or of legal, commercial, philosophical, ethical or political position regarding them.

The "Invariant Sections" are certain Secondary Sections whose titles are designated, as being those of Invariant Sections, in the notice that says that the Document is released under this License. If a section does not fit the above definition of Secondary then it is not allowed to be designated as Invariant. The Document may contain zero Invariant Sections. If the Document does not identify any Invariant Sections then there are none.

The "Cover Texts" are certain short passages of text that are listed, as Front-Cover Texts or Back-Cover Texts, in the notice that says that the Document is released under this License. A Front-Cover Text may be at most 5 words, and a Back-Cover Text may be at most 25 words.

A "Transparent" copy of the Document means a machine-readable copy, represented in a format whose specification is available to the general public, that is suitable for revising the document straightforwardly with generic text editors or (for images composed of pixels) generic paint programs or (for drawings) some widely available drawing editor, and that is suitable for input to text formatters or for automatic translation to a variety of formats suitable for input to text formatters. A copy made in an otherwise Transparent file format whose markup, or absence of markup, has been arranged to thwart or discourage subsequent modification by readers is not Transparent. An image format is not Transparent if used for any substantial amount of text. A copy that is not "Transparent" is called "Opaque".

Examples of suitable formats for Transparent copies include plain ASCII without markup, Texinfo input format, LaTeX input format, SGML or XML using a publicly available DTD, and standard-conforming simple HTML, PostScript or PDF designed for human modification. Examples of transparent image formats include PNG, XCF and JPG. Opaque formats include proprietary formats that can be read and edited only by proprietary word processors, SGML or XML for which the DTD and/or processing tools are not generally available, and the machine-generated HTML, PostScript or PDF produced by some word processors for output purposes only.

The "Title Page" means, for a printed book, the title page itself, plus such following pages as are needed to hold, legibly, the material this License requires to appear in the title page. For works in formats which do not have any title page as such, "Title Page" means the text near the most prominent appearance of the work's title, preceding the beginning of the body of the text.

A section "Entitled XYZ" means a named subunit of the Document whose title either is precisely XYZ or contains XYZ in parentheses following text that translates XYZ in another language. (Here XYZ stands for a specific section name mentioned below, such as "Acknowledgements", "Dedications", "Endorsements", or "History".) To "Preserve the Title" of such a section when you modify the Document means that it remains a section "Entitled XYZ" according to this definition.

The Document may include Warranty Disclaimers next to the notice which states that this License applies to the Document. These Warranty Disclaimers are considered to be included by reference in this License, but only as regards disclaiming warranties: any other implication that these Warranty Disclaimers may have is void and has no effect on the meaning of this License.

2. VERBATIM COPYING

You may copy and distribute the Document in any medium, either commercially or noncommercially, provided that this License, the copyright notices, and the license notice saying this License applies to the Document are reproduced in all copies, and that you add no other conditions whatsoever to those of this License. You may not use technical measures to obstruct or control the reading or further copying of the copies you make or distribute. However, you may accept compensation in exchange for copies. If you distribute a large enough number of copies you must also follow the conditions in section 3.

You may also lend copies, under the same conditions stated above, and you may publicly display copies.

3. COPYING IN QUANTITY

If you publish printed copies (or copies in media that commonly have printed covers) of the Document, numbering more than 100, and the Document's license notice requires Cover Texts, you must enclose the copies in covers that carry, clearly and legibly, all these Cover Texts: Front-Cover Texts on the front cover, and Back-Cover Texts on the back cover. Both covers must also clearly and legibly identify you as the publisher of these copies. The front cover must present the full title with all words of the title equally prominent and visible. You may add other material on the covers in addition. Copying with changes limited to the covers, as long as they preserve the title of the Document and satisfy these conditions, can be treated as verbatim copying in other respects.

If the required texts for either cover are too voluminous to fit legibly, you should put the first ones listed (as many as fit reasonably) on the actual cover, and continue the rest onto adjacent pages.

If you publish or distribute Opaque copies of the Document numbering more than 100, you must either include a machine-readable Transparent copy along with each Opaque copy, or state in or with each Opaque copy a computer-network location from which the general network-using public has access to download using public-standard network protocols a complete Transparent copy of the Document, free of added material. If you use the latter option, you must take reasonably prudent steps, when you begin distribution of Opaque copies in quantity, to ensure that this Transparent copy will remain thus accessible at the stated location until at least one year after the last time you distribute an Opaque copy (directly or through your agents or retailers) of that edition to the public.

It is requested, but not required, that you contact the authors of the Document well before redistributing any large number of copies, to give them a chance to provide you with an updated version of the Document.

4. MODIFICATIONS

You may copy and distribute a Modified Version of the Document under the conditions of sections 2 and 3 above, provided that you release the Modified Version under precisely this License, with the Modified Version filling the role of the Document, thus licensing distribution and modification of the Modified Version to whoever possesses a copy of it. In addition, you must do these things in the Modified Version:

A. Use in the Title Page (and on the covers, if any) a title distinct from that of the Document, and from those of previous versions (which should, if there were any, be listed in the History section of the Document). You may use the same title as a previous version if the original publisher of that version gives permission.

B. List on the Title Page, as authors, one or more persons or entities responsible for authorship of the modifications in the Modified Version, together with at least five of the principal authors of the Document (all of its principal authors, if it has fewer than five), unless they release you from this requirement.

C. State on the Title page the name of the publisher of the Modified Version, as the publisher.

D. Preserve all the copyright notices of the Document.

E. Add an appropriate copyright notice for your modifications adjacent to the other copyright notices.

F. Include, immediately after the copyright notices, a license notice giving the public permission to use the Modified Version under the terms of this License, in the form shown in the Addendum below.

G. Preserve in that license notice the full lists of Invariant Sections and required Cover Texts given in the Document's license notice.

H. Include an unaltered copy of this License.

I. Preserve the section Entitled "History", Preserve its Title, and add to it an item stating at least the title, year, new authors, and publisher of the Modified Version as given on the Title Page. If there is no section Entitled "History" in the Document, create one stating the title, year, authors, and publisher of the Document as given on its Title Page, then add an item describing the Modified Version as stated in the previous sentence.

J. Preserve the network location, if any, given in the Document for public access to a Transparent copy of the Document, and likewise the network locations given in the Document for previous versions it was based on. These may be placed in the "History" section. You may omit a network location for a work that was published at least four years before the Document itself, or if the original publisher of the version it refers to gives permission.

K. For any section Entitled "Acknowledgements" or "Dedications", Preserve the Title of the section, and preserve in the section all the substance and tone of each of the contributor acknowledgements and/or dedications given therein.

L. Preserve all the Invariant Sections of the Document, unaltered in their text and in their titles. Section numbers or the equivalent are not considered part of the section titles.

M. Delete any section Entitled "Endorsements". Such a section may not be included in the Modified Version.

N. Do not retitle any existing section to be Entitled "Endorsements" or to conflict in title with any Invariant Section.

O. Preserve any Warranty Disclaimers.

If the Modified Version includes new front-matter sections or appendices that qualify as Secondary Sections and contain no material copied from the Document, you may at your option designate some or all of these sections as invariant. To do this, add their titles to the list of Invariant Sections in the Modified Version's license notice. These titles must be distinct from any other section titles.

You may add a section Entitled "Endorsements", provided it contains nothing but endorsements of your Modified Version by various parties--for example, statements of peer review or that the text has been approved by an organization as the authoritative definition of a standard.

You may add a passage of up to five words as a Front-Cover Text, and a passage of up to 25 words as a Back-Cover Text, to the end of the list of Cover Texts in the Modified Version. Only one passage of Front-Cover Text and one of Back-Cover Text may be added by (or through arrangements made by) any one entity. If the Document already includes a cover text for the same cover, previously added by you or by arrangement made by the same entity you are acting on behalf of, you may not add another; but you may replace the old one, on explicit permission from the previous publisher that added the old one.

The author(s) and publisher(s) of the Document do not by this License give permission to use their names for publicity for or to assert or imply endorsement of any Modified Version.

5. COMBINING DOCUMENTS

You may combine the Document with other documents released under this License, under the terms defined in section 4 above for modified versions, provided that you include in the combination all of the Invariant Sections of all of the original documents, unmodified, and list them all as Invariant Sections of your combined work in its license notice, and that you preserve all their Warranty Disclaimers.

The combined work need only contain one copy of this License, and multiple identical Invariant Sections may be replaced with a single copy. If there are multiple Invariant Sections with the same name but different contents, make the title of each such section unique by adding at the end of it, in parentheses, the name of the original author or publisher of that section if known, or else a unique number. Make the same adjustment to the section titles in the list of Invariant Sections in the license notice of the combined work.

In the combination, you must combine any sections Entitled "History" in the various original documents, forming one section Entitled "History"; likewise combine any sections Entitled "Acknowledgements", and any sections Entitled "Dedications". You must delete all sections Entitled "Endorsements".

6. COLLECTIONS OF DOCUMENTS

You may make a collection consisting of the Document and other documents released under this License, and replace the individual copies of this License in the various documents with a single copy that is included in the collection, provided that you follow the rules of this License for verbatim copying of each of the documents in all other respects.

You may extract a single document from such a collection, and distribute it individually under this License, provided you insert a copy of this License into the extracted document, and follow this License in all other respects regarding verbatim copying of that document.

7. AGGREGATION WITH INDEPENDENT WORKS

A compilation of the Document or its derivatives with other separate and independent documents or works, in or on a volume of a storage or distribution medium, is called an "aggregate" if the copyright resulting from the compilation is not used to limit the legal rights of the compilation's users beyond what the individual works permit. When the Document is included in an aggregate, this License does not apply to the other works in the aggregate which are not themselves derivative works of the Document.

If the Cover Text requirement of section 3 is applicable to these copies of the Document, then if the Document is less than one half of the entire aggregate, the Document's Cover Texts may be placed on covers that bracket the Document within the aggregate, or the electronic equivalent of covers if the Document is in electronic form. Otherwise they must appear on printed covers that bracket the whole aggregate.

8. TRANSLATION

Translation is considered a kind of modification, so you may distribute translations of the Document under the terms of section 4. Replacing Invariant Sections with translations requires special permission from their copyright holders, but you may include translations of some or all Invariant Sections in addition to the original versions of these Invariant Sections. You may include a translation of this License, and all the license notices in the Document, and any Warranty Disclaimers, provided that you also include the original English version of this License and the original versions of those notices and disclaimers. In case of a disagreement between the translation and the original version of this License or a notice or disclaimer, the original version will prevail.

If a section in the Document is Entitled "Acknowledgements", "Dedications", or "History", the requirement (section 4) to Preserve its Title (section 1) will typically require changing the actual title.

9. TERMINATION

You may not copy, modify, sublicense, or distribute the Document except as expressly provided for under this License. Any other attempt to copy, modify, sublicense or distribute the Document is void, and will automatically terminate your rights under this License. However, parties who have received copies, or rights, from you under this License will not have their licenses terminated so long as such parties remain in full compliance.

10. FUTURE REVISIONS OF THIS LICENSE

The Free Software Foundation may publish new, revised versions of the GNU Free Documentation License from time to time. Such new versions will be similar in spirit to the present version, but may differ in detail to address new problems or concerns. See http://www.gnu.org/copyleft/.

Each version of the License is given a distinguishing version number. If the Document specifies that a particular numbered version of this License "or any later version" applies to it, you have the option of following the terms and conditions either of that specified version or of any later version that has been published (not as a draft) by the Free Software Foundation. If the Document does not specify a version number of this License, you may choose any version ever published (not as a draft) by the Free Software Foundation.

ADDENDUM: How to use this License for your documents

```
Copyright (c) YEAR YOUR NAME.
Permission is granted to copy, distribute and/or modify this document
under the terms of the GNU Free Documentation License, Version 1.2
or any later version published by the Free Software Foundation;
with no Invariant Sections, no Front-Cover Texts, and no Back-Cover Texts.
A copy of the license is included in the section entitled "GNU
Free Documentation License".
```

If you have Invariant Sections, Front-Cover Texts and Back-Cover Texts, replace the "with...Texts." line with this:

```
with the Invariant Sections being LIST THEIR TITLES, with the
Front-Cover Texts being LIST, and with the Back-Cover Texts being LIST.
```

If you have Invariant Sections without Cover Texts, or some other combination of the three, merge those two alternatives to suit the situation.

If your document contains nontrivial examples of program code, we recommend releasing these examples in parallel under your choice of free software license, such as the GNU General Public License, to permit their use in free software.